SEMI-PRESIDENTIALISM

COMPARATIVE POLITICS

Comparative Politics is a series for students, teachers, and researchers of political science that deals with contemporary government and politics. Global in scope, books in the series are characterized by a stress on comparative analysis and strong methodological rigour. The series is published in association with the European Consortium for Political Research. For more information visit www.ecprnet.eu

The Comparative Politics series is edited by Professor David M. Farrell, School of Politics and International Relations, University College Dublin, Kenneth Carty, Professor of Political Science, University of British Columbia, and Professor Dirk Berg-Schlosser, Institute of Political Science, Philipps University, Marburg.

OTHER TITLES IN THIS SERIES

Parliaments and Coalitions
The Role of Legislative Institutions in Multiparty Governance
Lanny W. Martin and Georg Vanberg

When Citizens Decide
Lesson from Citizens' Assemblies on Electoral Reform
Patrick Fournier, Henk van der Kolk, R. Kenneth Carty, André Blais, and Jonathan Rose

Platform or Personality?
The Role Of Party Leaders in Elections
Amanda Bittner

Political Leaders and Democratic Elections
Edited by Kees Aarts, André Blais, and Hermann Schmitt

The Politics of Party Funding
State Funding to Political Parties and Party Competition in Western Europe
Michael Koß

Designing Democracy in a Dangerous World
Andrew Reynolds

Democracy within Parties
Candidate Selection Methods and
Their Political Consequences
Reuven Y. Hazan and Gideon Rahat

Party Politics in New Democracies
Edited by Paul Webb and Stephen White

Intergovernmental Cooperation
Rational Choices in Federal Systems and Beyond
Nicole Bolleyer

The Dynamics of Two-Party Politics
Party Structures and the Management of Competition
Alan Ware

Cabinets and Coalition Bargaining
The Democratic Life Cycle in Western Europe
Edited by Kaare Strøm, Wolfgang C. Müller, and Torbjörn Bergman

Semi-Presidentialism

Sub-Types and Democratic Performance

ROBERT ELGIE

ecpr

OXFORD
UNIVERSITY PRESS

OXFORD
UNIVERSITY PRESS

Great Clarendon Street, Oxford OX2 6DP

Oxford University Press is a department of the University of Oxford.
It furthers the University's objective of excellence in research, scholarship,
and education by publishing worldwide in

Oxford New York

Auckland Cape Town Dar es Salaam Hong Kong Karachi
Kuala Lumpur Madrid Melbourne Mexico City Nairobi
New Delhi Shanghai Taipei Toronto

With offices in

Argentina Austria Brazil Chile Czech Republic France Greece
Guatemala Hungary Italy Japan Poland Portugal Singapore
South Korea Switzerland Thailand Turkey Ukraine Vietnam

Oxford is a registered trade mark of Oxford University Press
in the UK and in certain other countries

Published in the United States
by Oxford University Press Inc., New York

First published 2011

British Library Cataloguing in Publication Data
Data available

Library of Congress Cataloging in Publication Data
Data available

Typeset by SPI Publisher Services, Pondicherry, India

ISBN 978–0–19–958598–4

Table of Contents

Acknowledgements

Many different people and institutions have helped in the preparation and delivery of this book and I would like to take this opportunity to acknowledge their support.

First and foremost, I would like to thank the Irish Research Council for the Humanities and Social Sciences (IRCHSS) for the award of a Senior Research Fellowship in 2009–10. The book would not have been delivered without the support of this award.

I would also like to single out two people for their particular support. I would like to thank Shane Martin, who advised me some years ago to stick with the study of semi-presidentialism. This was, as ever, very sound professional advice and has also meant that I have pursued a really enjoyable research agenda in recent times. I would also like to thank David Farrell who supported the idea of this book right from the start and who has always shown interest in it.

There are many other people whose support I would also like to acknowledge. I would like to thank Shane Martin and Iain McMenamin for reading drafts of the original book proposal. I would also like to thank the anonymous referees of the proposal for their comments. In addition, I would like to thank David Doyle, Marek Hanusch, Carlos Jalali, Iain McMenamin, and Petra Schleiter for reading drafts of various chapters and for providing invaluable comments. I would also like to thank Petra Schleiter for arranging a period as a visiting researcher at Oxford University.

Thanks to the financial support of the IRCHSS, I was able to receive a total of twelve months of research assistance for this project. I would like to thank all of the research assistants who helped me in the preparation of material for this book: Lydia Beuman, Songul Cengiz, Marek Hanusch, and Michael Seifu.

Chapters 3 and 4 are derived from work that was originally conducted with Petra Schleiter and Iain McMenamin respectively. In particular, Petra Schleiter designed the first version of the event-history model that is presented in Chapter 3. It should be stressed, though, that they were not involved in the writing of these chapters or in the preparation of the models that are finally presented here. If there are any mistakes, or flaws, then they are solely and completely my responsibility.

I would like to thank Fernando Marques Pereira of the Directorate of Documentation, Information and Communication Services, Assembly of the Republic, Portugal, for supplying information about the Portuguese system.

I would like to thank the team at Oxford University Press, notably Dominic Byatt.

Finally, I would like to thank my family, Etain, Matthew, and Michael, for their support and forbearance.

List of Tables

1

The Perils of Semi-Presidentialism?

INTRODUCTION

On 25 March 2007, Sidi Mohamed Ould Cheikh Abdallahi was elected president of Mauritania. His election was the culmination of a process of democratization that had begun with a bloodless coup in August 2005 and that had brought down the autocratic regime of President Maaouya Ould Sid'Ahmed Taya. Immediately following the coup, the new regime, the Military Council for Justice and Democracy, committed itself to remaining in power for no more than two years during which time the conditions for democracy would be introduced. True to its word, the Military Council organized a constitutional referendum in June 2006 and then oversaw remarkably free and fair municipal and legislative elections in December 2006. At the 2007 presidential election, there were no fewer than twenty candidates at the first ballot with Ould Abdallahi finally winning 52.9 per cent of the vote at the second ballot. While there was certainly room for improvement in some aspects of the electoral process, the report of the EU's Election Assistance and Observation Mission stated that the elections 'constituted a remarkable democratic advance in a very short space of time' (Mission d'Observation electorale de l'Union europeenne en Mauritanie, 2007: 100)[1] and, for one observer at least, Mauritania's process of democratization provided the potential to serve as a 'regional model for political reform' (Zisenwine, 2007). It did not prove to be so. On 6 August 2008, President Ould Abdallahi was himself overthrown in a coup. General Mohamed Ould Abdel Aziz seized power at the head of a military-led High Council of State, placing President Ould Abdallahi under house arrest and bringing Mauritania's brief experience of electoral democracy to an end for the time being at least.

Why did electoral democracy collapse in Mauritania? Undoubtedly, the standard factors that are associated with the success or failure of democracy played their part. Mauritania is extremely poor with a GDP per capita of only US$893.08 in 2008.[2] The price of staple products, such as rice, sugar, and oil, is fundamental to social and political stability. In this context, democracy is sometimes seen as a costly luxury. Notwithstanding the general level of poverty, there is also considerable corruption that benefits particular individuals and groups. In 2008, Mauritania ranked 115th on Transparency International's Corruption Perceptions Index.[3] In terms of ethnic fragmentation, Mauritania is also highly divided (Alesina et al., 2003: 187). There are three main ethnic groups, though one, the Arab-Berber minority, has dominated the economic and political process. Moreover, within all groups, there are long-standing social and family rivalries that can supervene on standard political debates and that reinforce the neo-patrimonial nature of the state (Diaw, 1998). In addition to these economic and social factors, Mauritania had no experience of democracy prior to 2007. Military intervention in politics is standard practice. More than that, Mauritania is not situated in a part of the world where democracies are prevalent generally. Indeed, the fact that one observer thought that Mauritania might serve as a model was precisely because the roots of democracy in the region were shallow to say the least.

In this context, this book poses a general question – why is democratic performance better in some countries than in others? Why did democracy in Mauritania collapse when in other countries it has survived? In the case of Mauritania, all of the above factors no doubt help to explain why electoral democracy collapsed in 2008 and throughout this book these factors, or the majority of them, will consistently be shown to be part of the explanation for the relative performance of democracies. However, this book focuses on an additional explanation – the design of executive–legislative relations.

In the 2006 constitutional referendum, Mauritania adopted a semi-presidential form of government.[4] Moreover, it adopted a particular subtype of semi-presidentialism, known as president-parliamentarism. The main argument in this book is that democracies with this form of semi-presidentialism perform less well than those that have chosen the other subtype of semi-presidentialism, namely premier-presidentialism. The causal process underlying this argument will be presented in Chapter 2. Suffice to say for now that under premier-presidentialism, where the president does not have the power to dismiss the government, the president can only govern through the executive with the support of the legislature. Therefore, there is an incentive for the president to work with the legislature to reach a political deal. By contrast, under president-parliamentarism, where the government is responsible to both the president and the legislature, there is little incentive to broker a comprehensive deal. The president can tolerate a government supported by the legislature, knowing that the government can be dismissed at any time if there is a benefit to be gained from doing so. The problem is that the legislature can make the same calculation about a government supported by the president. With so few incentives for cooperation between the president and the legislature, there is likely to be instability that can be damaging for democratic performance. Indeed, in countries where democracy is not the 'only game in town', democracy itself may be the victim of such instability. The president may try to sideline the legislature and rule by decree, but at the cost of subverting democracy. Alternatively, the military may decide to restore stability by taking power, but again at the cost of democracy itself.

The perils of president-parliamentarism can clearly be seen in Mauritania.[5] Here, the 2006 legislative elections returned a very fragmented assembly. In a chamber with only ninety-five seats in total, no fewer than fifteen parties won representation and forty-one independents were elected (Aghrout, 2008). Following his election, President Ould Abdallahi was able to form a largely technocratic government that had the support of a number of small parties, but also the block of independents. In short, the government was not the result of a wide-ranging political deal. In February 2008, the president founded a new party, the National Pact for Democracy and Development, comprising many of those independents. Increasingly confident, President Ould Abdallahi decided to sideline the Prime Minister, Zeine Ould Zeidane, who stepped down in May 2008.[6] As a replacement, the president appointed one of his closest advisers, Yahya Ould Ahmed El Waghef. The new government included ministers associated with the regime of the former president, Ould Taya, who had been overthrown in the 2005 military coup, as well as two parties, the inclusion of at least one of which, Tawassoul, a moderate Islamist party, was extremely controversial. From this point on, President Ould Abdallahi's authority began to wane. So soon after the return of democracy, the most senior members of the military were concerned by the return of members from the Ould Taya era and by the president's attitude towards Islamism (N'Diaye, 2009). This discontent spread to deputies from the National Pact for Democracy and Development, many of whom joined with other parties in the legislature and lodged a motion of no-confidence in the government at the beginning of July. Faced with certain defeat, Prime Minister Ould Waghef resigned only for the president to reappoint him immediately. While the reconstituted government omitted some of the members of the former regime as well as the Tawassoul party, it was not the result of a comprehensive deal with the legislature. On 5 August 2008, opponents of the president within the National Pact for Democracy and Development abandoned the party, formally leaving the government without a majority.[7] Fearing that the military might intervene, on 6 August President Ould Abdallahi announced that he was removing a number of senior generals, including his own Chief of Staff, General Abdel Aziz. Later that morning, the president was arrested and General Abdel Aziz himself assumed power at the head of the High Council of State.

This book asks the question – why do some semi-presidential democracies perform better than others? The answer, it is contended, lies partly in whether a country has a president-parliamentary form of semi-presidentialism or a premier-presidential form. The Mauritanian case neatly captures the perils of president-parliamentarism. The deal between the president and the legislature was fragile. The president was willing to undermine a prime minister even at the expense of the latter stepping down. The president was happy to reappoint a prime minister, even when the government that he headed had clearly lost the confidence of the legislature. The president tried to use his powers to reshuffle the senior elements of the military even when it was clear that his authority in the legislature had all but disappeared. Overall, while the general economic, social, and political context in which Mauritania operated from 2007 to 2008 was likely to make any form of democracy difficult to establish, the precise circumstances in which the regime collapsed and the timing of that collapse can be explained at least partly by the organization of executive–legislative relations in the country, by the institutional dynamics associated with the country's president-parliamentary subtype of semi-presidentialism. This argument has important consequences. It implies that even a relatively minor constitutional amendment – a shift from president-parliamentarism to premier-presidentialism – is likely to improve the performance of democracies. Indeed, in some cases it may be the difference between the failure and success of democracy itself.

In Chapter 2, the distinction between president-parliamentarism and premier-presidentialism will be outlined and the reason why president-parliamentary countries are likely to be associated with a poorer democratic performance than premier-presidential countries will be presented in detail. To begin, though, the debate about institutional design and democratic performance needs to be placed in context. This is the aim of Chapter 1. First, the basic economic, social, historical, and international factors that affect the performance of democracy are identified. Then, the literature about the so-called perils of presidentialism and the virtues of parliamentarism is reviewed. Finally, the standard wisdom about semi-presidentialism is set out. The chapter will show that while semi-presidentialism has its supporters, there is a broad consensus that the disadvantages of semi-presidentialism outweigh the advantages. Whether or not there is evidence to back up the standard claims about semi-presidentialism is the focus of much of the empirical material in the chapters that then follow.

EXPLAINING THE PERFORMANCE OF DEMOCRACY

There are many ways to measure the relative performance of democracies. They might be judged in terms of the extent of corruption in a country, the level of equality/inequality in society, the level of women's representation in parliament, the degree of tolerance between social groups, and so on. While all of these measures may be perfectly valid, in this book performance is measured in terms of the level of democracy itself. The thorny issue of how democracy can be measured is addressed in subsequent chapters. Suffice to say for now that this book is concerned with two questions: firstly, why are some countries able to maintain at least some minimum standard of democracy whereas others collapse into authoritarianism and, secondly, assuming some minimum standard of democracy can be maintained, why do some countries hover just above this minimum standard whereas others enjoy a relatively high standard of democracy?

There is a voluminous literature that has tried to explain the relative performance of democracies understood in this way and there is an ongoing debate as to which variables have the greatest explanatory power. That said, the link between economic development and democracy is the most clearly established. In a well-known article, Lipset (1959) identified a positive correlation between economic development and democracy: 'the more well-to-do a nation, the greater the chance that it will sustain democracy' (Ibid.: 75). He explained this correlation in terms of the role that the middle class plays in reducing conflict, rewarding moderate parties, and penalizing extremist groups (Ibid.: 83). Many writers have tested the economic development hypothesis since this time. For example, Barro (1999) conducted a large-n statistical study and confirmed the relationship between economic development, measured as GDP per capita, and democracy. For their part, Przeworski et al. (2000) reached a slightly more nuanced conclusion. Their results (Ibid.: 106) showed that economic development does not explain why countries begin the process of democratization – in other words, there are countries that are economically developed and that remain authoritarian – but when a country, for whatever reason, has embarked upon the democratization process, the level of economic development is a strong predictor of whether or not democracy will survive. These findings, though, have been questioned. For example, Acemoglu et al. (2008) acknowledged the positive correlation between income and democracy, but found no evidence of any causal effect of the former on the latter. Instead, they argued, 'political and economic development paths are interwoven' (Ibid.: 836). Moreover, whatever the conclusions from all of these large-n statistical studies, there is no doubt that the link between economic development and democracy is not deterministic. As Lipset (1959: 24) put it, 'Many other variables can alter the expected impact of the development level on democracy in individual countries'. Thus, while any study of democratic performance needs to factor in the level of economic development, other explanations must also be considered.

This list of other explanatory variables is seemingly endless, ranging from macro-level generalizations about national political cultures (Almond and Verba, 1963) to specific arguments about the historical context of individual countries. Among the set of social, historical, and cultural variables that are commonly identified, the effect of homogenous populations vs. ethnic fractionalization is often emphasized. The explanatory logic behind this factor is simple: countries with ethnically divided populations are more likely to be faced with potentially irreconcilable demands. When a group finds that its demands have not been met, whereas those of a competing group have, then the excluded group is likely to question the very legitimacy of the regime itself. So, on the basis of case studies, Horowitz (1993) has claimed that 'ethnic conflict can be conducive to authoritarianism' (Ibid.: 20). In the context of Eastern Europe, he has argued that democracy has performed better in those countries where there are fewest ethnic cleavages (Ibid.: 19), stating that there is a 'direct relationship between ethnic conflict and nondemocratic development' (Ibid.) in the region. Similarly, on the basis of a large-n statistical study, Collier et al. (2009) have also found that social fractionalization significantly increases the risk of civil war. Building on their work, there is also evidence that the relationship is somewhat more complex, with highly homogenous and highly fractionalized countries being less susceptible to conflict than those that are polarized into two competing groups (Reilly, 2000). While, as with any argument about the determinants of democracy (Geddes, 1999: 119), there are also those who argue that the negative correlation between diversity and democracy is spurious (Fish and Kroenig, 2006), any study of the causes of the relative performance of democracy needs to include some consideration of the level of social fractionalization.

Students of democratization often emphasize historical factors. For example, there is a long-standing debate as to whether colonization affects the subsequent process of democratization and, assuming it does, whether different colonial powers have left behind different legacies in this regard. The fundamentally extractive nature of colonial rule means that former colonies are often poorly placed to manage their post-independence freedom. In addition, it is sometimes argued that the actions of certain colonizers were more conducive to the future prospects of democracy than others. For example, the British tended to tolerate civil society organizations more than other colonizers and also allowed a greater, though still limited, level of local representation. Arguably, this meant that there was a stronger tradition of competitive democracy in the post-independence regimes of former British colonies than in those of some of their colonial counterparts. In a large-n study, Bernhard et al. (2004) have shown that former colonies are indeed more likely to collapse than countries that were never colonized. They also provide some evidence to show that former British colonies are more likely to perform better than French colonies. Equally, Huber et al. (1993) have shown, via case studies, that colonial rule was an important factor explaining why democracy has tended to be stronger in former British colonies in the Caribbean than in former Spanish colonies of Central America. Again, though, it must be stressed that, even if valid, these findings are not deterministic. Examples of poorly performing democracies in former British colonies are not hard to find.

Another set of factors comprises the international determinants of democracy. These factors are extremely wide-ranging.[8] For example, there is some evidence that democracies and autocracies are spatially clustered (O'Loughlin et al., 1998), with the more successful democratizers being geographically closer to existing consolidated democracies (Kopstein and Reilly, 2000). This finding suggests that there are 'neighbourhood' or 'democratic diffusion' effects. In other words, countries with democracies on their borders are themselves likely to face pressure to democratize. More specifically, there is an ongoing debate as to whether democracy can be successfully imposed by external actors. Some large-n studies show that there may be beneficial effects, but only in individual countries (Peceny, 1999). Moreover, there is only moderate support for the claim that the successful imposition of democracy in one country is likely to have a domino effect throughout a region as a whole (Leeson and Dean, 2009). By contrast, there is perhaps better evidence that democracy can be encouraged, or promoted. So, small-n case studies seem to suggest that conditionality can have beneficial effects for democracy. The most obvious example here is the effects of prospective EU membership on former communist countries in Central and Eastern Europe. Whatever the shortcomings of EU policies, there is little doubt that conditionality had a generally positive democratic effect on candidate countries in the region (Pridham, 2005).

These factors are just a sample of those that have been proposed to explain the relative performance of democracies. Throughout the book, in the statistical models and in the case studies, these and other variables will be included in the analysis. However, the aim of this book is to focus on a different factor – the impact of a particular form of executive/legislative relations. There is a long-standing belief that the design of government institutions can have an effect on democratic performance. In the past, this debate concerned the relative merits of presidentialism vs. parliamentarism. In more recent times, the advantages and disadvantages of semi-presidentialism have also been considered. This book focuses solely on the effects of semi-presidentialism on democratic performance, specifically the effects of institutional variation within semi-presidentialism. However, to place the study of semi-presidentialism in its appropriate intellectual context, the literature on the impact of presidentialism and parliamentarism is first briefly reviewed.

PRESIDENTIALISM VS. PARLIAMENTARISM

The debate about the respective merits of presidentialism and parliamentarism has a long history. For example, in the late nineteenth century, Woodrow Wilson (1884) wrote an essay extolling the virtues of British-style parliamentary government and criticizing the US system. In the 1940s, Don Price (1943) defended the presidential system in the United States, provoking a reply from Harold Laski (1944).[9] While the debate continued after this time, it became more urgent in the late 1980s and early 1990s. At this time, there was an 'institutional turn' in political science (March and Olsen, 1984). The so-called 'new institutionalism' prioritized the explanatory power of institutions over other factors. Around the same time, the third wave of democratization began. The break-up of the Soviet Union and the democratization of large parts of Central and Eastern Europe, Africa, Latin America, and Asia meant that many countries were actively debating which form of government they wanted. As a result, the political science research agenda and the broader political agenda were, at least temporarily, aligned.

Institutions were central to the discussion about how best to construct successful democracies, while the relative merits of presidentialism and parliamentarism were central to the debate about which institutions were most likely to help or hinder the process of democratization.

In the context of the debate at this time, the most influential author was Juan Linz (1990*a*, 1994). He was an opponent of presidentialism and he put forward a number of arguments against this system of government. For example, he stressed the potential problems of dual legitimacy (Linz, 1994: 6–8). In presidential systems, the president is directly elected and so too is the legislature. When the majority in the legislature is opposed to the president, then who, asks Linz, 'on the basis of democratic principles, is better legitimated to speak in the name of the people[?]' (Ibid.: 7). There is no answer to this question. The result, Linz fears, is that the military may intervene as a way of resolving the matter. Linz is also concerned with the 'rigidity' of presidentialism (Ibid.: 8–10). In presidential systems, the president serves for a fixed term and so does the legislature. The problem, Linz argues, is that the political process 'therefore becomes broken into discontinuous, rigidly determined periods without the possibility of continuous readjustments as political, social, and economic events might require' (Ibid.: 8). The worry is that, in order to introduce some element of flexibility into the system, either the legislature may resort to impeaching the president, thus intensifying the crisis, or the president may use his/her powers to govern over and above the legislature, thereby threatening the rule of law. A further problem concerns the winner-takes-all/loser-loses-all nature of presidential elections (Ibid.: 14–16). Presidential elections can often be closely fought with the victorious candidate winning only slightly more than a plurality of the votes cast. Whatever the margin of victory, the successful candidate enjoys the full spoils of executive office, whereas the losing candidates receive nothing. Especially when elections are closely contested, there is the fear that the unsuccessful candidates may call into question the conduct of the election and the legitimacy of the president's mandate, encouraging their supporters to take to the streets and overturn the result, and democracy, by force.

For Linz, parliamentarism is a much better option for young democracies, though he stressed that he did not want to argue that '*any* parliamentary system is *ipso facto* more likely to ensure democratic stability than *any* presidential system' (Linz, 1990*b*: 84). Under parliamentarism, where only the legislature is directly elected, there can be no problem of dual legitimacy. In addition, Linz argues (1994: 8–10) that parliamentary systems are much more flexible than presidential systems. Here, the cabinet is the source of executive power, but the cabinet is responsible to the legislature. Therefore, if circumstances change, the legislature can remove the government by way of a vote of no confidence. What is more, often the prime minister may have the power to dissolve the legislature and bring about change that way, though Linz worries that this option may compound any problems that the regime is already facing (Ibid.: 9). Finally, while Linz acknowledges that parliamentary systems, where one party gains an absolute majority of seats in the legislature, may resemble a winner-takes-all situation, he also argues that even in this situation there is invariably a 'leader of the opposition', who has certain parliamentary privileges (Ibid.: 15). In fact, what often happens in parliamentary systems is that coalition governments are formed, allowing parties who do less well to enter government and still feel that they have a stake in the governance of the system as a whole.

Linz clearly established the terms of the debate about presidentialism vs. parliamentarism. However, his arguments have been criticized and others have since added to the debate. For example, Mainwaring (1993) argued that it is not presidentialism per se that is dangerous, but the interaction of presidentialism and a multiparty system. This combination, he argues, 'is more likely to produce immobilizing executive/legislative deadlock than either parliamentary systems or two-party presidentialism' (Ibid.: 200). Following on from this article and in an explicit critique of Linz's work, Mainwaring and Shugart (1997: 469) argue that Linz 'understated the importance of differences among constitutional and institutional designs within the broad category of presidential systems and in doing so overstated the extent to which presidentialism is inherently flawed'. They argue that 'providing the president with limited legislative power, encouraging the formation of parties that are reasonably disciplined in the legislature, and preventing extreme fragmentation of the party system enhance the viability of presidentialism' (Ibid.). By the same token, Sartori argued that parliamentarism can operate in very different ways, ranging from UK-style premiership-dominated systems to extreme assembly government, such as in the French Third and Fourth Republics, 'that makes governing a near-impossibility' (1997: 101). Thus, Sartori rejected pure parliamentarism as strongly as he rejected pure presidentialism (Ibid.: 135).

The theoretical arguments about the relative merits of presidentialism vs. parliamentarism were soon well rehearsed. Consequently, in recent years, attention has focused mainly on whether there is evidence to support the contention that countries with presidential systems are likely to perform less well than those with parliamentary regimes. The earliest studies, including Linz's work, tended to rely on anecdotal evidence from individual countries. So, while Linz (1990*a*, 1990*b*) could give examples of presidential collapses and parliamentary successes, equally Horowitz (1990) was able to give examples of presidential successes and parliamentary collapses. Somewhat later, Stepan and Skach (1993) provided descriptive statistics, including rudimentary controls for variables such as economic development, to show that presidentialism's record was worse than that of parliamentarism. Recent studies have employed more datapoints and used more sophisticated statistical models. For example, Przeworski et al. (2000) found evidence that presidential regimes were indeed likely to survive less long than parliamentary systems. In a recent study, Norris (2008) has confirmed this basic result. Similarly, on the basis of a large-n study, Gerring et al. (2009: 353) concluded that 'parliamentary systems offer significant advantages over presidential systems' and that in 'most policy areas, particularly in the areas of economic and human development, parliamentary systems are associated with superior governance'. By contrast, Power and Gasiorowski's study (1997) of fifty-six transitions to democracy in developing countries from 1930 to 1995 concluded that the 'breakdown rates of presidential and parliamentary democracies are nearly identical' (Ibid.: 137). Equally, Cheibub (2007: 136) confirmed that 'democracies tend to have shorter lives when they are presidential'. However, he showed that 'the fragility of presidential democracies is a function not of presidentialism per se but of the fact that presidential democracies have existed in countries where the environment is inhospitable for any kind of democratic regime' (Ibid.). Specifically, democracies are generally more prone to breakdown when they have been preceded by a military regime and presidential democracies are much more likely to have a military legacy than parliamentary systems.

The power of the theoretical arguments and the general results of the empirical studies mean Linz's initial scepticism about presidentialism remains the dominant attitude within the academic community. Indeed, Lijphart (2004: 102) states that 'there is a strong scholarly consensus in favor of parliamentary government'. What about semi-presidentialism? As will be seen in the next section, even though there is much less work on semi-presidentialism than on presidentialism vs. parliamentarism, there is an equivalent academic consensus. For most observers, semi-presidentialism is inherently perilous. This book makes no claims about the performance of semi-presidentialism relative to that of presidentialism or parliamentarism. Instead, the focus is solely on semi-presidentialism, specifically the relative effects of president-parliamentarism and premier-presidentialism. In Chapter 2, the concept of semi-presidentialism is defined and the differences between these two subtypes of semi-presidentialism are identified. However, to place Chapter 2 in its proper context, the remainder of this chapter outlines the existing work on semi-presidentialism and identifies the reasons why there is a consensus against this general form of government.

THE PROS AND (MAINLY) CONS OF SEMI-PRESIDENTIALISM

The concept of semi-presidentialism was identified rigorously only in the 1970s, and the relationship between semi-presidentialism and democratization was first discussed only as late as the 1990s. So, there is a much longer history to the debate about presidentialism and parliamentarism than to the debate about semi-presidentialism. Moreover, even since this time, writers have focused much more on the two standard forms of government than on semi-presidentialism. The net result is that much less work has been conducted on semi-presidentialism than on either presidentialism or parliamentarism. While the theoretical impact of semi-presidentialism on democratic performance is now well documented, there are still very few studies that systematically assess the empirical evidence for and against these theoretical claims.

There are three main criticisms of semi-presidentialism. The first, the problem of the dual executive, flows directly from the basic institutional features of this type of system. However semi-presidentialism is defined, all writers agree that semi-presidential countries have both a directly elected president and a prime minister who is responsible to the legislature. Thus, the configuration of the executive is fundamentally different under semi-presidentialism than under both presidentialism and parliamentarism. Under semi-presidentialism, there can be two competing actors within the executive – the president and the prime minister. Under presidentialism and parliamentarism, there can only be one such actor – the president under presidentialism and the prime minister under parliamentarism. For critics of semi-presidentialism, the dual nature of the executive can lead to problems of executive coordination that may weaken the performance of democracy or even threaten its very existence.

Again, Juan Linz was one of the first to write systematically about the pros and cons of semi-presidentialism. He was almost as opposed to semi-presidentialism as he was to presidentialism and the problem of the dual executive was one of the main reasons why he opposed semi-presidentialism. Linz argues (1994: 55) that 'instability and inefficiency' are present under semi-presidentialism even during the most favourable political circumstances, meaning when the president, prime minister, and ministers are all from the same party and when that party has a majority in the legislature. He worries both that the president will develop policies that are different from those of the prime minister and that ministers will appeal to the president when they have not received what they consider to be favourable treatment from the prime minister. The inevitable result, Linz argues (Ibid.), 'is a lot of politicking and intrigues that may delay decision making and lead to contradictory policies due to the struggle between the president and the prime minister'. In addition, Linz points to a very specific problem that may result from the dual nature of the semi-presidential executive. He is concerned that there will be no clear lines of political control over the military (Ibid.: 57). Under semi-presidentialism, he states (Ibid.), there are likely to be 'at least three major actors and very often four: the president, the prime minister, the minister of defense, and generally a joint chief of staff who has the immediate command of the forces. The hierarchical line that is so central to military thinking acquires a new complexity'. Whereas the general nature of the dual executive leads Linz to believe that decision-making may be inefficient, this element, he states (Ibid.: 59), 'has room for constitutional ambiguities regarding one of the central issues of many democracies: the subordination of the military to the democratically elected authorities and hopefully to civilian supremacy'. In other words, for Linz, the problem of the dual executive means that it is not just the quality of democracy that may be at stake under semi-presidentialism but democracy itself.

The second criticism of semi-presidentialism is a variant of the dual legitimacy problem that was encountered under presidentialism. As in presidential systems, in semi-presidential countries both the president and the legislature are directly elected. When the president fails to enjoy majority support in the legislature, there is the potential for institutional conflict. Under semi-presidentialism, the dual legitimacy problem takes two forms. The first is the problem of cohabitation, meaning the situation where the president and prime minister are from opposing parties and where the president's party is not represented in the cabinet. Given the prime minister and cabinet are responsible to the legislature in semi-presidential countries, if the legislative majority is opposed to the president, then that majority can approve a prime minister and cabinet that are equally opposed. One of the most influential articles on cohabitation was by Roy Pierce (1991), who examined the experience of the French case from 1986 to 1988 when the Socialist President, François Mitterrand, cohabited with the right-wing Prime Minister, Jacques Chirac. Pierce argued that cohabitation 'produced severe strains between the president and the prime minister, but it did not produce a fundamental political or constitutional crisis' (Ibid.: 287). However, he also argued that cohabitation 'worked as well as it did' (Ibid.) because of four contingent factors that might not be replicated in the future. Indeed, he argued that 'the experience of 1986–1988 took place under favorable circumstances, perhaps the most favorable that can be imagined, and that problems avoided then might not be avoided at a later time . . .' (Ibid.: 290–1). Thus, by focusing on the experience of cohabitation in a specific case, Pierce produced a general argument about the risks of cohabitation in other circumstances.

In their highly influential book, Shugart and Carey (1992) cited Pierce's argument and warned explicitly against the 'perils of cohabitation' (Ibid.: 56). Transferring Pierce's logic from France to the domain of democratizing countries, Shugart and Carey argued that when either the president or the cabinet with assembly support 'fail to recognize the claim to executive authority made by the other, cohabitation could generate regime crisis' (Ibid.: 57). Linz and Stepan (1996) make exactly the same argument. They say: 'when supporters of one or other component of semipresidentialism feel that the country would be better if one branch of the democratically legitimated structure of rule would disappear or be closed, the democratic system is endangered and suffers an overall loss of legitimacy, since those questioning one or the other will tend to consider the political system undesirable as long as the side they favor does not prevail' (Ibid.: 286–7). More succinctly, they say that 'in a semipresidential system, policy conflicts often express themselves as a conflict between two branches of democracy' (Ibid.: 287). In sum, Linz's argument against semi-presidentialism is very similar to his argument against presidentialism. Under presidentialism, crises of government can soon become crises of regime and democracy can be threatened as a result (Linz, 1990*a*: 65). Under semi-presidentialism, cohabitation can quickly degenerate from a conflict about policies to a conflict about the very legitimacy of the political process itself.

The second form of the dual legitimacy problem under semi-presidentialism is a divided minority government. Whereas the problem of cohabitation focuses on the conflict within the executive between the president and the prime minister, the problem of divided minority government stresses the conflict between the executive and the legislature. Specifically, it stresses the problems that can arise from the situation where the legislature is highly fragmented and where there is no stable or coherent legislative majority. The general worry about this situation is that governing becomes difficult for anyone, for the president, for the prime minister, and for the legislature. In other words, a stalemate, or power vacuum, emerges. In this context, the president (or the military) may be tempted to fill the vacuum and rule by decree. As a consequence, the rule of law may be violated and democracy may collapse.

Again, Linz warned against this scenario. He argued that the 'most difficult situation arises in a stalemated party system in which there is a very unstable or no majority in the legislature and the president cannot have either support or influence on a party or party coalition . . .' (Linz, 1997: 11). Speaking of the president, he continues: 'The temptation to govern without or against the legislature, to dissolve it and seek a new majority and, in case of failure, even to disband the legislature thereby turning to an *autogolpe* strategy, cannot be excluded' (Ibid.). While Linz warned against problems of this sort, Cindy Skach (2005) actually coined the term 'divided minority government'. Defined as where 'neither the president nor the prime minister, nor any party or coalition, enjoys a substantive majority in the legislature' (Ibid.: 17), she calls this scenario 'semi-presidentialism's most conflict-prone subtype' (Ibid.). She outlines the causal process in the following terms: 'divided minority government is characterized by legislative immobilism, on the one hand, and continuous presidential dominance, on the other. Presidential domination usually takes the form of extensive rule by executive decree as a substitute for a legislative majority. It is often accompanied by a narrowing of the decision-making arena to a small group of handpicked, nonparty ministers. This narrowing of the decision-making arena violates the democratic principles of inclusion and contestation, and delegitimizes the democratically elected legislature' (Ibid.: 124). Thus, Skach warns against the introduction of semi-presidentialism in young democracies, especially those without a stabilized party system.

The third criticism of semi-presidentialism is a variant of the winner-takes-all problem that was encountered under presidentialism. Here, there is the problem that presidential elections are zero-sum. The loser loses everything. Exactly the same situation occurs under semi-presidentialism. Only one person can hold the presidency. Therefore, the stakes at the presidential election are very high. In addition, semi-presidentialism can compound the winner-takes-all problem because of the cabinet's responsibility to the legislature. If the president's party also wins a large majority in the legislature, then the cabinet is not only safe in office but the chances are very high that the legislature and the cabinet will be loyal to the president and will faithfully enact the president's programme. In this context, the legislature fails to act as a check on the executive or, more specifically, the president. When the system becomes so personalized, then there is always the danger that the very existence of democracy is in the hands of one individual. If that individual's commitment to democracy is, or becomes, questionable, then democracy can collapse. So, Lijphart (2004: 102) warns that semi-presidential systems 'actually make it possible for the president to be even more powerful than in most pure presidential systems'. In this context, he resolutely defends parliamentarism against both presidentialism and semi-presidentialism.

All told, the criticisms of semi-presidentialism seem powerful. Certainly, the critics of semi-presidentialism seem to be more numerous, or at least more vociferous, than its supporters. However, what about the benefits of semi-presidentialism? Essentially, there are two basic advantages of this general form of government.

The first advantage concerns the potential for power-sharing under semi-presidentialism. This argument is a counterpoint to, or perhaps even a rebuttal of, the winner-takes-all criticism of semi-presidentialism and makes a virtue out of the dual executive. Under semi-presidentialism, the executive comprises both the president and a prime minister and cabinet. Thus, even if the presidency is a winner-takes-all institution, the executive as a whole does not have to be. In the context of a society that is polarized between two opposing groups, semi-presidentialism offers the opportunity for representatives of both groups to have a share of power, one as the president and one as the prime minister heading a coalition government. Given members of both groups share decision-making responsibility, both feel that they have a stake in the regime as a whole. Therefore, there is greater support for democracy under semi-presidentialism than there would be under presidentialism and parliamentarism, both of which are headed by only a single person, the president and prime minister respectively.

The argument from power-sharing has an intuitive logic. However, it is difficult to find people who explicitly propose this argument, though Sartori (1994: 109) includes power-sharing as one of the reasons for his limited support for semi-presidentialism.[10] Nonetheless, it is certainly the case that power-sharing has been the motivation behind the creation of a semi-presidential system. For example, in Kenya the position of prime minister was created by way of a constitutional amendment in 2008 following highly disputed legislative elections in which the opposition party challenged the victory of the president's party. After a period of violence, the two sides reached a compromise whereby the president would remain in office, but the post of prime minister would be created and would be held by the leader of the opposition to the president. Thus, in Kenya, semi-presidentialism was created explicitly to allow for a system of power-sharing, precisely because the previous presidential system could not.[11]

The second advantage of semi-presidentialism emphasizes the flexibility of this form of government. This argument is a counterpoint to the problem of cohabitation. It is particularly associated with the work of Giovanni Sartori. Whereas the problem of cohabitation emphasized the likelihood of conflict when the legislature was opposed to the president, the argument from flexibility suggests that cohabitation is likely to lead to a 'rebalancing' (Sartori, 1997: 125) of the executive diarchy. Under cohabitation, power within the executive shifts from the president (assuming the legislative majority supported the president previously) to the prime minister, who is appointed with the backing of the legislature. Thus, semi-presidentialism allows for the oscillation of power between the president and the prime minister, generating a '*flexible* dual authority structure' (Ibid.). It must be stressed that Sartori's support for semi-presidentialism is equivocal. Certainly, he prefers it to presidentialism, but he refuses to choose between semi-presidentialism and forms of parliamentarism (Ibid.: 135–7). Moreover, Sartori notes that there are potential problems with the dual authority structure. He states, 'any dual authority structure can become confrontational and thereby stalemated by an executive divided against itself . . . Still one must recognize that in this formula the problem of divided majorities finds a solution by "head shifting", by reinforcing the authority of whoever obtains the majority. And this is a most brilliant, if unintended, piece of constitutional witchcraft' (Ibid.: 125).

In addition to Sartori, the argument from flexibility is also associated with Samuels and Shugart (2010). They state (Ibid.: 260): '. . . the most important potential advantage is the prospect of cohabitation, which does not necessarily offer parties the "best of both worlds" but at least offers the possibility to oscillate between the presidential and parliamentary worlds . . .'. To use their terms (Ibid.), the 'parliamentarization' of the system under cohabitation can act as a counterweight to the presidency. That said, though, like Sartori, they do not have a strong preference for semi-presidentialism.[12] They see some potential advantages, but state that 'none of the truly hybrid formats combines the "best of both worlds"' (Ibid.: 261).

Overall, there are fewer arguments in favour of semi-presidentialism than against. Moreover, the people who are explicitly associated with the arguments in favour are often still reticent to support the explicit adoption of this system of government. All told, to the extent that there is a consensus, then it is a consensus against the adoption of semi-presidentialism.

While the theoretical arguments about semi-presidentialism are well rehearsed, there is still very little empirical work to determine whether semi-presidentialism really is as perilous as its critics would suggest. Indeed, in comparison with studies of presidentialism and parliamentarism, this is the aspect of semi-presidential studies that really lags behind.

The vast majority of work on the performance of semi-presidential democracies comprises case studies of individual countries or small-n comparisons of particular regions. There are plenty of country case studies that confirm the intuition about the inherent perils of semi-presidentialism. For example, Shoesmith (2003: 252) concluded his study of East Timor by saying that the 'fault line established by a semi-presidential system complicates the already formidable task of establishing an effective and at the same time democratic system of governance'. Speaking of Russia, Huskey (1996: 466) states that 'semi-presidentialism contains an added danger that is often overlooked in the comparative literature: the politics of the dual executive. The logic of semi-presidentialism in the Second Russian Republic suggests that the president's ability to hire and fire the prime minister will ensure the cooperation of presidency and government. Such is not the case. Yeltsin has frequently chosen to rule around rather than through the government'. Colton and Skach (2005) also note the problems that have been caused by semi-presidentialism in Russia. Surveying the Polish party system after 1990, Freeman (2000: 277) argues that although 'coalition building was clearly not going to be easy, the semi-presidential system in Poland made matters worse', concluding that 'coalition building was impeded by the "dual executive" nature of semi-presidential systems' (Ibid.). In Ukraine, Birch (2008: 236) stressed various issues that have made the consolidation of democracy difficult, but concluded that semi-presidentialism has also been 'a barrier to its achievement'. Equivalent conclusions have been drawn about other countries, including Guinea-Bissau (Akokpari and Azevedo, 2007), Weimar Germany (Skach, 2005), and sub-Saharan Africa generally (Kirschke, 2007).

That said, there is also some evidence that semi-presidentialism has helped the performance of democracy. For example, Fish (2001: 331) wrote that 'Mongolia's choice of semipresidentialism has been a boon to democratization'. Frison-Roche (2005: 455), writing about Central and Eastern Europe, concluded that the semi-presidential model 'showed at the end of the 1980s that it was well suited to the circumstances that were present in the countries of former communist Europe, that it was able to mould itself to the geopolitical context that each country faced, and that it was able to adapt to the different phases of the transition process that occurred over little more than a decade'. Pasquino (2007: 18) argued that in France 'the overall political assessment of the working of semi-presidentialism seems to be quite positive' and concluded that Portugal and Poland 'are democracies where, also thanks to semi-presidentialism, there is no undemocratic challenge by significant actors against the rules of the game' (Ibid.: 24). Overall, while there is evidence to support semi-presidentialism, on balance country studies and small-n regional comparisons tend to emphasize the negative effects that it has had on democratic performance.

Where the study of semi-presidentialism is really deficient is in terms of large-n comparisons and rigorous statistical tests. There are some studies of the performance of 'mixed systems' relative to both presidential and parliamentary regimes (Cheibub, 2007; Norris, 2008: ch. 6), but often the countries that are classed as 'mixed' are not the same as those that are defined in this book as 'semi-presidential'.[13] In fact, Moestrup (2007) provides perhaps the only large-n statistical study to date whose explicit aim is to compare the performance of presidential, parliamentary, and semi-presidential regimes. She concludes that 'the statistical results . . . cast doubt on the general applicability of Sartori's positive judgement [about semi-presidentialism]. On average, semi-presidential young democracies have not performed better than presidential regimes, either in terms of average Freedom House scores, or when considering the propensity to democratic breakdown' (Ibid.: 43). Thus, to the extent that there have been any large-n comparisons, the evidence reinforces the general consensus about the inherent perils of semi-presidentialism.

CONCLUSION

This book starts from the assumption that, all else equal, institutions matter, though not deterministically. Specifically, it starts from the assumption that, while many factors affect the performance of democracy, the design of executive/legislative relations is an important consideration. To date the literature linking executive/legislative relations and democratic performance has emphasized the negative effects of presidentialism relative to those of parliamentarism. By contrast, the literature on semi-presidentialism is less developed. Even so, to the extent that semi-presidentialism has been the focus of empirical attention, then the literature has tended to assert the problems of semi-presidentialism. By combining large-n comparisons and small-n country studies, this book provides the most rigorous empirical study of semi-presidentialism and democratic performance so far. The aim is not to compare the performance of semi-presidentialism with that of presidentialism or parliamentarism. Instead, the study confines itself solely to the performance of countries with semi-presidential constitutions, comparing the relative effects of the two main subtypes of semi-presidentialism, namely president-parliamentarism and premier-presidentialism. The argument is that democracies with a president-parliamentary form of semi-presidentialism are likely to perform less well than those with a premier-presidential form. Why this should be the case is the subject of Chapter 2.

NOTES

1. All translations, except where noted, are by the author.
2. World Bank, World Development Indicators, GDP per capita current US$, accessed 21 September 2009.

3. See http://www.transparency.org/policy_research/surveys_indices/cpi/2008 (accessed 22 September 2009).
4. Technically, amendments to the 1991 constitution were adopted. The text is available at: http://democratie.francophonie.org/IMG/pdf/mauritanie.pdf (accessed 21 September 2009).
5. Article 30 of the 1991 Mauritanian constitution, as amended in 2006, stated that the prime minister and ministers are responsible to the president. As will be outlined in Chapter 2, this is the key element of the president-parliamentary subtype of semi-presidentialism.
6. *Le Calame*, 13 May 2008, available at: http://www.lecalame.mr/index.php?option=com_content&task=view&id=1406&Itemid=38 (accessed 21 September 2009).
7. *Le Calame*, 5 August 2008, available at: http://www.lecalame.mr/index.php?option=com_content&task=view&id=1596&Itemid=38 (accessed 21 September 2009).
8. For an overview and case studies, see Zielonka and Pravda (2001).
9. Laski took issue with Price's description of the British system. He did not recommend the introduction of parliamentarism in the United States.
10. Jean Blondel (1984: 80–1) suggested that power-sharing is one of the advantages of a system of dual leadership. However, his definition of dual leadership is very different from the definition of semi-presidentialism that is used in this book. So, Blondel's work in this regard is not considered as part of the literature on semi-presidentialism.
11. In 2010, Kenya adopted a new constitution with a presidential form of government.
12. Their discussion is in relation to premier-presidentialism rather than semi-presidentialism in general.
13. For example, Norris (2008: 133) includes Hungary and Albania in her category of 'mixed systems', whereas few people would class these countries as semi-presidential.

2

Variation Within Semi-Presidentialism

INTRODUCTION

Over the years, the concept of 'semi-presidentialism' has been hotly contested. Indeed, it would scarcely be an exaggeration to say that more time has been spent debating the meaning of the term and arguing whether particular countries are semi-presidential than has been spent studying the effects of semi-presidential institutions on political life. That said, over time the term has been defined more and more rigorously to the point where, now, the concept can be understood and, more importantly, operationalized in a methodologically reliable manner. This has allowed the systematic and largely uncontroversial identification of a set of semi-presidential countries. Within this general category, though, there is still considerable institutional variation. One way of capturing this variation is to distinguish between countries with a president-parliamentary form of semi-presidentialism and those with a premier-presidential form. There are good theoretical reasons to believe that the performance of democracy in president-parliamentary countries should be worse than in premier-presidential countries. Whether or not there is evidence to support such reasoning is the subject of the next chapters. To set the scene, this chapter begins by defining the concept of semi-presidentialism and identifying the set of semi-presidential countries. Then, it distinguishes between the concepts of president-parliamentarism and premier-presidentialism, sets out the reasons why president-parliamentary countries are expected to perform less well than premier-presidential countries, and reviews the literature on this topic to date. The chapter ends by specifying the methods of inquiry by which the relationship between the variation within semi-presidentialism and democratic performance will be tested in the next chapters.

DEFINING SEMI-PRESIDENTIALISM

The term 'semi-presidential' has a surprisingly long history. The first mention of the word dates at least as far back as 1857.[1] In the 1920s, it was used to refer to the style of leadership adopted by the British Prime Minister David Lloyd George (Smith,

1923: 35). By the early 1950s, the term was employed relatively regularly in both English and French to refer to the role of the leader in particular countries, notably France itself (Wright, 1950: 48). At this time, the term was also used in a number of articles (e.g. Cumming, 1953: 28; Schiller, 1953: 382) relating to the Eritrean constitution of 1952, mainly because this was how the UN Commissioner described the system that had been put in place there. By the end of the 1950s, the term was now being commonly used to refer to the institutions of the French Fifth Republic, which was established in late 1958 (e.g. Beuve-Méry in 1958, reprinted as Beuve-Méry, 1987). Moreover, by the early 1960s it was beginning to be employed comparatively, particularly in the context of the newly independent countries in Francophone Africa (Blondel, 1960: 514). What is common to all of these examples is that no definition of the term 'semi-presidential' was provided and there was no concept of 'semi-presidentialism'. Instead, at least from the 1920s onwards, the term was being used adjectivally to refer to the situation where there was either a powerful prime minister or a fairly powerful president. The term implied either that a prime minister was acting beyond the normal bounds of the office and in a presidential-like manner or that a president, though more than a figurehead, was nonetheless not behaving as powerfully as the traditional image of US presidents.

In 1970, the use of the term was transformed and the concept of 'semi-presidentialism' took shape. In the 11th edition of his university textbook, Maurice Duverger (1970: 198–201) systematically identified a set of what he called 'semi-presidential regimes'. Duverger had used the adjective 'semi-presidential' on many occasions prior to this time (e.g. Duverger, 1967: 431) and he had used it loosely in much the same way that it was being employed by his contemporaries. In 1970, though, he started to use the phrase more rigorously, providing a definition of the concept (Duverger, 1970: 198) and distinguishing semi-presidential regimes from both presidential and parliamentary regimes. Over the next few years, Duverger tweaked his definition, arriving at his stock description of a semi-presidential regime in 1978 (Duverger, 1978: 17). In 1980, he provided his English-language statement of the concept:

> [a] political regime is considered as semi-presidential if the constitution which established it combines three elements: (1) the president of the republic is elected by universal suffrage; (2) he possesses quite considerable powers; (3) he has opposite him, however, a prime minister and ministers who possess executive and governmental power and can stay in office only if the parliament does not show its opposition to them. (Duverger, 1980: 166)

This definition soon became the standard way of understanding the concept of semi-presidentialism and was adopted by writers generally (e.g. Nogueira Alcalá, 1986).

As noted in Chapter 1, the general process of democratization in the 1990s coincided with a renewed interest in the study of institutions. In this context, and given so many countries in the third wave of democratization decided to adopt a semi-presidential form of government, there was further debate as to how semi-presidentialism should be understood. Many people, including Linz, implicitly or explicitly accepted Duverger's definition. By contrast, Cheibub (2007) rejected the term, preferring to compare what he called 'mixed' regimes with presidential and parliamentary regimes. For his part, O'Neil (1993: 197) accepted the concept of semi-presidentialism but rephrased Duverger's definition and, in so doing, ended up using the term in a way that was very similar to how it had been used in the 1950s and 1960s. More ambitously, Sartori (1997: 131–2) reframed the concept, stating that a system was semi-presidential if:

> the following properties or characteristics jointly apply:
>
> (i) The head of state (president) is elected by popular vote – either directly or indirectly – for a fixed term of office.
>
> (ii) The head of state shares the executive power with a prime minister, thus entering a dual authority structure whose three defining criteria are:
>
> (iii) The president is independent from parliament, but is not entitled to govern alone or directly and therefore his will must be conveyed and processed via his government.
>
> (iv) Conversely, the prime minister and his cabinet are president-independent in that they are parliament-dependent: they are subject to either parliamentary confidence or no-confidence (or both), and in either case need the support of a parliamentary majority.
>
> (v) The dual authority structure of semi-presidentialism allows for different balances and also for shifting prevalences of power within the executive, under the strict condition that the 'autonomy potential' of each component unit of the executive does subsist.

Sartori's definition was not widely adopted. In essence, though, it is entirely compatible with Duverger's understanding of the concept and, indeed, with the general interpretation of semi-presidentialism at this time. According to this interpretation, semi-presidentialism involved a certain institutional structure, even if there was some disagreement as to precisely what that structure comprised, although it usually involved a directly elected president. Within such a structure, and this was a point on which everyone agreed, there was a fairly powerful president, though there was disagreement as to how powerful the president had to be in order for a country to qualify as semi-presidential.

This way of understanding semi-presidentialism was challenged in the late 1990s (Elgie, 1998). The challenge was both empirical and theoretical. Empirically, the concept of semi-presidentialism was problematic because it was inherently unreliable. For example, using Duverger's definition, in order to decide whether or not a country is semi-presidential, a judgement call has to be made as to whether a president possesses 'quite considerable powers'.[2] But what constitutes 'quite considerable powers'? Each writer has room to decide for himself/herself. One result was a seemingly endless flow of papers by country experts arguing that country *x* was or was not semi-presidential on the basis of whether the president was interpreted as having 'quite considerable powers'. Another result was that comparativists identified slightly different lists of semi-presidential countries. Consequently, when comparisons were made about the performance of semi-presidential regimes, writers were not always comparing like with like (Elgie, 1999). To end the essentially fruitless debates of country experts and to ensure effective comparison, a definition was required that allowed the reliable identification of semi-presidential countries.

Theoretically, the concept of semi-presidentialism was problematic because it encouraged case-selection bias. For example, Sartori's definition stipulated that for a country to be semi-presidential, the president must, in practice, share executive power with the prime minister in a system of dual authority. In Chapter 1, though, it was noted that the problem of dual authority is a common criticism of semi-presidentialism. Semi-presidential countries with a dual authority structure were observed to exhibit potentially destabilizing presidential/prime ministerial conflict. However, when based on Sartori's definition, this criticism suffers from an endogeneity problem. If the only countries that are classed as semi-presidential are those that are observed to have a dual authority structure, then it is hardly surprising that the problems associated with a dual authority structure are observed in semi-presidential countries.[3] To avoid case-selection bias, a definition of semi-presidential was required that avoided the endogeneity problem.

The solution to the problems of unreliability and endogeneity was to define semi-presidentialism in a way that avoided any reference to the observed powers of the president or any other political actor and, instead, to rely solely on the wording of the constitution.[4] In addition, the number of constitutive elements in the definition was reduced to a minimum. This method has provided a much more systematic way of understanding semi-presidentialism. Constitutions are publicly available. Therefore, no specialized information about a country is required to determine whether or not it is semi-presidential. Similarly, by minimizing the number of constitutive elements, very little constitutional interpretation is required when identifying semi-presidential countries. For both reasons, the definition is inherently reliable. Equally, by avoiding any reference to the observed behaviour of political actors, the problem of endogenous case selection is avoided. As a result, when a country is identified by one writer as semi-presidential, it will most likely be identified by another writer as semi-presidential and the set of countries identified as semi-presidential raises no worries about case-selection bias.

Thus, by the end of the 1990s the concept was defined as follows:

> Semi-presidentialism is the situation where a constitution makes provision for both a directly elected fixed-term president and a prime minister and cabinet who are collectively responsible to the legislature. (Elgie, 1999: 13)

This definition was soon adopted by various writers (Shugart, 2005: 331; Skach, 2005: 13; Samuels, 2007: 705). Indeed, this has now become the standard definition of semi-presidentialism in political science (Schleiter and Morgan-Jones, 2009: 875).[5] This is the definition that will be used in the rest of this book and that provides the basis for the identification of semi-presidential countries.[6]

IDENTIFYING SEMI-PRESIDENTIAL COUNTRIES

Using Duverger's definition, or Sartori's, it is unclear whether Bulgaria should be classed as semi-presidential. Art. 1 (1) of the 1991 constitution states that Bulgaria is a republic 'with a parliamentary form of government'. The Bulgarian president has 'mostly ceremonial powers' (Andreev, 2008: 32) and 'there has been virtually no disagreement among the country's specialists that Bulgaria has been a parliament-dominated regime throughout most of its transition' (Ibid.). At the same time, 'the president has been an active player, helping the political system emerge stronger and arguably more democratic' (Ibid.: 47). Indeed, during the early years of the transition to democracy, there were 'ample opportunities for clashes between the president and prime minister' (Ibid.: 48)' and at times there has been a 'balanced version of semi-presidentialism' (Ibid.: 32). While most academics would probably include Bulgaria in their list of semi-presidential countries, this is not necessarily the case and at least one country expert has designated Bulgaria's political system as being 'parliamentary with reinforced presidential powers' (Karasimeonov, 1996: 47). So, is Bulgaria semi-presidential or not?

Using the definition of semi-presidentialism in this book, Bulgaria is unequivocally semi-presidential. Art. 93 (1) of the constitution states that the 'President shall be elected directly by the voters for a period of five years'. Art. 97 (1) lists the circumstances under which the president's term of office can be terminated before the end of this period. They comprise resignation, illness, impeachment, or death. They do not include any ways of dismissing the president in the normal course of parliamentary business. Therefore, in effect, the president serves for a fixed term. Art. 108 (1) states that the 'Council of Ministers shall consist of a Prime Minister, Deputy Prime Ministers and ministers'. In other words, there is a constitutionally designated post of prime minister. Art. 111 (1) includes the clause: 'The authority of the Council of Ministers shall expire upon any of the following occurrences: 1. A vote of no confidence in the Council of Ministers or the Prime Minister . . . '. This indicates that the government is collectively responsible to the legislature. In addition, Art. 122 states: '(1) The Council of Ministers shall be free to ask the National Assembly's vote of confidence in its overall policy, its programme declaration, or on a specific issue. A resolution shall require a majority of more than half of the votes of the National Assembly Members present. (2) Should the Council of Ministers fail to receive the requested vote of confidence, the Prime Minister shall hand in the government's resignation.' In short, there is a directly elected fixed-term president and a prime minister and cabinet that are collectively responsible to the legislature. This is the very epitome of a semi-presidential constitution.

On the basis of this definition, Table 2.1 provides a list of countries that currently have semi-presidential constitutions and records the year in which the constitution or the constitutional amendment that established the current system was adopted.[7] In addition, various other countries have had semi-presidential constitutions at some point in the past, but have now changed to another system. Moreover, some countries had a semi-presidential constitution in the past, but abandoned this form of government at some point, perhaps because the constitution was formally suspended in a coup, only to readopt a semi-presidential constitution at a later date. Table 2.2 lists all historic cases of semi-presidentialism and the dates when a semi-presidential constitution was operational.

The list of countries includes cases that almost everyone would agree to be semi-presidential, including France, Lithuania, Poland, and Portugal. However, the list also includes some surprising examples of contemporary semi-presidentialism, for example Egypt and Yemen, as well as some remarkable historic cases, notably Cuba and South Vietnam. Are all of these cases really semi-presidential? Is the definition of semi-presidentialism used in this book too permissive? On the basis of the rules for identifying semi-presidentialism outlined above, all of these

TABLE 2.1 *Countries with a semi-presidential constitution (as of December 2010)*

Algeria (1989)	Guinea-Bissau (1993)	Russia (1993)
Armenia (1995)	Haiti (1987)	Rwanda (2003)
Austria (1945)	Iceland (1944)	São Tomé e Príncipe (1990)
Azerbaijan (1995)	Ireland (1937)	Senegal (1991)
Belarus (1996)	Kazakhstan (1993)	Serbia (2006)
Bulgaria (1991)	Kyrgyzstan (1993)	Slovakia (1999)
Burkina Faso (1991)	Lithuania (1992)	Slovenia (1992)
Cameroon (1991)	Macedonia (1991)	Sri Lanka (1976)
Cape Verde (1990)	Mali (1992)	Taiwan (1996)
Central African Rep. (2005)	Mauritania (2009)	Tanzania (1995)
Chad (1996)	Mongolia (1992)	Timor-Leste (2002)
Congo-Kinshasa (2006)	Montenegro (2006)	Togo (1992)
Croatia (1991)	Mozambique (1990)	Tunisia (1988)
Egypt (2007)	Namibia (1990)	Turkey (2007)
Finland (1919)	Peru (1993)	Ukraine (1996)
France (1962)	Poland (1990)	Yemen (1994)
Gabon (1991)	Portugal (1976)	
Georgia (2004)	Romania (1990)	

TABLE 2.2 *Historic cases of countries with a semi-presidential constitution*

Angola	1992–2010
Austria	1929–33
Burkina Faso/Upper Volta	1970–4, 1978–83
Burundi	1992–6
Central African Republic	1981, 1992–2003
Comoros	1979–85, 1992–9
Congo-Brazzaville/Republic of Congo	1992–7
Congo-Kinshasa/Dem. Rep. of Congo	1990–7
Cuba	1940–52, 1955–9
Germany (Weimar Republic)	1919–33
Kenya	2008–10
Madagascar	1992–2009
Mauritania	1991–2005, 2006–8
Moldova	1994–2001
Niger	1992–6, 1999–2009
Peru	1979–92
Rwanda	1991–93
Senegal	1970–83
South Vietnam	1967–75

countries are, or were, semi-presidential. In Egypt, following the 2007 amendment to the constitution, Art. 76 states that 'The President shall be elected by direct, public, secret ballot', Art. 153 states that the government 'shall consist of the Prime Minister, his deputies, the Ministers and their deputies', while Art. 127 elaborates the way in which the People's Assembly may pass a vote of no-confidence in the government that forces its collective resignation. In Yemen, Art. 107 of the 1994 constitution sets out the rules for directly electing the president, while Art. 140 states that 'if the House of Representatives withdraws confidence from the Council of Ministers . . . the Prime Minister is obliged to tender the resignation of his government to the President of the Republic'. In Cuba, Art. 140 of the 1940 constitution stated that the 'President of the Republic shall be elected by universal, equal, direct, and secret suffrage . . . for a term of four years . . . '. Art. 151 stated that there was a Council of Ministers and that one of the ministers 'shall hold the title of Prime Minister'. Arts. 164–169 detailed the relations between the Congress and Government and included Art. 168, which stated: 'In any case in which a vote of confidence is refused the Government . . . must resign within forty-eight hours following the parliamentary decision . . . '. In South Vietnam, Art. 52 of the 1967 constitution stated that the president and vice-president were elected 'at large through universal suffrage by direct and secret ballot'. Art. 58, among others, made it clear that there was a prime minister. Art. 42 stated that the National Assembly had the right to recommend the replacement of the government by a two-thirds majority and that if the president refused the recommendation then the National Assembly had 'the right to vote final approval of the recommendation by a three-quarters majority vote of the total number of Representatives and Senators'. Thus, all of these cases are constitutionally semi-presidential.

Using constitutions as the basis of the definition of semi-presidentialism allows the most reliable possible identification of semi-presidential countries. However, constitutions are not always as neat and tidy as they might be and some countries are not always quite as straightforwardly semi-presidential as Bulgaria. Therefore, even when the number of constitutive elements in the definition is as parsimonious as possible, a degree of interpretation is sometimes required. For example, for the purposes of this study, countries that meet the other requirements of semi-presidentialism but where there is merely individual accountability of ministers or the prime minister to the legislature are excluded from the list. So, in Argentina, Art. 101 of the constitution states that the 'Chief of the Ministerial Cabinet [prime minister] may be removed by the vote of the absolute majority of the members of each House'. However, Argentina is not classed as semi-presidential because responsibility to the legislature is purely individual. Similarly, cases where the legislature may recommend the dismissal of the government, but where the president may refuse the recommendation, are also excluded because the ultimate decision is the president's and not the legislature's. So, South Korea, where there is only individual responsibility and where the legislature may only recommend the dismissal of the prime minister, is also excluded. By contrast, countries such as Mozambique and Sri Lanka, where the president is constitutionally specified as the head of the executive and/or the head of government, are included as cases of semi-presidentialism. In these countries the constitution explicitly provides for a fixed presidential term. Thus, even if the government falls, the president remains in office. Given that these countries have both a directly elected fixed-term president and a prime minister, and that the prime minister and cabinet are collectively responsible to the legislature, then they are classed as semi-presidential. Finally, countries where a supermajority is required in the legislature to dismiss the government are also included. Even though a supermajority requirement may, in practice, make it extremely difficult to remove the government, the possibility still exists. In presidential countries, by contrast, it does not.[8] Therefore, countries such as Egypt, Mali, Rwanda, and, historically, South Vietnam are classified as semi-presidential, even though their constitutions contain a supermajority requirement for the dismissal of the government.[9]

The main observation to be made about the list of semi-presidential countries in Tables 2.1 and 2.2 is that there is a tremendous variety to the set of cases. For example, there are cases that have never experienced any reasonable level of democracy, such as Cameroon, Chad, and Rwanda, but whose constitutions nonetheless formally meet the requirements of semi-presidentialism. However, many countries with semi-presidential constitutions have experienced some form of democracy. There are cases where democracy has been fully consolidated for a long period of time, including Finland, France, and Portugal. Equally, there are countries that have experienced at least a minimal level of democracy but have never managed fully to consolidate. Examples might include Sri Lanka and Ukraine. Finally, there are also countries that have experienced at least a minimal level of democracy at some point but have since collapsed. These cases include Madagascar, Russia, and Weimar Germany. Therefore, there is a puzzle. Why have some semi-presidential democracies performed better than others?

Another element of variety among the set of countries with semi-presidential constitutions concerns the relations between the president, prime minister, and the legislature. There are countries that have consistently had a strong president, a weak prime minister, and a weak legislature. Mozambique and Namibia are cases in point. There are countries that have regularly had a weak president, a strong prime minister, and often an active legislature. Austria, Ireland, and Slovenia could be included in this category. There are also countries where the relationship between the president, the prime minister, and the legislature has varied considerably over time. Cases include France, Mongolia, and Poland. While in the last chapter it was noted that the performance of democracy depends on many different factors, this book explores the extent to which variations in presidential, prime ministerial, and legislative relations are systematically associated with the democratic performance. In the next section, one way of capturing the institutional differences within semi-presidentialism is identified and the reasons why democratic performance might vary as a function of such differences are identified.

PRESIDENT-PARLIAMENTARY AND PREMIER-PRESIDENTIAL FORMS OF SEMI-PRESIDENTIALISM

A key observation about semi-presidentialism is that there is great variation across the set of countries with semi-presidential constitutions. A consequence of such variation is that semi-presidential countries as a whole should not be expected to be systematically associated with any particular outcomes, including the performance of democracy. Indeed, Cheibub and Chernykh (2008, 2009) confirm that there is no evidence for any such association. To put it another way, the variation within semi-presidential countries means that there is no reason to expect semi-presidentialism to have any power as an explanatory variable. This implies that comparisons of the performance of the full set of semi-presidential democracies relative to that of presidential and/or parliamentary democracies lack foundation. Therefore, in order to explore the consequences of semi-presidentialism, it is necessary to capture any systematic variation within the set of semi-presidential democracies and determine whether such variation is itself associated with particular outcomes.

There are various ways of identifying variation within semi-presidentialism. Crucially, though, to avoid the problems of unreliability and endogeneity, the logic that underpinned the definition of semi-presidentialism itself should also serve as the basis for the identification of variation within semi-presidentialism. In other words, there should be no reference to the observed powers of political actors. Instead, the variation should be based solely on the wording of the constitution, and it should involve as few constitutive elements as possible. A common way of capturing variation on this basis is to distinguish between semi-presidential countries in terms of the constitutional powers of their presidents (Shugart and Carey, 1992; Metcalf, 2000; Roper, 2002; Siaroff, 2003). In the chapters that follow, this method will be utilized to test particular arguments. However, this book focuses on a more parsimonious way of capturing variation within semi-presidentialism, and one that is still based on the same principles as the definition of semi-presidentialism itself. Here, a distinction is made between countries with a president-parliamentary form of semi-presidentialism and those with a premier-presidential form.

This distinction was first identified by Shugart and Carey (1992).[10] On the basis of this and subsequent work,[11] the distinction between the two forms, or subtypes, of semi-presidentialism can be expressed as follows:

> President-parliamentarism is a form of semi-presidentialism where the prime minister and cabinet are collectively responsible to both the legislature and the president.
>
> Premier-presidentialism is a form of semi-presidentialism where the prime minister and cabinet are collectively responsible solely to the legislature.

As with semi-presidential countries generally, president-parliamentary and premier-presidential countries can be reliably identified on the basis of this distinction. For example, Art. 111 (1) of the 1991 Bulgarian constitution states in full: 'The authority of the Council of Ministers shall expire upon any of the following occurrences: 1. A vote of no confidence in the Council of Ministers or the Prime Minister; 2. The resignation of the Council of Ministers or the Prime Minister; 3. The death of the Prime Minister'. Thus, the circumstances under which the government must end are explicitly set out and they do not include any mention of the president's ability to dismiss the cabinet. As a result, Bulgaria is an example of a premier-presidential form of semi-presidentialism. By contrast, following the 2005 constitutional amendments, Art. 73 (1 c) of the constitution of the Republic of Georgia states that the president is 'entitled, on his/her own initiative or in other cases envisaged by the Constitution, to dissolve the Government . . . '. In addition, Art. 78 (1) explicitly states that 'The Government shall be responsible before the President and the Parliament of Georgia'. This is a very clear statement of

TABLE 2.3 *President-parliamentary and premier-presidential countries*

President-parliamentary	Premier-presidential
Angola	Algeria
Armenia (1995–2005)	Armenia (2006–)
Austria	Bulgaria
Azerbaijan	Burkina Faso (1970–4)
Belarus	Cameroon
Burkina Faso (1978–83, 1991–)	Cape Verde
Burundi	Chad
Central African Republic	Congo-Brazzaville
Comoros	Croatia (2001–)
Croatia (1991–2000)	Dem. Rep. of Congo
Cuba	Egypt
Gabon	Finland
Georgia	France
Germany (Weimar Republic)	Haiti
Guinea-Bissau	Ireland
Iceland	Kenya
Kazakhstan	Lithuania
Kyrgyzstan	Macedonia
Madagascar (1996–2009)	Madagascar (1992–5)
Mauritania (2006–8, 2009–)	Mali
Mozambique	Mauritania (1991–2005)
Namibia	Moldova
Peru	Mongolia
Portugal (1976–82)	Montenegro
Russia	Niger
Rwanda	Poland
São Tomé e Príncipe (1990–2002)	Portugal (1983–)
Senegal (1970–83, 2001–)	Romania
South Vietnam	São Tomé e Príncipe (2003–)
Sri Lanka	Senegal (1991–2000)
Taiwan	Serbia
Tanzania	Slovakia
Tunisia	Slovenia
Turkey	Timor-Leste
Ukraine (1996–2006)	Togo
Yemen	Turkey
	Ukraine (2007–)

president-parliamentarism. Table 2.3 identifies all the cases of president-parliamentarism and premier-presidentialism within the set of countries with semi-presidential constitutions. In a small number of cases, countries have amended their constitution and switched from one subtype of semi-presidentialism to the other. The dates of these switches are also recorded in Table 2.3.

THE PERILS OF PRESIDENT-PARLIAMENTARISM

There would be little point in distinguishing between president-parliamentary and premier-presidential forms of semi-presidentialism unless there was some reason to expect that the distinction mattered. This book is premised on the idea that it does matter. Indeed, since Shugart and Carey first identified these forms of government, it has been assumed that they do have consequences for political outcomes. For example, referring to the distinction between the two types of government, Shugart has stated: 'These seemingly small changes in the formal definition of executive-legislative relations are in fact crucial' (Shugart, 1993: 30). Indeed, in the last paragraph of their study of executive-legislative relations, Shugart and Carey (1992: 287) explicitly warn constitution-makers 'to stay away from president-parliamentary designs'. What is the basis for such an unequivocal recommendation?

In their 1992 study, Shugart and Carey compare the effects of presidentialism, parliamentarism, premier-presidentialism, and president-parliamentarism. Their general conclusion is that when 'the electorate has two agents, it becomes critical for the relative powers to be spelled out clearly in the constitution' (Ibid.: 273). In relation to both premier-presidentialism and president-parliamentarism, they 'underscore the danger of institutional arrangements that do not provide clear mechanisms for the resolution of conflict between presidents and opposition assemblies' (Ibid.: 56). More specifically, they state that 'ambiguity will increase the danger that either a president or an opposition assembly majority will reject the claims to executive authority of the other' (Ibid.: 75). They include president-parliamentarism among the set of regimes that 'might be labeled "confused," in that the responsibility of cabinet ministers is unclear and quite possibly contradictory' (Ibid.: 121). Thus, for Shugart and Carey, relative to parliamentarism, both premier-presidentialism and president-parliamentarism may display an ambiguity that can be damaging for democratic performance. However, relative to premier-presidentialism, president-parliamentarism is likely to be more damaging. The reason why flows directly from the simple constitutional difference that separates the two forms of semi-presidentialism. Under president-parliamentarism the accountability of the government to both the president and the legislature creates greater institutional confusion and ambiguity than under premier-presidentialism.

Shugart and Carey spell out the causal mechanisms that result from the inherent ambiguity within president-parliamentarism. The system of dual responsibility, Shugart argues, creates the situation where 'there is no institutionally defined authority over the cabinet' (Shugart, 1993: 30). For Shugart and Carey (1992: 165), this is 'one of the most basic elements to any democracy' and when this authority principle is violated then 'conflicts of a very basic nature are likely' (Ibid.). In other words, conflict over the appointment and dismissal of the cabinet is likely to lead to a conflict of legitimacy over the regime itself. This is because under president-parliamentarism, there is no satisfactory answer to the question 'Are the ministers the president's ministers, or are they the assembly's?' (Ibid.). Moreover, the conflict between the president and the assembly is likely to be ongoing. On the assumption that both the president and the legislature have some role in the process of appointing a new cabinet, then, they argue, neither institution can blame the other if there is a 'prolonged standoff' (Ibid.: 121). In this case, the dominant strategy for both the president and the legislature 'is to make the next move, creating an appointment-dismissal game in which there is no stable equilibrium' (Ibid.). While Shugart and Carey do not specify the consequences of such disequilibrium, the likelihood is that either the president or the majority in the legislature will try to seize power unilaterally and, in so doing, will precipitate the collapse of democracy. Alternatively, the military will intervene to restore some sort of equilibrium, but, again, at the expense of democracy. By contrast, the situation under premier-presidentialism is likely to be more positive. Shugart and Carey say much less about the causal mechanism in this regard. However, they do assert that the 'majoritarian tendencies of presidential executives' (Ibid.: 282) may be diminished. Specifically, they emphasize the potentially beneficial effects of cohabitation,[12] arguing that it may reduce the 'presidential "pull" on assembly elections, and thus on the cabinet' (Ibid.).

This book proposes a similar but nonetheless different causal mechanism. The argument is that the two forms of semi-presidentialism provide different incentive structures for political actors and that the incentives under premier-presidentialism are likely to be less damaging for the performance of democracy than those under president-parliamentarism. The key intuition in this regard is the idea that under premier-presidentialism the president can maximize influence over the government only by working with the legislature. Given the president cannot dismiss a government once it has been formed, to maximize influence the president has an incentive to negotiate with the legislature and reach a deal about government formation. Thus, the president may have to cede some power to the legislature, but in return the president receives an ongoing influence over the political process, perhaps by securing the position of prime minister for someone from the president's party. The president could try to avoid ceding power and impose a presidential government on the legislature. However, under premier-presidentialism, there is little incentive for the president to engage in such a strategy. The president knows that such an act will only antagonize the legislature and that, in all likelihood, the legislature will vote the president's government down. In this event, the president can either try to impose another presidential government on the legislature with in all likelihood the same outcome, or negotiate with the legislature after all. If the president persists in trying to impose a government on the legislature, the blame for failing to form a stable government will lie squarely with the president for refusing to negotiate. At some point, the president will realize that the costs of being blamed for the failure to form a stable government are too politically damaging, and will calculate that it is better to negotiate after all.

By this point, though, the president is likely to have antagonized the legislature so much that the legislature will either not wish to negotiate and will try, instead, to form an anti-presidential government, or the president's negotiating position will now be so weak that the government will contain only the bare minimum level of representation from the president's supporters. The president will, by definition, have no opportunity to dismiss any such government. As a result, any presidential influence over the government will either be lost altogether or will be greatly reduced compared with what it would have been had the president decided to negotiate in the first place. Thus, under premier-presidentialism the president has a direct incentive to negotiate with the legislature in order to maximize influence over the government. Indeed, the president will be aware of the consequences of failing to negotiate with the legislature right from the start and will realize that there is an incentive to begin negotiations immediately.

Under premier-presidentialism, the legislature also has an indirect incentive to negotiate with the president. Given, by definition, only the legislature has the power to vote down a government, the legislature could decide to ignore the president's attempts to negotiate and simply try to impose a government on the president. With the president being unable to dismiss the government, this might be the way for the legislature to maximize its influence over the political process. However, this is a very high-risk strategy. Given the president has an incentive to negotiate, the formation of a legislative government in opposition to the president means that the blame for any subsequent government instability or, indeed, any adverse political outcome is likely to lie squarely with the legislature and the parties that opposed the negotiations with the president. While the president will be unable to oppose a legislature that is unwilling to negotiate and can form its own government, the legislature may calculate that it is best to negotiate and cede some power to the president because the legislature will still be able to maintain influence over the government and political blame will also be shared more broadly. Thus, under premier-presidentialism the legislature will find that it too has an indirect incentive to negotiate with the president and reach a deal about government formation. Only when a legislative election returns a new majority that is actively opposed to the president can the legislature legitimately refuse to negotiate with the president and insist on forming a cohabitation government. True, subsequently the cohabitation government will receive all the blame for any poor political performance, but at least the government will not be blamed for not having negotiated with the president in the first place. After all, by returning an opposition majority, the voters collectively signalled that negotiations with the president were unnecessary.

Under premier-presidentialism, where, outside cohabitation, both the president and the legislature have a direct or indirect incentive to negotiate over the process of government formation, the result is that both the president and the legislature are likely to have a stake in the government. Moreover, it should be appreciated that the process of government formation involves more than merely the choice of a prime minister. It involves negotiations about the partisan composition of the government as a whole, appointments to senior public sector posts, the distribution of resources in the legislature, agreement over policies, and so on. Thus, the president and the legislature are likely to have a stake in the regime more broadly. This does not mean that inter-institutional relations will necessarily be consensual or even cordial. However, it does mean that both actors will have an incentive to stick to the original bargain. With considerable costs sunk into the political deal, the benefits needed to motivate an actor to renege on the deal will have to be great. This generates a degree of stability in the political process. All else equal, stability is likely to be more beneficial to democratic performance than instability. Stability is likely to reassure foreign governments, international organizations, and the markets, facilitating the flow of aid and/or allowing governments to borrow at beneficial interest rates and encouraging investment in the economy and society that generates support for the political system as a whole. The prospect of relative stability is also likely to reassure political actors, providing political security, the promise of access to state resources, and perhaps even the prospect of physical security in a post-conflict situation. Overall, relative to president-parliamentarism, premier-presidentialism should be associated with negotiations between the president and the legislature, which means that both actors have a stake in the government and, indeed, the regime generally and which, in turn, generates a degree of stability in the political process that helps the prospects of democratic performance.

Under president-parliamentarism, the situation is likely to be very different. Here, by definition, both the president and the legislature retain the power to dismiss the government. In this situation, each institution may calculate that the best way to maximize influence over the government is to work against the other institution. The president may calculate that the best way to maximize influence is to form a non-partisan presidential government or a government with partisan ministers serving in a personal capacity against the wishes of their party leaders. This calculation is based on the assumption that ultimately the legislature will receive the blame for voting down a presidential government. The president reasons that if the legislature were to vote down the government and the president were simply to nominate another presidential government, then the legislature would be faced with the prospect of either having to tolerate that government or voting it out of office again. The president knows that, at some point, the legislature will realize that the political costs of persistently voting down the president's government are too great and that it will be left with no alternative but to accept the government, thus allowing the president to maximize influence over the process. The problem is that the legislature may make exactly the same calculation. The legislature may try to propose its own government, calculating that if the president refuses to accept it then the legislature can simply propose another. If the president persists in refusing the legislature's proposal, then the legislature reasons that ultimately the president will take the blame for the ongoing instability. If neither side concedes, then this is the unstable equilibrium that Shugart and Carey identified in their causal mechanism.

Most likely, though, at a certain point the costs of persistent instability, or the potential costs associated with the threat of persistent instability, are likely to lead to the formation of a government. It may be a presidential government, or, perhaps less likely, a legislative government, or it may be a government that is the result of a deal between the president and the legislature. The problem is that the legislature will have little incentive to tolerate a presidential government. By the same token, the president will have little incentive to tolerate a legislative government. Moreover, if the president and the legislature do reach a deal, it is likely to be a fragile one. This is because, by definition, each side retains the opportunity to dismiss the government and, crucially, each side has the incentive to do so, or at least to threaten to do so, in the hope of forcing the appointment of a new government over which it can exercise more influence. With few costs sunk into the process of government formation, few incentives will be needed to motivate a movement away from the status quo. The result, though, is likely to be political instability at least relative to premier-presidentialism. Again, under president-parliamentarism, instability is likely to be observed across the political system generally. For example, there may be frequent changes of prime minister. Even if there is no change of prime minister, there may be constant ministerial reshuffles. There may be a battle for control of public sector appointments. The president may veto legislation to prevent the passage of the legislature's policy programme and, in turn, the legislature will try to override the president's veto.

Instability is likely to be damaging for democratic performance. If actors feel insecure and under threat, then they will manoeuvre to protect their interests. For example, external actors may have material interests in the country and may intervene in the domestic arena to secure those interests, but at the expense of democracy. International financial actors may decide that instability requires an interest rate premium. This may mean that the country can borrow less than it needs, creating economic and social difficulties that the government may be unable to resolve and that generate popular unrest that the government cannot control. If there is persistent political instability, the military may decide to intervene to restore order. Perhaps most likely of all, with both the president and the legislature believing that there are gains to be made from a change in the status quo and with each side having an incentive to act against the other in order to make those gains, the president or the legislature may start to behave in a way that subverts the democratic process. There may be changes to the internal organization of the legislature as the president's supporters try to use procedural rules to gain control there. There may be constitutional reform as actors try to change the rules of the game to their advantage. The president may try to bypass the legislature and rule by decree. The president may propose a referendum, again with the aim of taking decision-making power out of the hands of the legislature. For its part, the legislature may try to rid itself of what it perceives to be the problem by impeaching the president. As actors skew the process in their favour, authoritarianism may emerge. To sum up, under president-parliamentarism the president and the legislature have an incentive to act against each other, which means there is little incentive to maintain the status quo and which in turn generates instability that is likely to undermine democratic performance and, in the worst-case scenario, lead to the collapse of democracy.

This book suggests that there is a direct causal link between the form of semi-presidentialism that a country has chosen and the democratic performance of that country. This link is not based on the general powers of the president. Whether or not the president has the power to issue decrees or the right to negotiate treaties is not integral to this causal link. Instead, the causal process is based on whether the prime minister and government under semi-presidentialism are collectively responsible to both the president and the legislature or solely to the legislature. In the former case under president-parliamentarism, neither the president nor the legislature has an incentive to negotiate over the formation of the government. Political deals are likely to be fragile. This means that there is likely to be political instability, which will be damaging for the performance of democracy. By contrast, under premier-presidentialism the president has an incentive to negotiate with the legislature over the formation of the government and the legislature is likely to have an interest in reciprocating. Both the president and the legislature have a stake in the government and the regime generally. The result is greater political stability relative to president-parliamentarism. This stability is likely to be conducive to better democratic performance. Overall, premier-presidential democracies should be less likely to collapse than president-parliamentary democracies and, within the set of democracies, the performance of democracy should be better under premier-presidentialism than under president-parliamentarism.

THE EXISTING LITERATURE ON THE TWO FORMS OF SEMI-PRESIDENTIALISM

The distinction between premier-presidentialism and president-parliamentarism is now more than a decade old and from the outset there was a very clear warning about the perils of president-parliamentarism (Shugart and Carey, 1992: 287). Since this time, various writers have operationalized the distinction between these two forms of semi-presidentialism and some of this work has found evidence that it makes a difference. However, the majority of this work has not been concerned with the performance of democracy. Moreover, even when it has, predictions about the performance of president-parliamentarism relative to that of premier-presidentialism have not been the subject of rigorous empirical testing. There is, therefore, an empirical gap that this book aims to fill.

The distinction between premier-presidentialism and president-parliamentarism has been operationalized by various writers. For example, Reiter and Tilman (2002) hypothesize that premier-presidential countries are less likely to initiate conflict than presidential and president-parliamentary countries, but that they are more likely to do so than parliamentary countries. They find only limited support for this hypothesis. In a similar study, Clark and Nordstrom (2005) also failed to find that premier-presidentialism had any significant impact.

More usually, though, the distinction between these two forms of semi-presidentialism has been operationalized in the context of intra-executive politics, namely relations between the president and the prime minister and cabinet, and particularly in the context of comparative studies of former communist countries in Central and Eastern Europe and the former Soviet Union. For example, Protsyk (2005: 742) found that 'the choice of prime minister in premier-presidential regimes more consistently reflected the preferences of the parliamentary majority than the choice of prime minister in president-parliamentary regimes reflected the preferences of the president' and concluded that 'the outcomes of cabinet formation in premier-presidential regimes are much more predictable' (Ibid.). That said, in a separate article, Protsyk (2006: 239) found that, contrary to the hypothesized relationship, there was 'no significant relationship between the type of semi-presidential system and the likelihood of intra-executive conflict'. Sedelius (2006) also studied whether the form of presidentialism affects the level of conflict between the president and prime minister/cabinet. In contrast to Protsyk, he concluded that 'premier-presidential systems have great governance potential provided that the party systems develop and consolidate' (Ibid.: 5) and he found that levels of conflict were higher under president-parliamentarism. For his part, Roper (2002: 269) focused solely on premier-presidential regimes, finding that there was variation within this set of countries and concluding that 'premier-presidential regimes that are considered to be the most presidential have the greatest level of cabinet instability'. Similarly, Morgan-Jones and Schleiter (2004) conducted a case study of Russia and whether president-parliamentary system there was associated with government instability. They concluded that there was variation within this form of semi-presidentialism as well and that, in the Russian case, it was not the main cause of cabinet instability. Protsyk (2003: 1091) provides a similar study of Ukraine, demonstrating how the president-parliamentary system there 'contributed to high levels of intra-executive conflict, cabinet instability and executive–legislative confrontation'.

In addition to this work on intra-executive conflict, Samuels and Shugart (2010) have recently conducted a large-n study of regime types and party organization. They state that regime type is the 'missing variable' in the comparative study of political parties (Ibid.: 7) and focus on the effects of presidentialism, president-parliamentarism, premier-presidentialism, and parliamentarism in this regard. They found that regime type does make a difference to party organization with a greater tendency towards intra-party dilemmas in countries with directly elected presidents (Ibid.: 251). In general terms, they found that parties are more presidentialized under both premier-presidentialism and president-parliamentarism than under parliamentarism. However, they also identified differences between the two forms of semi-presidentialism in relation to issues such as the incidence of cohabitation and the presidentialization of political parties (Ibid.: 106–8).

While all of these studies have focused more or less directly on the effects of premier-presidentialism vs. president-parliamentarism, none of them have been concerned explicitly with the consequences for democratic performance. That said, a small number of comparative studies have addressed this topic as part of a broader study. For example, in their recent book, Samuels and Shugart (2010: 260) state that they 'see some potential advantages to premier-presidentialism', not least because, on the basis of their definition of democracy, 'no premier-presidential democracy has ever been replaced by an authoritarian regime' (Ibid.). However, as noted previously, they were overwhelmingly concerned with party organization as the dependent variable. They only addressed the issue of democratic performance in passing and, when they did so, there was no controlled comparison of the effects of different regime types. The same point applies to Sedelius (2006). He was concerned with nascent democracies, but his focus was on the level of intra-executive conflict. To the extent that the presence of such conflict was deemed to be deleterious to democracy, then Sedelius was concerned with democratic performance. So, he concluded that the level of intra-executive conflict under president-parliamentarism was such that 'the adoption of this system is an important factor in relation to the failed democratisation in many post-Soviet countries' (Ibid.: 5). Again, though, this was an indirect finding of his work rather than the specific aim.

In addition, a small number of comparative studies have focused explicitly on the relative impact of the two forms of semi-presidentialism and democratic performance. For example, as noted previously, Shugart and Carey (1992) made a strong theoretical case against president-parliamentarism. However, there was no controlled comparison of the relative effects of the two forms of semi-presidentialism to back up their predictions.[13] Instead, they relied on indicative case studies of particular countries, pointing to the success of premier-presidentialism in Finland and France relative to the failure of president-parliamentarism in Weimar Germany. In another study (see Chapter 1), Moestrup (2007) provided a controlled statistical test of the performance of semi-presidentialism relative to presidentialism and parliamentarism. In this study, she also tested the impact of premier-presidentialism vs. president-parliamentarism, relying on descriptive statistics and finding some evidence to suggest that countries with president-parliamentary systems did indeed perform worse than those with premier-presidential systems. Elgie (2007) has also provided descriptive statistics to suggest that president-parliamentarism may be problematic for new democracies, but, again, this was part of a broader study of the reasons for the collapse of semi-presidentialism.

Over and above this comparative work, various writers have provided studies of democratic performance in individual countries and have placed these studies in the context of a premier-presidential/president-parliamentary framework. These studies are the source of rich descriptive material, but, for the most part, they are not concerned with testing the predictions about the relative performance of the two types of semi-presidentialism. Instead, they are interested in the dynamics of specific cases. For example, Matsuzato (2005) explained the choice of president-parliamentarism in Ukraine and outlined the problems caused by this form of semi-presidentialism. Elgie and Cavatorta (2010) discussed the problems caused by president-parliamentarism on the system of governance in the Palestinian Authorities. By contrast, Pugačiauskas (1999) emphasized the negative effects of the premier-presidential form of semi-presidentialism in Lithuania and Poland.

Overall, while the theoretical predictions about the effect of premier-presidentialism vs. president-parliamentarism on democratic performance have been articulated for a considerable time, for the most part the empirical support for these predictions has been assumed rather than demonstrated. This book aims to provide the first systematic comparative empirical study of this topic. To what extent is there evidence to support the argument that the performance of democracy is likely to be worse under president-parliamentarism than under premier-presidentialism? The next section briefly outlines the methods of inquiry that will be used to provide a rigorous answer to this question.

RESEARCH STRATEGY

This book aims to test the hypothesis that democracies with a president-parliamentary form of semi-presidentialism perform less well than those with a premier-presidential form. Thus, the dependent variable in this study is democratic performance. This variable is operationalized in two general ways: first, countries that were once democratic but have since collapsed are deemed to have performed less well than those where democracy still survives; second, among the set of democracies that have survived, the countries that remain quasi-democracies are deemed to have performed less well than those that are more consolidated. These concepts will be specified in future chapters. It should be clear by now that the main explanatory variable in this study is the form of semi-presidentialism that a country has adopted: president-parliamentarism vs. premier-presidentialism. However, as noted in Chapter 1, the book rests on the assumption that other factors are likely to determine the performance of democracy as well. Therefore, where possible, standard control variables will always be included in the analysis to maximize the chances that any findings about the effect of the two different forms of semi-presidentialism are not merely spurious.

To determine whether democracies with a president-parliamentary form of semi-presidentialism perform less well than those with a premier-presidential form, a mix of research methods will be employed. Various types of statistical analysis will be used, including descriptive statistics, cross-sectional analysis, multivariate regression, and event history models. Chapter 3 provides statistical evidence to show that democracy in president-parliamentary countries is more likely to collapse than democracy in premier-presidential countries. Chapter 4 provides equivalent evidence to demonstrate that president-parliamentary countries are more likely to have a lower standard of democracy than premier-presidential countries.

In addition to the statistical analysis, the book includes in-depth qualitative analysis. While the statistics indicate associations between variables, the in-depth analysis helps to identify the causal process at work. Chapter 5 presents two in-depth analytic narratives – one that concerns the collapse of democracy in a president-parliamentary country and another that describes the survival of democracy in a premier-presidential country. Again, these cases are chosen with a view to keeping as many other variables as possible constant, so allowing more purchase on the key explanatory variable under consideration. Chapter 6 considers two 'natural-like' experiments – a country that switched from president-parliamentarism to premier-presidentialism and one that switched from premier-presidentialism to president-parliamentarism. Both of these countries remained democratic after the switch, but in the case of the switch to premier-presidentialism the performance of democracy improved, whereas in the other case it disimproved. Again, when constructing the narratives, account is taken of other factors that may be associated with the improvement/disimprovement of democracy so as to highlight as best as possible the independent institutional effects of the two types of semi-presidentialism.

Chapters 3 and 4 rely on large-n statistical analysis with no reference to individual cases. By contrast, Chapters 5 and 6 focus on a small number of in-depth country studies. However, there are currently over fifty countries with semi-presidential constitutions as well as a number of historic cases of semi-presidentialism. In this context, Chapter 7 provides a more general overview of democratic performance under semi-presidentialism. It presents a set of indicative case studies to demonstrate that the basic dynamics of premier-presidentialism vs. president-parliamentarism can be identified generally. At the same time, it reflects on a number of seemingly anomalous cases, including, for example, premier-presidential democracies that have collapsed and president-parliamentary democracies that have survived, to determine whether these cases provide a fundamental challenge to the argument presented in the book generally. The Conclusion addresses some of the issues that are often associated with semi-presidentialism, such as the impact of cohabitation, minority government, and super-presidentialism, and discusses why, contrary to the existing literature, there was so little evidence to suggest that these factors affected the performance of democracy.

Throughout the book, a key concern is the issue of the endogenous selection of institutions. It may be the case that president-parliamentary democracies perform less well than premier-presidential countries because of the conditions under which the particular forms of semi-presidentialism were chosen at the outset. In short, countries that were likely to perform poorly may have chosen president-parliamentarism and countries that were likely to perform better may have chosen premier-presidentialism. If so, then the subsequent performance of democracy would not be a function of the particular form of semi-presidentialism that a country operated under, but of the circumstances in which that form of semi-presidentialism was adopted in the first place. In this way, the endogenous selection of semi-presidentialism would provide a real challenge to the validity of the argument presented in this book. The challenge provided by the endogenous selection of institutions is acknowledged throughout the book. By adopting an appropriate case-selection strategy, by including models that test for the endogenous selection of institutions, and by providing sufficient background information about the circumstances in which particular forms of semi-presidentialism were chosen, the aim is to minimize the endogeneity problem and make the conclusions of the book as robust as possible.

CONCLUSION

In Chapter 1, it was shown that semi-presidentialism is usually considered to be a problematic choice for new democracies. This chapter has defined the concept of semi-presidentialism and identified the countries that have, or have had, semi-presidential constitutions. The most noticeable feature of this set of countries is how varied they are. They vary in terms of their democratic performance. Crucially, though, they also vary in terms of their institutional arrangements. In other words, semi-presidentialism is a very heterogenous regime type and for this reason it is unlikely to be associated *in toto* with any specific political consequences. Instead, to understand the politics of semi-presidential countries, it is necessary to distinguish between different forms of semi-presidentialism. This book operationalizes Shugart and Carey's distinction (1992) between president-parliamentary and premier-presidential subtypes of semi-presidentialism. There are good theoretical reasons to believe that democracies with the former subtype of semi-presidentialism are likely to perform worse than those with the latter. To date, there is only indicative evidence to show that this is actually the case. This book explores the impact of premier-presidential vs. president-parliamentary forms of semi-presidentialism on democratic performance using a mix of methods of inquiry. What is the empirical evidence to support the claim that president-parliamentarism is a more perilous subtype of semi-presidentialism than premier-presidentialism? This question is the focus of the rest of this book.

NOTES

1. See web.me.com/relgie/The_Semi-presidential_One/Blog/Entries/2010/6/4_Is_this_the_first_reference_to_semi-presidentialism_(10)_2.html
2. There is a sense in which Duverger had a difficulty in making such a judgement call. Persistently, he includes Austria, Iceland, and Ireland in his list of semi-presidential countries even though he acknowledges that, in practice, the president has very few powers in any of these countries. In other words, Duverger seems to ignore the second element of his own definition when it comes to classifying these countries. Most people who rely on Duverger's definition exclude all three countries from the list of semi-presidential regimes. See, for example, Stepan and Skach (1993: 9).
3. The same logic applies to Duverger's definition. If the only countries that are classed as semi-presidential are those where the president is observed to have quite considerable powers, then it is hardly surprising that the problems associated with conflict between a fairly powerful president and the prime minister are also observed.
4. Even though Cheibub prefers the concept of 'mixed' regimes rather than semi-presidentialism, he, too, insists that constitutions should be the basis of a classification (Cheibub, 2007: 39).
5. Among those trained in constitutional law, the term 'semi-presidentialism' is almost universally rejected. This book does not engage with the literature in the discipline of constitutional law.
6. This book does not compare semi-presidentialism with either presidentialism or parliamentarism, but both of these regimes can be defined using the same principles. So, a presidential regime is where there is a directly elected fixed-term president and where cabinet members are not collectively responsible to the fixed-term legislature, while a parliamentary regime is where there is either a monarch or an indirectly elected president and where the prime minister and cabinet are collectively responsible to the legislature.
7. In addition, a number of sub-national units of government or non-recognized states currently have semi-presidential constitutions. They include the Republika Srpska within Bosnia and Herzegovina in the former category and the Palestinian Authorities in the latter.
8. In semi-presidential countries where no supermajority requirement exists, but where a disciplined party dominates the legislature, then, in practice, the government is as safe in office as a government in a presidential system. This situation occurred in France from 2002 to 2007 and after the 2007 election. Presumably, no one would wish to classify France as presidential during this time, even though in reality the government faced absolutely no risk of being

brought down. Thus, the key distinction between regime types is constitutional. In countries with a supermajority requirement, there is still the possibility, depending on the configuration of the party system, for the government to be dismissed by the legislature, whereas, constitutionally, this cannot be the case in a presidential regime whatever the configuration of the party system may be. Therefore, countries like Mali are classed as semi-presidential and not presidential.

9. For more information about the interpretation of particular cases, see Elgie and Moestrup (2008) and Elgie (2010*a*).
10. In their book, Shugart and Carey (1992: 23) state that 'what Duverger refers to as semi-presidential, we designate as premier-presidential', implying that president-parliamentarism is not a form of semi-presidentialism. However, in subsequent work, Shugart has made it clear that he considers both types of government to be forms of semi-presidentialism (Shugart, 2005; Samuels and Shugart, 2010).
11. The definition of president-parliamentarism has changed since its first appearance. Compare, for example, Shugart and Carey (1992: 24) where the president's power to dissolve the legislature is a requirement for president-parliamentarism with Shugart (2005: 334) where any such requirement is explicitly omitted and considered separately.
12. As noted in Chapter 1, a similar point was recently reiterated by Samuels and Shugart (2010: ch. 9, 337).
13. The only table that records the survival and collapse of democracies is provided on pp. 40–1 and it includes Ecuador as a case of president-parliamentarism. Ecuador is no longer included in Shugart's list of such countries.

3

Varieties of Semi-Presidentialism and Democratic Survival

Having identified the difference between president-parliamentarism and premier-presidentialism and having established why democracy should perform less well in the former when compared with the latter, this chapter provides an overview of the evidence linking the two subtypes of semi-presidentialism with democratic survival or collapse. Doing so provides an immediate challenge. If the concept of semi-presidentialism has often been contested, then identifying successful and failed democracies has proved to be an even more controversial exercise still. Therefore, the first part of this chapter sets out the strategy that will be adopted throughout this book to identify the set of semi-presidential democracies so that their performance can be evaluated. The second section provides some descriptive statistics to show both that there is *prima facie* evidence that president-parliamentary democracies have been more likely to collapse than premier-presidential democracies and that this is the case even when controlling for the endogenous selection of institutional structures. Having done so, a controlled statistical test of the relative performance of the two subtypes of semi-presidential democracies is then conducted, using a Cox proportional hazards model that was developed by Petra Schleiter (Elgie and Schleiter, 2011). The results show unequivocally that concerns about the perils of president-parliamentarism are empirically justified.

IDENTIFYING DEMOCRATIC SUCCESSES AND FAILURES

There is a long-standing debate about what constitutes democracy. Given this issue has been discussed since the time of the ancient Greeks, it should come as no surprise that contemporary scholars have failed to resolve the matter definitively. While the theoretical debate continues, recently there have been various attempts to operationalize the concept of democracy. This work posits certain observable elements of democracy and then examines various countries at a given time to determine whether or not these elements are present. If they are, or if a sufficient number of them are, then the country can be classed as democratic. What emerges from such an exercise is a list of democracies and non-democracies. If a country enters such a list at a certain point but exits from it at a later time, then democracy in that country can be said to have collapsed. This chapter is founded on the logic of an exercise of this sort.

There are now many competing frameworks for estimating whether or not a country is democratic. They differ in terms of the elements they consider to be constitutive of democracy, the countries they examine, and the time period they cover. Perhaps the most well known is Freedom House's classification of all the countries in the world as Free, Partly Free, or Not Free and in their classification of countries as Electoral Democracies or not. This exercise has been undertaken annually since 1972, though a list of Electoral Democracies is only available from 1989 onwards.[1] In academia, perhaps the most widely used framework is Polity IV, which also has its origins in the mid-1970s. The Polity IV data set examines all countries with a population of more than 500,000, providing an overall score for each country on a twenty-one-point scale that ranges from –10 (an hereditary monarchy) to +10 (a consolidated democracy). The exercise is updated periodically and the most recent 2010 update covers the period 1800–2009.[2] In addition to Freedom House and Polity IV, there are many other competing frameworks. For example, the Vanhanen index of democratization, now referred to as the Polyarchy data set, is based on the degree of party competition in a country and the level of voter participation. Almost all countries in the world are covered for the period 1810–2008.[3] As its name suggests, the Vanhanen index results in a discrete score for each country that allows the relative degree of democracy in those countries to be assessed for any given year. By contrast, the Alvarez, Cheibub, Limongi, Przeworski (ACLP/DD) methodology generates a dichotomous classification of dictatorships and democracies with no intermediate categories or scores. The original ACLP/DD data set has recently been updated and now covers 199 countries from 1946 to 2008.[4] Similarly, building on work by Boix and Rosato, Milan Svolik has recently produced an equivalent data set. Again, no intermediate categories or scores are recorded, merely democracies and, by extension, non-democracies. The Svolik data set covers the period 1789–2001.[5]

There are two points to note about these and other indicators of democracy. The first is that all of the indicators raise conceptual problems. As Munck and Verkuilen (2002: 28) note, 'no single index offers a satisfactory response to all three challenges of conceptualization, measurement, and aggregation' and 'even the strongest indices suffer from weaknesses of some importance'. Therefore, whatever the claims made by the supporters of any given index, there is no single industry-standard indicator. The second point is that while there is often a fairly high degree of correlation between the various indices, there are always differences between them and sometimes there is considerable variation, especially in the classification of particular countries. So, for example, Cheibub et al. (2010: 11) show that both Polity and Freedom House correctly predict 87 per cent of the cases classified as democracies in the ACLP/DD data set and 93 per cent of those classified as dictatorships. However, they also note that when the most autocratic and most democratic Polity and Freedom House countries are excluded, then Polity predicts only 65 per cent of the cases classified as democracies in the ACLP/DD data set whereas Freedom House predicts 73 per cent with both predicting 87 per cent of dictatorships. Another recent study has shown that there is a high degree of correlation between the countries that are given the most democratic scores by both Polity and Freedom House (Committee on Evaluation of USAID Democracy Assistance Programs, 2008: 80). However, they also found that 'the average correlation between the annual Freedom House and Polity scores for autocratic countries (those with a Polity score ≤–6) during 1972–2002 was only .274' (Ibid.). In addition, they showed that in the case of certain countries and particular regions of the world, such as the former USSR and the Middle East, the correlation between the scores on the two indices was very low (Ibid.: appendix C).

The identification of democracies and non-democracies is central to the analysis in this chapter. Given there is no industry-standard way of identifying such countries, it would be unsatisfactory to rely on a particular indicator of democracy as the results may be sensitive to the idiosyncratic classifications of that indicator. At the same time, there is little point in trying to develop a new indicator of democracy from scratch given there are already so many competing indicators and given the essentially contestable nature of the exercise. Therefore, the solution is to use a variety of different indicators. If substantively similar results are obtained using the same model across a range of indicators, then confidence in the findings of the model can be maximized. In this chapter, five indicators of democracy are operationalized at some point or another: two are based on the work of Freedom House, two are derived from the Polity IV scores, and one uses the ACLP/DD methodology.

The choice of these five indicators is driven at least partly by the fact that Freedom House, Polity IV, and ACLP/DD are commonly used in the political science literature. More importantly, the choice is motivated by Collier and Adcock's dictum (1999) that the decision to use a particular indicator of democracy should be as specific as possible and that it should be related to the particular research question that is being addressed. As noted above, the research design in this chapter requires the ability to distinguish between democracies and non-democracies. The Freedom House Electoral Democracy (FH ED) indicator and the ACLP/DD indicator are based on such a dichotomy. Therefore, they are well suited to the task at hand. However, Collier and Adcock (1999) also note that one of the major issues in the debate about how best to capture democracy is whether it should be considered as a dichotomous concept (democracy vs. non-democracy) or a graded concept (levels of democracy and non-democracy). Given that neither way is inherently more reliable than the other, this chapter also uses Freedom House and Polity

IV scores, both of which are based on gradations of democracy. When a graded indicator of democracy is used, a boundary point separating democracies from non-democracies needs to be identified. However, there is no a priori way of determining where that boundary should lie. For the purposes of this chapter, it is assumed that countries classed by Freedom House as Free and Partly Free (FH F & PF) are democracies and that countries classed as Not Free are non-democracies. On the basis of this logic, democracy is deemed to have collapsed if at some point Freedom House classes a country as either Free or Partly Free and then at some subsequent point the country is classed as Not Free. The same logic applies to the Polity IV scores. Here, two boundary points are identified. The first Polity indicator (Polity ≥+1) records a democracy when a country reaches a score ≥+1 on the scale from –10 to +10. If a score ≤0 is recorded at any subsequent time, then democracy in that country is considered to have collapsed. The second Polity indicator (Polity ≥+6) records a democracy when a country reaches a score ≥+6. If a score ≤+5 is recorded at any subsequent time, then democracy is deemed to have collapsed. Whereas the other three indicators of democracy allow the identification of democracies and non-democracies on the basis of different constitutive criteria, the Polity ≥+1 and Polity ≥+6 indicators allow the identification of democracies and non-democracies on the basis of the same criteria but with a different boundary point. Together, these five indicators provide a comprehensive set of ways of identifying successful and unsuccessful periods of democracy.

Accordingly, Table 3.1 records the periods when countries with semi-presidential constitutions have been classed as democratic using the five indicators of democracy identified above. Table 3.2 records the cases of semi-presidential collapse using each of the indicators. There are common elements to both tables. For example, in Bulgaria an ongoing episode of democracy is recorded as beginning in 1991 by all five indicators. Similarly, all five indicators record the collapse of democracy in Niger in 1996. That said, as a function of both the methodology used by each indicator and the time period covered, there is considerable variation across the different indicators in terms of both the country coverage and the cases of democratic collapse. Using countries as the unit of observation and distinguishing between different units of democracy in the same country as a function of time (e.g. classing Algeria 1989–91 as Algeria 1 and giving it a value of '1' for the FH F & PF data set and '0' for all of the other data sets because only FH F & PF records a democratic episode around that time), then the highest positive and statistically significant correlation between the list of semi-presidential cases and any two of the data sets is a fairly modest 0.56 between Polity ≥+1 and Polity ≥+6[6] (see Table 3.3). The correlations between the semi-presidential collapses in the different data sets are even weaker. Here, there is only one positive and statistically significant correlation, which is between the Polity ≥+1 data set and ACLP/DD at 0.58 (see Table 3.4). For the purposes of this chapter, modest positive correlations and correlations that are not significant are useful. If the correlations

TABLE 3.1 *Periods of democracy in countries with semi-presidential constitutions (various indicators and data set coverage in years inclusive)*

Country	Polity ≥+1 (1919–2008)	Polity ≥+6 (1919–2008)	FH F & PF (1972–2009)	FH ED (1989–2009)	ACLP/DD (1946–2008)
Algeria	2004–		1989–91		
Armenia	1991–5 1998–	1991–4	1995–	1999–2002	1991–
Austria	1929–32 1945–	1929–32 1946–	1972–	1989–	1946–
Azerbaijan			1991–2 1997–9		
Bulgaria	1991–	1991–	1991–	1991–	1991–
Burkina Faso	1978–9		1972–4 1978–80 1992–		
Burundi					1993–5
Cape Verde			1992–	1992–	1992–
Central African Republic	1993–2002		1993–2002 2005–	1993–2000 2005–7	1993–2002
Comoros	1992–4 1996–8		1979–84 1992–9		1990–4
Congo-Brazzaville	1992–6		1992–6	1992–6	1992–6
Congo-Kinshasa	2006–				
Croatia	1999–	2000–	1991–	1991–	1991–
Cuba	1940–51				1946–51
East Timor	2002–	2002–	2002–	2002–	2002–
Finland	1919–	1919–30 1944–	1972–	1989–	1946–
France	1962–	1969–	1972–	1989–	1962–
Gabon			1991–2008		
Georgia	2004–	2004–	2004–	2004–7	2004–
Germany	1919–32	1919–32			
Guinea-Bissau	1994–7 1999–2002 2005–	2005–	1994–	1994–2002 2005–	2000–2 2004–
Haiti	1994–9 2006–	1994–8	1994–9 2006–	1994–9 2006–	
Iceland			1972–	1989–	1946–
Ireland	1937–	1937–	1972–	1989–	1946–
Kazakhstan			1993		
Kenya	2008–	2008–	2008–		2008–
Kyrgyzstan	2005–		1993–9 2005–8	1995–9	2005–
Lithuania	1992–	1992–	1992–	1992–	1992–
Macedonia	1992–	1992–	1992–	1992–	1992–
Madagascar	1992–	1992–	1992–	1993–2008	1993–
Mali	1992–	1992–	1992–	1992–	1992–

Continued

TABLE 3.1 *Contined*

Country	Polity ≥+1 (1919–2008)	Polity ≥+6 (1919–2008)	FH F & PF (1972–2009)	FH ED (1989–2009)	ACLP/DD (1946–2008)
Mauritania	2007		2001–2 2006–7	2007	2007
Moldova	1994–2000	1994–2000	1994–2000	1995–2000	1994–2000
Mongolia	1992–	1992–	1992–	1992–	1992–
Montenegro	2006–	2006–	2006–	2006–	
Mozambique	1994–	1994–	1991–2 1994–	1994–2008	
Namibia	1990–	1990–	1990–	1990–	
Niger	1993–5 1999–	1993–5 2004–	1993–5 1999–	1993–5 1999–2008	1993–5 2000–
Peru	1980–91 1993–	1980–91 2001–	1980–91 1993–	1989–91 2001–	1980–9 2001–
Poland	1990–	1991–	1990–	1990–	1990–
Portugal	1976–	1976–	1976–	1989–	1976–
Romania	1991–	1996–	1991–	1992–	1991–
Russia	1993–	2000–6	1993–2003	1993–2003	
São Tomé			1990–	1991–	1991–
Senegal	2000–	2000–	1975–83 1991–	2000–	2000–
Serbia	2006–	2006–	2006–	2006–	2006–
Slovakia	1999–	1999–	1999–	1999–	1999–
Slovenia	1992–	1992–	1992–	1992–	1992–
S. Vietnam			1972–4		
Sri Lanka	1978–	1978–81 2001–2 2006–	1978–	1989–	1989–
Taiwan	1997–	1997–	1997–	1997–	1997–
Tanzania			1995–		
Togo			1999–2001 2007–		
Tunisia			1988–91		
Turkey	2007–	2007–	2007–	2007–	2007–
Ukraine	1991–	1991–2 1994–	1996–	1996–	1991–
Yemen			2003–8		
Total	53	43	66	46	43

were highly positive and strongly significant across all of the data sets, then there would be little point in focusing on more than one of them. However, given the significant correlations are only ever positive at a relatively modest level and that sometimes the data sets are, in effect, uncorrelated, particularly regarding semi-presidential collapses, then the strategy of testing the same model on different data sets as a way of determining the robustness of the results is justified.

TABLE 3.2 *Collapses of democracy (year) in countries with semi-presidential constitutions (various indicators and data set coverage in years)*

Country	Polity ≥+1 (1919–2008)	Polity ≥+6 (1919–2008)	FH F & PF (1972–2009)	FH ED (1989–2009)	ACLP/DD (1946–2008)
Algeria			1992		
Armenia	1996	1995		2003	
Austria	1933	1933			
Azerbaijan			1993 2003		
Burkina Faso	1980		1981		
Burundi					1996
Central African Republic	2003		2003	2001 2008	2003
Comoros	1995 1999		1985		1995
Congo-Brazzaville	1997		1997	1997	1997
Cuba	1952				1952
Finland		1931			
Gabon			2009		
Georgia				2008	
Germany	1933	1933			
Guinea-Bissau	1998 2003			2003	2003
Haiti	2000	1999	2000	2000	
Kazakhstan			1994		
Kyrgyzstan			2000–9	2000	
Madagascar				2009	
Mauritania	2008		2003 2008	2008	2008
Mozambique			1993	2009	
Niger	1996	1996	1996	1996 2009	1996
Peru	1992	1992	1992	1992	1990
Russia		2007	2004	2004	
S. Vietnam			1975		
Sri Lanka		1982 2003			
Togo			2002		
Tunisia			1992		
Ukraine		1993			
Yemen			2009		
Total	15	11	22	15	9

TABLE 3.3 *Correlation between the coverage of the five indicators of democracy (countries and discrete democratic episodes in those countries as the units of observation)*

	Polity ≥+1	Polity ≥+6	FH F & PF	FH ED	ACLP/DD
Polity ≥+1	1.0000				
Polity ≥+6	0.5574*	1.0000			
FH F & PF	–0.0504	0.0346	1.0000		
FH ED	0.5094*	0.5211*	0.4026*	1.0000	
ACLP/DD	0.5574*	0.4469*	0.1666	0.5211*	1.0000

Note: $N = 80$ country episodes of democracy.

*Significant at $p < 0.01$.

TABLE 3.4 *Correlation between the collapses of democracy on the basis of the five indicators of democracy (countries and discrete episodes of democratic collapse as the units of observation)*

	Polity ≥+1	Polity ≥+6	FH F & PF	FH ED	ACLP/DD
Polity ≥+1	1.0000				
Polity ≥+6	0.2258	1.0000			
FH F & PF	–0.1065	–0.2100	1.0000		
FH ED	0.1590	–0.0028	–0.0050	1.0000	
ACLP/DD	0.5759*	–0.0551	0.0202	0.2089	1.0000

Note: $N = 41$ separate cases of democratic collapse across the five data sets.

*Significant at $p < 0.01$.

THE COLLAPSE OF PREMIER-PRESIDENTIAL AND PRESIDENT-PARLIAMENTARY DEMOCRACIES – BASIC EMPIRICAL EVIDENCE

In Chapter 2, the complete set of countries with semi-presidential constitutions was identified and within this set of countries those with a president-parliamentary form of semi-presidentialism were distinguished from those with a premier-presidential form. It was hypothesized that democracy in president-parliamentary countries was likely to perform less well than in premier-presidential countries. In this chapter, various sets of semi-presidential democracies and democratic collapses have been identified on the basis of different indicators of democracy. What is the evidence that president-parliamentary democracies have been more likely to collapse than premier-presidential democracies?

The cross-tabulations in Table 3.5 provide the most basic indication that democracies with a president-parliamentary form of semi-presidentialism run a greater risk of collapse than their premier-presidential counterparts. Here, for each of the five indicators of democracy, the unit of observation is a semi-presidential country that has experienced an episode of democracy, however long that episode may have lasted. For example, using the FH ED indicator, there is one unit of observation for Austria, because, as indicated in Table 3.1, it has been classed as an Electoral Democracy since 1989. There is also one unit of observation for Congo-Brazzaville, because it was classed as an Electoral Democracy from 1992 to 1996 only for it to lose that status in 1997 when democracy collapsed. However, there are two units of observation for Peru because it was classed as an Electoral Democracy from 1989 to 1991 and then again from 2001 onwards. Calculated this way, there have been forty-six episodes of semi-presidential democracy since 1989 using the FH ED indicator, nineteen (41.3 per cent) of which have occurred in countries with a president-parliamentary form of semi-presidentialism and twenty-seven (58.7 per cent) in countries with a premier-presidential form.[7] So, using this indicator there was a relatively even distribution of the two forms of semi-presidentialism across the set of observations as a whole. Of the forty-six democratic episodes, fifteen (32.6 per cent) resulted in a collapse of Electoral Democracy. Of those fifteen collapses, eleven (73.3 per cent) occurred in countries with a president-parliamentary form of semi-presidentialism and only four (26.7 per cent) in countries with a premier-presidential form. To put it in the language of the way the figures are reported in Table 3.5, eleven of nineteen (57.9 per cent) cases of president-parliamentarism collapsed, whereas only four of twenty-seven (14.8 per cent) cases of premier-presidentialism collapsed. Across the five indicators of democracy, the descriptive statistics are very clear. President-parliamentary democracies are always much more likely to collapse than premier-presidential democracies. Thus, without controlling for any other potential explanatory variables, the descriptive statistics show that president-parliamentarism is considerably more dangerous for democracy than premier-presidentialism.

While these results are reassuring, as John Carey (2000: 751) puts it, '[a] persistent challenge confronting comparative institutional research is the issue of endogeneity'. This research assumes that institutions affect the behaviour of political actors. However, institutions are themselves the creation of political actors. Therefore, they reflect the preferences of those actors. If so, then institutions cannot explain political behaviour. They are themselves explained by such behaviour. The argument in this book suffers from a potential endogeneity problem. It is posited that president-parliamentary institutions are likely to induce certain types of behaviour in political actors and that such behaviour is liable to be detrimental to democratic performance. However, what if those actors already exhibited behaviour that was liable to be detrimental to democracy and the choice of president-parliamentarism merely reflected it? If this were the case, then even if there was a strong association between president-parliamentarism and, in this chapter, the collapse of semi-presidential democracies, it would be wrong to conclude that president-parliamentarism caused the collapse.

TABLE 3.5 *Cross-tabulations of semi-presidential subtype and democratic collapses/survivals*

	President-parliamentary	Premier-presidential	Total
Polity ≥+1			
Collapses	12 (48.0)	3 (10.7)	15 (28.3)
Survivals	13 (52.0)	25 (89.3)	38 (71.7)
Total	25 (100.0)	28 (100.0)	53 (100.0)
Polity ≥+6			
Collapses	8 (42.1)	3 (12.5)	11 (25.6)
Survivals	11 (57.9)	21 (87.5)	32 (74.4)
Total	19 (100.0)	24 (100.0)	43 (100.0)
FH F & PF			
Collapses	17 (50.0)	5 (15.6)	22 (33.3)
Survivals	17 (50.0)	27 (84.4)	44 (66.7)
Total	34 (100.0)	32 (100.0)	66 (100.0)
FH ED			
Collapses	11 (57.9)	4 (14.8)	15 (32.6)
Survivals	8 (42.1)	23 (85.2)	31 (67.4)
Total	19 (100.0)	27 (100.0)	46 (100.0)
ACLP/DD			
Collapses	7 (38.9)	2 (8.0)	9 (20.9)
Survivals	11 (61.1)	23 (92.0)	34 (79.1)
Total	18 (100.0)	25 (100.0)	43 (100.0)

Note: For all tables, the frequencies are presented with the percentages in parentheses.

As Carey (2000: 754) notes, the existence of a potential endogeneity problem has to be conceded. Given institutions are not actors, they are, by definition, the product of actor preferences. However, this does not mean that the effect of institutions cannot be studied. It simply means that the endogeneity problem needs to be confronted. In this book, the endogeneity problem is addressed mainly by way of the in-depth case studies in the chapters that follow. In these chapters, the founding circumstances of the particular type of semi-presidentialism under consideration are always outlined. This allows the endogeneity issue to be placed in its appropriate context and the impact of initial actor preferences to be assessed. At this point, though, a basic test for the potential impact of endogenous institutional selection is conducted. If the impact of president-parliamentarism fails to pass a basic endogeneity test, then it can safely be assumed that the choice of president-parliamentarism is purely endogenous and that this particular institutional structure has no independent impact on the survival of semi-presidential democracies. However, if the basic test is passed, then it is reasonable to move on to a more sophisticated test of the impact of the various types of semi-presidentialism.

When testing for the impact of a given institutional structure, there is no standard way of controlling for the endogeneity problem. Moreover, it is usually very difficult to capture the endogeneity problem directly. Instead, a plausible proxy is required. Here, the proxy relates to the percentage of votes cast for the winning candidate at the presidential election prior to the choice of the particular type of semi-presidentialism, or at the first presidential election immediately thereafter if there was no prior contest. The logic behind the choice of this proxy is that in a nascent democracy, there is likely to be a great deal of political competition. Therefore, if the winning candidate is able to secure a very large percentage of the vote at what might be considered the 'founding' election, then that candidate may be in a position to choose a set of institutions that consolidate their hold over the political process. In the context of this book, they may be in a position to choose a president-parliamentary form of semi-presidentialism. In this event, the choice of president-parliamentarism may reflect an existing desire for autocratic rule. If so, this type of semi-presidentialism would not have an independent effect on any subsequent collapse of democracy.

Table 3.6 reports the results of a logistic regression with heteroskedasticity-robust standard errors. The unit of observation is an episode of democracy in a country with a semi-presidential constitution. The dependent variable is a binary variable coded '1' when democracy has survived and '0' when democracy has collapsed. The explanatory variable is the subtype of semi-presidentialism in each episode of democracy. This is a binary variable coded '1' for premier-presidentialism and '0' for president-parliamentarism. The control variable is a proxy variable for the endogenous selection of institutions. This is the score won by the winning candidate at the first ballot (if there was more than one ballot) of the presidential election immediately prior to the selection of the semi-presidential subtype.[8] This is a continuous variable bounded at 100. If no such election was held prior to the choice of semi-presidentialism, then the score at the first presidential election after the selection of semi-presidentialism is recorded if the election was held in the period soon after the choice of institutional subtype.[9] Clearly, Table 3.6 indicates that the negative impact of president-parliamentarism relative to premier-presidentialism is still strong. In all five models, the relationship between president-parliamentarism and the collapse of semi-presidential democracies is still significant at conventional levels. Indeed, two models are significant at the 1 per cent level and three at the 5 per cent level. These models cover a range of different ways of identifying democracy, including dichotomous vs. graded indicators, different constitutive criteria, and different boundaries using the same criteria. Therefore, while the issue of the endogenous selection of president-parliamentarism does need to be addressed, the results show that president-parliamentarism does seem to exert a negative effect on democratic survival even when controlling for the endogeneity problem.

Overall, these results suggest three preliminary conclusions. The first is that the impact of the particular subtype of semi-presidentialism on the survival or collapse of democracy is not deterministic. Democracies that have chosen a premier-presidential form of semi-presidentialism have collapsed and they have done so on the basis of whatever way the concept of democracy is operationalized.

Examples include Congo-Brazzaville in 1997, Niger in 1996, and Haiti in 1999 or 2000 depending on the indicator used. Equally, democracies that have chosen a president-parliamentary form of semi-presidentialism have survived. They include Taiwan, which has been classed as a democracy since 1996 by all five indicators, and Namibia, which has been classed as a democracy since 1990 by four of the five indicators. This conclusion implies that in addition to the subtype of semi-presidentialism, attention needs to be paid to other factors that affect the collapse and survival of democracies, such as the ones that were identified in Chapter 1. The second conclusion is that, taken solely in isolation from any other potentially important explanatory factors, countries with a president-parliamentary form of semi-presidentialism are much more likely to collapse than those with a premier-presidential form. Again, this conclusion applies to whatever indicator of democracy is used. Thus, there is basic empirical evidence to support the hypothesis that is central to this book. The third conclusion is that the impact of the endogenous selection of semi-presidential institutions does need to be systematically addressed. This issue will be confronted in the in-depth country studies that are included in subsequent chapters. In the rest of this chapter, though, a more sophisticated statistical test is undertaken in which the impact of president-parliamentarism on the survival of democracy is identified controlling for other potentially important explanatory factors.

TABLE 3.6 *Results of logistic regressions of democratic survival by form of semi-presidentialism controlling for endogenous institutions*

	Outcome is survival of semi-presidential democracy				
	Polity ≥+1	Polity ≥+6	FH F & PF	FH ED	ACLP/DD
Odds ratio					
Prem-pres	8.9	5.2	4.6	10.7	8.5
Pres election	1.0	1.0	1.0	1.0	1.1
Confidence interval (95%)					
Prem-pres	(2.1, 38.1)	(1.1, 24.7)	(1.4, 15.0)	(2.4, 48.6)	(1.3, 55.2)
Pres election	(1.0, 1.1)	(1.0, 1.0)	(1.0, 1.0)	(1.0, 1.1)	(1.0, 1.1)
Robust standard error					
Prem-pres	6.6***	4.1**	2.8**	8.3***	8.1**
Pres election	0.0**	0.0	0.0	0.0*	0.0***
R^2	24.8	10.2	9.3	22.8	35.8
N	51	41	63	44	41

Note: *significant at $p < 0.1$, **significant at $p < 0.05$, ***significant at $p < 0.01$.

Legend: Prem-pres = premier-presidentialism; Pres election = first-round score for winning candidate at the presidential election.

THE COLLAPSE OF PREMIER-PRESIDENTIAL AND PRESIDENT-PARLIAMENTARY DEMOCRACIES – A SURVIVAL MODEL

The evidence in this section relies wholly on a baseline model that was developed by Petra Schleiter (Elgie and Schleiter, 2011). This model is founded on what is known as survival, duration, or event-history analysis. This type of analysis identifies a hazard function, namely the likelihood that a given event will occur after a particular period of time. In the context of this book, the survival model is primarily designed to estimate how long president-parliamentary democracies are likely to survive relative to premier-presidential democracies. Specifically, the evidence in this section relies on a Cox proportional hazards model, which is based on a semi-parametric method. This means that the model makes no assumptions about how the hazard function is dependent upon time itself as a factor (or covariate), but assumptions are made about how other covariates, such as the economy and ethnic fragmentation, affect the hazard function. Thus, the model allows an estimation of the likely duration of president-parliamentary democracies relative to premier-presidential democracies, while controlling for all other factors and without making the assumption, for example, that democracies are more or less likely to collapse as time advances. Survival analysis has become standard for addressing certain issues in political science and international relations and has been applied to determine the effect of various factors, including regime types, on democratic survival (e.g. Bernhard et al., 2004).

The unit of observation is an episode of semi-presidential democracy in a given country. Thus, a country enters a data set in the year when it has both a semi-presidential constitution and when it is classed as a democracy on the basis of a given indicator. A country exits the data set in the year when it is deemed to have collapsed on the basis of that indicator. Thus, there can be multiple entries for a given country if democracy collapses and is then restored at a later date. The baseline model will be tested on three of the five indicators of democracy identified earlier in this chapter: Polity $\geq$+1, which was the indicator used in the original model (Elgie and Schleiter, 2011), Polity $\geq$+6, and FH ED. For each of the three indicators, there are fifty-two, forty-two, and forty-six episodes of democracy respectively. The frequency of observation is annual. This generates 740, 590, and 532 country years for the Polity $\geq$+1, Polity $\geq$+6, and FH ED data sets respectively. The logic behind the choice of these three indicators is similar to the one identified earlier in the chapter. The FH ED indicator is based on a dichotomous classification of countries as either democracies or non-democracies. Therefore, it is tailored to the purposes of this exercise. Moreover, the FH ED indicator is restricted to the post-1989 period. Therefore, it helps to keep constant various exogenous international historical factors. The Polity indicators are based on a graded classification of countries using different constitutive criteria.

Therefore, they provide a test based on an alternative conceptualization of democracy. Moreover, the use of two Polity indicators allows a test based on the same constitutive criteria but using a different boundary point. Again, therefore, given the identification of democracies vs. non-democracies is essentially contestable, using these three indicators provides a rounded set of tests to determine the impact of premier-presidentialism vs. president-parliamentarism.

For all three indicators, the dependent variable is both whether or not democracy survives in a given country and the duration of the democratic episode in that country. Thus, the model is not simply estimating whether, all else equal, premier-presidential democracies are more or less likely to collapse than president-parliamentary democracies. It is estimating, all else equal, how much longer democracy is likely to last in premier-presidential countries relative to president-parliamentary countries. Thus, the strongest possible results would be generated by a data set where the democratic episode successfully continued through to the end of the time period in all of the premier-presidential countries in the data set, but where it collapsed the year after it was first recorded in all of the president-parliamentary countries. Given democracy continues to endure in many countries at the point when a data set ends, these countries are deemed to be 'right-censored' in the language of survival analysis. The Cox model takes account of right-censored cases. As per Table 3.2, for the Polity ≥+1, Polity ≥+6, and FH ED indicators, there are fifteen, eleven, and fifteen democratic collapses respectively.[10]

The main explanatory variable in the baseline model is the subtype of semi-presidentialism. President-parliamentary democracies are expected to survive less long than premier-presidential democracies. The subtype of semi-presidentialism is coded as a binary variable with president-parliamentarism coded '1' and premier-presidentialism coded '0'. The classification of countries as premier-presidential or president-parliamentary was provided in Table 2.3. The percentage of premier-presidential observations in the Polity ≥+1, Polity ≥+6, and FH ED data sets is 59.1, 64.9, and 59.4 per cent respectively.

While the main aim of this chapter is to estimate the relative impact of the two forms of semi-presidentialism on democratic survival, in Chapter 1 a number of other criticisms of semi-presidentialism were also outlined. If the only test of the arguments against semi-presidentialism is related to the subtype of this form of government, then even if a positive result were to be found for this variable, it is possible that the result would simply be masking the effect of other supposedly problematic situations that are often associated with semi-presidentialism. If so, then the seemingly positive result for this variable would be spurious. Therefore, a range of potentially problematic aspects of semi-presidentialism will be tested too.

In Chapter 1, it was shown that semi-presidentialism has been associated with the problem of the dual executive. Therefore, the model includes a dummy variable for a divided executive. This is defined as the situation where the president is from one party and the prime minister is from another party, but where the president's party is represented in government, that is, where there is a coalition government and the president's party is represented in the coalition but does not hold the premiership. If the existing literature is correct, then semi-presidential democracies that experience a divided executive should not survive as long as those with a unified executive, that is, when the president and prime minister are from the same party. If a country experienced a divided executive for six months or more during any given year, then a value of '1' was recorded. If there was a unified executive, then a value of '0' was recorded.

Semi-presidentialism has also been associated with the problem of dual legitimacy. There were two manifestations of this problem: cohabitation and divided minority government. To address the first, the model includes a binary variable for cohabitation. In contrast to a divided executive, cohabitation is defined as the situation where the president is from one party and the prime minister is from another party, but where the president's party is absent from government. In other words, the president is isolated within the executive. According to this literature, semi-presidential democracies are likely to survive less long if they experience cohabitation. Again, if a country experienced a period of cohabitation for six months or more during any given year, then a value of '1' was recorded. If not, then a value of '0' was recorded. To address the problem of divided minority government, the model includes a dummy variable for this situation. The concept of divided minority government is associated with the work of Cindy Skach (2005). According to her logic, semi-presidential democracies are likely to survive less long if they experience a minority government situation. A potential problem, though, is that Skach does not make it very clear whether the term refers to the situation where the government parties simply fail to enjoy majority support in the legislature or whether it is the combination of cohabitation as defined here and minority government. Here, a binary variable is reported that records whether or not there is a minority government (coded '1' if so and '0' if not).

To identify periods of divided executive and cohabitation in semi-presidential democracies, the main source is 'worldstatesmen.org'. This website lists the names of all presidents and prime ministers and provides their party affiliation. Cross-checking the information with country-specific literature, the website seems to be extremely reliable.[11] It should be noted that if a country has either a non-partisan president or a non-partisan prime minister, then a period of divided executive or cohabitation cannot be generated. These situations are assumed to be problematic because of the partisan competition that they encourage and so non-partisan leaders are discounted and recorded as a '0'. The episodes of divided executive and cohabitation in semi-presidential democracies are recorded in Table 3.7. To identify periods of divided minority government, the World Bank's Database of Political Institutions (DPI) is used.[12] The MAJ variable in the DPI records the fraction of seats held by the government. If the figure is 50 per cent or lower, then a value of '1' is recorded for divided minority government, otherwise a '0' is recorded.

The final problem with which semi-presidentialism has been associated is the problem of hyperpresidentialism. In effect, this argument suggests that semi-presidential democracies with powerful presidents are likely to survive less long than those with weaker presidents. As a proxy for this problem, a continuous variable is used. Specifically, Siaroff's index (2003) of presidential power is used. This index is based on nine indicators of presidential power, including whether the president chairs cabinet meetings, whether the president can veto legislation passed by parliament, whether the president can invoke emergency powers, and so on. Siaroff then examines the actual power of presidents in a large set of countries, and records a score of '1' if the president in that country enjoys the particular power in question and '0' otherwise. Thus, countries emerge with a presidential power score somewhere in a range from 0 to 9. That said, given one of his indicators is whether or not the president is directly elected, in the data set used here the range is from 1 to 9. In his article, Siaroff provides scores for most countries with semi-presidential constitutions. If a country is missing, then Siaroff's method is replicated and the resulting score is included in the data set.

In the previous section, it was demonstrated that the link between semi-presidential subtype and democratic survival or collapse was not deterministic. In Chapter 1, a number of standard variables associated with the survival and collapse of democracies were identified. To determine the effect of the subtype of semi-presidentialism, it is important to control for the impact of these variables. The most important factor associated with the survival or collapse of democracy is the economy. To capture the effect of this factor, two controls for the economy are included in the baseline model. They are, firstly, the level of GDP per capita and, secondly, the level of economic growth. The literature suggests that countries with low levels of GDP per capita are likely to survive less long than those with higher levels, though after a certain point higher levels of income are, in practice, unlikely to make a country any more stable. Therefore, a variable recording the log of GDP per capita is included in the model. Equally, the literature suggests that countries with low growth rates are likely to survive less long than those with positive growth. So, the annual level of growth is also included in the model. The primary source for these data is the Angus Maddison Statistics on World Population, GDP and Per Capita GDP, 1–2008 AD data set.[13] Here, the GDP per capita figures are measured in 1990 International Geary-Khamis dollars. For the FH ED data set, the source for economic data is the ERS International Macroeconomic Data Set, which provides annual figures for Real 2005 GDP Per Capita in US dollars.[14]

Another variable that is often associated with the survival and collapse of democracies is the level of social fragmentation in a country. This work has generated conflicting conclusions about the relationship between fragmentation and democratic performance. For some, the likelihood of collapse is a simple function of the level of fragmentation: the greater the level of fragmentation, the sooner a country is likely to collapse. For others, countries that are divided into a small number of competing groups are likely to collapse sooner than either more

TABLE 3.7 *Periods of divided executive and cohabitation lasting more than two months in semi-presidential democracies (various indicators of democracy and various time periods to end 2009)*

Country	Divided executive	Cohabitation
Austria	Sep 1929–Sep 1930	
	April 1945–Dec 1950	
	June 1951–Jan 1957	
	May 1957–Feb 1965	
	June 1965–April 1966	April 1966–April 1970
	Jan 1987–Feb 2000	July 2004–Jan 2007
Bulgaria		Jan 1995–Jan 1997
		July 2001–Aug 2005
		July 2009–
Burundi	July 1993–July 1996	
Central African Republic	Dec 1992–Oct 1993	
	June 1996–Jan 1997	
Comoros	Jan 1993–June 1993	
Congo-Brazzaville	June 1993–Oct 1997	
Congo-Kinshasa	Dec 2006–	
Cuba	Oct 1951–March 1952	
Finland	March 1920–April 1921	
	Nov 1922–Jan 1924	
	May 1924–Dec 1925	Dec 1926–Dec 1927
	July 1930–Dec 1940	Dec 1928–Aug 1929
	March 1943–Aug 1944	March 1946–Nov 1953
	Nov 1953–May 1954	May 1954–Feb 1956
	Feb 1956–May 1957	
	Aug 1958–Jan 1959	
	May 1966–May 1970	Feb 1972–Sep 1972
	Sep 1972–June 1975	
	May 1977–Jan 1982	
	April 1987–April 1991	April 1991–April 1995
	April 2003–April 2007	April 2007–
France	May 1974–Aug 1976	March 1986–May 1988
		March 1993–May 1995
		June 1997–May 2002
Georgia	Feb 2004–Nov 2007	
Germany		June 1920–May 1921
	May 1921–Nov 1922	
	Aug 1923–Nov 1923	
		Nov 1923–May 1925
Iceland		Aug 1952–July 1956
	July 1956–Dec 1958	
	Nov 1959–Aug 1968	
		Aug 1996–May 2007
	May 2007–Feb 2009	
Ireland		Feb 1948–June 1951
		June 1954–March 1957
		Mar 1973–July 1977

Continued

TABLE 3.7 Contined

Country	Divided executive	Cohabitation
		June 1981–March 1982
		Dec 1982–March 1987
		Dec 1990–Jan 1993
	Jan 1993–June 1997	June 1997–Sep 1997
Kyrgyzstan	Aug 2005–April 2006	
	March 2007–Nov 2007	
Lithuania		Nov 1996–Feb 1998
		Feb 2003–April 2004
Macedonia		Nov 2002–May 2004
		Aug 2006–April 2009
Madagascar	Aug 1991–Oct 1995	
	May 1996–Sep 1996	
Mongolia		June 1993–July 1996
		June 1997–July 2000
	Aug 2004–Jan 2006	
	June 2009–	
Niger	April 1993–Sep 1994	Feb 1995–Jan 1996
Peru	July 2000–Nov 2000	
	Oct 2008–July 2009	
	Jan 1991–Dec 1991	
		Dec 1991–Dec 1995
Poland		Oct 1997–Oct 2001
		Nov 2007–
Portugal		March 1986–Oct 1995
		April 2002–March 2005
		March 2006–
Romania	Dec 2004–April 2007	April 2007–Dec 2008
São Tomé and Príncipe		July 1996–Sep 2001
		March 2004–June 2005
	June 2005–April 2006	
	June 2008–Dec 2009	
Senegal	April 2000–March 2001	
Serbia	May 2007–July 2008	Nov 2006–May 2007
Slovakia	June 1999–June 2004	
Slovenia	Dec 2004–Jan 2006	
Sri Lanka		Aug 1994–Nov 1994
		Dec 2001–April 2004
Taiwan	May 2000–Oct 2000	
Togo	Sep 2006–Dec 2007	
Ukraine	Jan 2005–Sep 2005	
	Aug 2006–	

Note: For more information about particular cases, go to www.semipresidentialism.com

homogenous or very fractionalized countries. To control for this factor, the model includes two variables. The first simply records the level of ethnic fragmentation as measured by Alesina et al. (2003). This measure is used to test the argument that democracies with higher levels of fragmentation are likely to collapse sooner than those with lower levels. This is a continuous measure but it is stationary for any given country. The second variable assumes that fragmentation expresses itself through party competition. To capture different levels of fragmentation in this way, the effective number of parliamentary parties (ENPP) is calculated. The source for these calculations is Michael Gallagher's data set with additional calculations where a country is not recorded.[15] This measure is used to test the argument that countries with particular forms of fragmentation are likely to collapse sooner than others. To this end, the figures are divided into quartiles: low fragmentation (ENPP to 2.46), moderate fragmentation (2.47–3.06), high fragmentation (3.07–4.37), and extreme fragmentation (≥4.38). Using low fragmentation as the base category, three binary variables are generated for each of the three remaining measures. It is assumed that countries with high levels of fragmentation are likely to collapse sooner than countries with extreme levels of fragmentation.

The final set of control variables captures a range of historical and contextual factors. In Chapter 1, it was noted that colonization is often considered to have an impact on subsequent political performance. For some writers, former colonies are less likely to democratize successfully than countries that were never colonized. Therefore, the model includes a dummy variable capturing whether or not a country has experienced colonization at any point after 1918. It assumed that democracy in former colonies (recorded as 1) is likely to last less long than in countries that were never colonized. Another historical factor concerns whether or not a country has a democratic history when it begins to democratize. According to this line of argument, democracy is both difficult to impose and takes time to learn. Therefore, countries that have an existing democratic tradition are likely to survive for a longer period of time than those without any such tradition. To capture this potential effect, both Polity models include a variable that records the number of previous Polity ≥+1 and Polity ≥+6 years of democracy respectively that a country experienced prior to the beginning of the period recorded in the data set. Given the FH ED indicator only records Electoral Democracies from 1989 and given there is no way of knowing whether Freedom House would have recorded an Electoral Democracy prior to this time in any of the countries in the data set, this variable is omitted from the FH ED model. In addition, recent literature has stressed the importance of democratic diffusion in particular regions or a democratic domino effect. In other words, countries that democratize in regions with an already high percentage of democracies are likely to survive for longer than those that democratize in regions without any democratic tradition. Therefore, the model records the percentage of democracies in any given year in different regions of the world (Western Europe, Central and Eastern Europe, sub-Saharan Africa, and so on). Finally, given democracy has generally performed less well in Africa than elsewhere, the model includes a dummy variable for sub-Saharan African countries. This variable is coded '1' if a country is located in sub-Saharan Africa and '0' otherwise. It is assumed that democracy will be more likely to collapse in countries in this region than in those elsewhere.

Table 3.8 presents the results of the baseline model applied to the three indicators of democracy (Polity ≥+1, Polity ≥+6, and FH ED). For each model, the table reports the hazard ratio, which in the case of a binary variable is the ratio of the hazard rate for one coding of the covariate (1) to the hazard rate for the other coding (0). If the hazard ratio for a covariate is greater than 1, then it indicates that the greater the covariate, the greater the hazard. Conversely, if the hazard ratio for a covariate is less than 1, then it indicates that the greater the covariate, the less the hazard. For the purposes of this model, the hazard is the length of time that a democracy is likely to survive. So, for a dummy variable a hazard ratio greater than 1 suggests that democracy in countries where a particular covariate is coded 1 is likely to survive less long than in countries where the covariate is coded 0. By the same token, a hazard rate less than 1 implies that a covariate is associated with democratic episodes that last for a longer period of time.

The results are both very clear and remarkably consistent across the three models. They show that, all else equal, president-parliamentarism increases the likely failure rate of democracy relative to premier-presidentialism. For example, the results of the FH ED model suggest that at any given time, countries with a president-parliamentary form of semi-presidentialism are more than ten times more likely to collapse than premier-presidential countries. In addition, the results for the Polity ≥+1 and Polity ≥+6 models are very similar to the results for the FH ED model. This finding is reassuring, given that the various indicators of democracy are constituted in very different ways and cover very different periods. In all three models, the findings are significant at the 1 per cent level. It should be noted, though, that, using Schoenfeld residuals, the Polity ≥+1 model violates the proportional hazards assumption. This result weakens the validity of the findings for this model. Generally, though, these results provide good empirical support for the central hypothesis of this book. Moreover, they also provide little support for any of the other hypothesized problems of semi-presidentialism. There is absolutely no evidence that the presence of either a divided executive or cohabitation is likely to decrease the survival chances of a semi-presidential democracy. In other words, even though much ink has been spilt about the dangers of cohabitation for semi-presidential democracies, there is no statistical evidence to support such an argument. Furthermore, there is no support for the divided minority government hypothesis. In the Polity ≥+6 model, the presence of a minority government is statistically significant, but the result is in the opposite direction to one that was hypothesized. Minority government is associated with a higher survival rate. The only other semi-presidential variable that is associated with the collapse of democracy at conventional levels of significance is the presidential power variable in the Polity ≥+6 model. Here, there is evidence that countries with more powerful

TABLE 3.8 *Baseline model: type of semi-presidentialism and the survival of democracy (various indicators of democracy)*

	Polity ≥+1	Polity ≥+6	FH ED
President-parliamentarism	8.76***	11.74***	10.25***
	(3.09)	(2.88)	(3.69)
Divided executive	2.06	4.35	1.00
	(0.56)	(1.37)	(–0.01)
Cohabitation	2.29	7.36	0.84
	(0.62)	(1.38)	(–0.12)
Minority government	3.32	0.16*	0.66
	(1.17)	(–1.93)	(–0.33)
Presidential power	1.11	3.97**	1.16
	(0.27)	(2.39)	(0.55)
Log GDP per capita	0.31**	0.11**	0.33**
	(–2.24)	(–1.99)	(–2.34)
Growth GDP per capita	0.96**	0.97	1.03
	(–2.47)	(–0.81)	(0.68)
Ethnic fragmentation	0.04***	0.00	0.43
	(–2.89)	(–1.27)	(–0.34)
ENPP (low)	1.94	19.03**	0.45
	(0.88)	(2.02)	(–0.70)
ENPP (medium)	8.11**	15.12*	9.06**
	(2.17)	(1.88)	(2.51)
ENPP (high)	0.43	5.24	2.04
	(–0.87)	(1.12)	(0.73)
Former colony	4.41	0.46	2.61
	(1.28)	(–0.72)	(0.77)
Proportion of democracies in region	0.97	0.98	1.00
	(–0.87)	(–0.96)	(–0.24)
Previous years of democracy	1.0	0.99	N/A
	(–0.10)	(–0.51)	
Africa	7.54*	0.04**	0.51
	(1.84)	(–2.01)	(–0.57)
Log (partial) likelihood	–33.96	–22.72	–38.28
Linktest hat(2)	0.01	–0.28	–0.10
	$p = (0.912)$	$p = (0.181)$	$p = (0.529)$
Test of proportional hazards assumption – Global Test chi(2)	28.61 (15df) $p = (0.0180)$	10.47 (15df) $p = (0.7890)$	7.55 (14df) $p = (0.9116)$
No. of subjects	52	42	46
No. of failures	15	11	15
No. of observations	740	590	532

Note: *significant at $p < 0.1$, **significant at $p < 0.05$, ***significant at $p < 0.01$ based on country-clustered standard errors.

presidents are likely to survive less long than those with weaker presidents. This result is significant at the 5 per cent level.

Over and above the findings for semi-presidentialism, the results also confirm the importance of two of the more general factors associated with the survival and collapse of democracies. They show that countries with higher levels of GDP per capita are likely to survive for a longer period of time than those with lower levels. This variable is significant at the 5 per cent level in all three models. This result is highly reassuring. Indeed, such is the strength of the argument that there is a link between economic development and democratic collapse that if a result of this sort had not been obtained, then the whole model could have been called into question. In addition, the results also provide some evidence for the impact of social fragmentation. All three models show that democracy is likely to last less long in countries with a high but not extreme degree of party fragmentation. This finding is consistent with one interpretation of the established wisdom about social fragmentation and democratic performance, namely that democracy is more fragile in countries where political competition takes places between a relatively small number of opposing groups rather than in the context of just two competing groups or a multitude of them. There are two slightly puzzling results. In the Polity ≥+1 model, high levels of ethnic fragmentation were found to have a positive effect on democratic survival. This result runs counter to the standard wisdom. In addition, while in the Polity ≥+1 model countries in sub-Saharan Africa were shown to be associated with a higher risk of collapse, in the Polity ≥+6 model they were associated with a lower risk. This is because in the latter only one semi-presidential democracy in sub-Saharan Africa collapsed (Niger 1996), yet in a number of countries it survived. By contrast, in the former, nine sub-Saharan democracies collapsed. This suggests that democracy can endure in sub-Saharan African democracies, but that it is rarely able to do so in weakly consolidated countries. Overall, the results are intuitive, increasing the degree of confidence in the finding about president-parliamentarism.

To maximize the robustness of the results, a number of other tests were carried out, though the results are not reported. For example, few writers provide a specific definition of cohabitation.[16] For example, Kirschke's argument (2007) about the problem of cohabitation in sub-Saharan Africa includes examples both of cohabitation, as defined above, and of what, here, has been termed a 'divided executive'. Therefore, to make sure that this aspect of the problem of dual legitimacy was being properly captured, a binary variable was introduced that recorded periods when there was either divided executive or cohabitation as defined in this book. Similarly, given the slight confusion about Skach's concept of divided minority government, another binary variable was included that captured the interaction of cohabitation and minority government. The introduction of these variables did not affect the substantive results. In addition, 'worldstatesmen.org' records various presidents as non-partisan. However, sometimes would-be leaders hide behind the non-partisan label as a vehicle for their populist policies. Therefore, a binary variable was included that recorded whether or not a president was non-partisan. Again, the baseline results were not challenged. Similarly, the result for the effect of semi-presidential subtype was robust to the substitution of the several party fragmentation variables by a single variable reporting the effective number of political parties. Equally, when the presidential power variable based on full Siaroff (2003) scores was replaced by a variable based on only the president's legislative powers as recorded by Siaroff, the results were also substantively unaffected. Also, to ensure that the results were not sensitive to the inclusion of individual countries, the models were re-estimated excluding countries on a case-by-case basis. Once more, the results did not challenge the central findings presented in Table 3.8. The FH ED model was also re-estimated excluding all those countries, such as Austria, France, and Portugal, that were already electoral democracies prior to the beginning of the observations in this data set. Thus, the model is robust to the inclusion of only those countries that began to be classed as democratic after 1989. Finally, the VIF test showed that there is no problem of colinearity among the variables.

Having presented a set of baseline models, Table 3.9 presents the results of a reduced model for each indicator of democracy. In these models the variables that did not reach statistical significance in the full model are excluded. Again, the results are reassuring. Across all three indicators of democracy, the results confirm that democracies with a president-parliamentary form of semi-presidentialism are likely to survive considerably less long than their premier-presidential counterparts and that democracies with lower levels of GDP per capita are also very vulnerable to collapse. In addition, the negative effect of a high degree of party competition remains present in all three models. In the Polity $\geq$+6 model the variable for minority government loses significance, though the negative effect of the presidential power variable remains significant. Overall, the subtype of semi-presidentialism is strongly and consistently associated with the survival of democracies. Indeed, in the reduced form of the estimation, the Polity $\geq$+1 model no longer violates the proportional hazards assumption.

Overall, both the full model and the reduced model confirm the importance of the standard factor associated with collapse or survival of democracies, namely economic development. They also suggest that of all the potential problems of semi-presidentialism, whether or not countries have chosen a president-parliamentary form or a premier-presidential form of semi-presidentialism is by far and away the most important determinant of the collapse or survival of democracy. Indeed, the results suggest that countries that have opted for a president-parliamentary form of semi-presidentialism have potentially made a very dangerous choice indeed.

TABLE 3.9 *Reduced model: premier-presidentialism, president-parliamentarism, and the survival of democracy (various indicators of democracy)*

	Polity ≥+1	Polity ≥+6	FH ED
President-parliamentarism	9.24***	4.70*	6.84***
	(3.13)	(1.85)	(2.85)
Minority government		0.41	
		(–0.95)	
Presidential power		1.58**	
		(2.00)	
Log GDP per capita	0.34**	0.38***	0.46***
	(–2.38)	(–3.08)	(–4.50)
Growth	0.98		
	(–0.88)		
Ethnic fragmentation	0.05***		
	(–3.09)		
ENP (low)		1.90	
		(0.66)	
ENP (medium)	8.03***	1.65	5.07**
	(3.14)	(0.58)	(2.32)
Africa	3.44	0.04*	
	(1.52)	(–1.91)	
Log (partial) likelihood	–37.20	–29.11	–40.48
Linktest hat(2)	–0.05	–0.17	–0.05
	p = (0.660)	p = (0.535)	p = (0.672)
Test of proportional hazards assumption – Global Test chi(2)	5.66 (6df)	3.50 (7df)	1.03 (3df)
	p = (0.4624)	p = (0.8354)	p = (0.7949)
No. of subjects	52	42	46
No. of failures	15	11	15
No. of observations	740	590	532

Note: *significant at $p < 0.1$, **significant at $p < 0.05$, ***significant at $p < 0.01$ based on country-clustered standard errors.

CONCLUSION

Chapter 2 outlined a set of reasons why democracies that adopted a president-parliamentary form of semi-presidentialism were more likely to collapse than countries that adopted a premier-presidential form. This chapter has provided statistical evidence to test the validity of these reasons. Using a Cox proportional hazards model that was developed by Petra Schleiter (Elgie and Schleiter, 2011), the tests have conclusively shown that president-parliamentarism is much more perilous for the survival of semi-presidential democracies than premier-presidentialism. This is the general finding of the basic descriptive statistics, the model that controlled for the endogenous selection of the particular subtype of semi-presidentialism, and the survival model that controlled both for the standard range of other variables associated with the collapse of democracy and for the other reasons that are commonly thought to be problematic for democratic survival under semi-presidentialism. Certainly, the findings are probabilistic rather than deterministic. The results also need to address more systematically the potential problem of the endogenous selection of president-parliamentarism. Nevertheless, strong support has been found for the hypothesis that is central to this book. In subsequent chapters, in-depth case studies will illustrate the causal chain of events linking premier-presidentialism and president-parliamentarism with the success and failure of democracy respectively. In Chapter 4, though, the performance of semi-presidential democracies will be assessed. Within the set of democracies, to what extent do premier-presidential countries perform better than president-parliamentary countries?

NOTES

1. Various annual reports and the time-series data are available at: www.freedomhouse.org/template.cfm?page=15 (accessed 12 March 2010).
2. The time-series data are available at: www.systemicpeace.org/inscr/inscr.htm (accessed 12 March 2010).
3. The time-series data are available at: www.fsd.uta.fi/english/data/catalogue/FSD1289/meF1289e.html (accessed 12 March 2010).
4. The time-series data are available at: https://netfiles.uiuc.edu/cheibub/www/DD_page.html (accessed 12 March 2010).
5. The time-series data are available at: https://netfiles.uiuc.edu/msvolik/www/research/research.html (accessed 12 March 2010).
6. If there are minor differences in the start or end dates for the democratic episode, then only one episode of democracy is recorded. For example, all five indicators of democracy identify the beginning of a democratic episode in Niger sometime between 1999 and 2004. Therefore, for the purposes of this exercise, all five indicators are treated as recording the same episode of democracy. Similarly, if a country is classed as democratic continuously from the time when the indicator of democracy starts to record countries, then only one democratic episode is recorded. For example, Ireland is recorded as having one democratic episode, even though democracy is recorded as starting sometime between 1937 and 1989 depending on the indicator of democracy. In other words, it is assumed that if, for example, the FH ED indicator had begun to classify countries in 1937, then Ireland would have been classed as an electoral democracy at that time. The different democratic episodes and collapses that are the basis of the pairwise correlations can be discerned in Tables 3.1 and 3.2.
7. If a country has switched from one form of semi-presidentialism to the other, the most recent institutional configuration is recorded.

8. This may be a direct presidential election, or it may be an indirect election by parliament.
9. Mongolia and Macedonia are omitted for this reason. Data is not available for the election of the president prior to the choice of semi-presidentialism and the first presidential election under semi-presidentialism was held up to three years after the choice of institutions. Yemen is also omitted because of the absence of data.
10. If a country switches from semi-presidentialism to another form of government without collapsing (e.g. Moldova in 2000), then this case is also treated as if it is right-censored.
11. There is one error: www.worldstatesmen.org/Finland.html (accessed 12 March 2010) records Finland's President Pehr Evind Svinhufvud as being from the Social Democratic Party, whereas he was a member of the conservative party (KOK). However, this site correctly records him as a member of KOK during his time as prime minister. The mistake relating to his affiliation as president has been rectified in the data set.
12. See http://econ.worldbank.org/WBSITE/EXTERNAL/EXTDEC/EXTRESEARCH/0,,contentMDK:20649465pagePK:64214825piPK:64214943theSitePK:469382,00.html (accessed 27 October 2010).
13. Available at: www.ggdc.net/maddison/ (accessed 15 March 2010).
14. Available at: http://www.ers.usda.gov/Data/Macroeconomics/ (accessed 28 October 2010).
15. Available at: www.tcd.ie/Political_Science/staff/michael_gallagher/ElSystems/index.php (accessed 15 March 2010).
16. Samuels and Shugart (2010) are an exception. They define cohabitation in exactly the same way as it is defined here.

4

Varieties of Semi-Presidentialism and the Performance of Democracy

Chapter 3 examined the general evidence linking premier-presidentialism and president-parliamentarism with democratic survival or collapse. The findings clearly showed that democracy was more likely to collapse in countries with a president-parliamentary form of semi-presidentialism than in those with a premier-presidential form. In this chapter, the focus is solely on semi-presidential democracies. Within the set of democracies, what is the general evidence to suggest that democratic performance is likely to be worse in president-parliamentary countries than in premier-presidential countries? The chapter begins by outlining the strategy that will be adopted to measure the performance of democracy. The second section presents some descriptive statistics to demonstrate that premier-presidential democracies have performed better than president-parliamentary democracies. The third section presents the results of a wide range of controlled statistical tests. As in Chapter 3, the results are very clear: premier-presidential democracies are clearly shown to perform much better than president-parliamentary democracies.

IDENTIFYING DEMOCRATIC PERFORMANCE

In Chapter 3, the case selection was limited to the set of countries with semi-presidential constitutions that were classed as democracies measured in various ways. While some countries remained within the set of democracies, others exited at some point. Therefore, it was possible to distinguish between countries where democracy had survived and those where it had collapsed. In this chapter, the case selection is also limited to the set of semi-presidential countries that have been classed as democracies. Here, though, the aim is to 'discriminate between better and worse democratic units' (Altman and Pérez-Liñán, 2002: 95). To what extent are premier-presidential countries associated with the better units of democracy and president-parliamentary countries with the worse units?

According to Altman and Pérez-Liñán (2002: 87), there are two general ways of discriminating between better and worse democratic units. The first is familiar from Chapter 3 and places the emphasis on the relative level of democratization within the set of democracies. For example, Polity and Freedom House provide a range of scores across virtually all countries. On the basis of these scores, it is possible to identify the relative performance of all the countries that have crossed some minimum threshold for democracy. This allows the better-performing democracies to be distinguished from those that have performed less well.

The second general way of discriminating between better and worse democratic units for Altman and Pérez-Liñán is to focus on the quality of democracy. For example, Morlino (2004: 6–7) defines a good democracy as 'one presenting a *stable institutional structure that realizes the liberty and equality of citizens through the legitimate and correct functioning of its institutions and mechanisms*' (emphasis in the original). On this basis, he identifies five dimensions along which the quality of democracy may vary, comprising the rule of law, accountability, the responsiveness of government, freedom, and equality. For their part, Diamond and Morlino (2004: 21) identify eight dimensions, incorporating the previous five plus participation, competition, and horizontal accountability. More parsimoniously, Altman and Pérez-Liñán (2002) themselves measure the quality of democracy on the basis of three dimensions – effective civil rights, effective participation, and effective competition. Whereas Morlino, and Diamond and Morlino do not quantify the quality of democracy, Altman and Pérez-Liñán provide a score that tracks the quality of democracy in eighteen Latin American countries from the late 1970s to the mid-1990s. Foweraker and Krznaric (2003) engage in a similar exercise, identifying twenty-one indicators of democracy across two dimensions – rule of law and sovereignty of the people – for forty countries from 1970 to 1998, and comparing the quality of democracy in Western countries with countries elsewhere.

While Altman and Pérez-Liñán identify two main ways of discriminating between better and worse units of democracy, there are other ways of measuring performance as well. Some authors have constructed their own index of democratic performance. For example, Negretto (2006) has built an index of executive–legislative conflict and has identified whether or not the level of support for the president in Latin American legislatures is associated with the amount of conflict in the system. Other authors have operationalized standard measures of political, economic, and social performance, treating them as a test of democratic performance. For instance, Cheibub and Chernykh (2008, 2009) have provided a battery of tests to try to establish whether democratic performance is worse under semi-presidentialism than other constitutional arrangements, notably parliamentarism. They focus on indicators such as government stability, accountability to economic outcomes, economic reforms (Cheibub and Chernykh, 2009), as well as legislative effectiveness (Cheibub and Chernykh, 2008). In the same way, Lijphart (1999) identifies a number of indicators of democratic performance, including a range of macroeconomic variables, as well as various indicators relating to the control of violence. Finally, there are off-the-shelf indicators of performance more broadly, such as the Human Development Index or the Gini coefficient that could be used to judge the performance of semi-presidential democracies.

Faced with a variety of different ways of assessing democratic performance, this chapter follows the strategy adopted in Elgie and McMenamin (2008) and focuses on the level of democratization within the set of semi-presidential democracies. The decision to focus on the level of democratization as the most appropriate measure of democratic performance was taken for three reasons. Firstly, this choice is consistent with the strategy adopted in Chapter 3. There, it was noted that there are plenty of existing measures of democracy and that they are all more or less problematic at a conceptual and/or an empirical level. Therefore, rather than developing a new and in all likelihood equally problematic measurement of democracy, the decision was taken to rely on existing measures. Here, rather than developing a completely new index of democratic performance, like Foweraker and Krznaric or Negretto, this chapter also relies on an established way of distinguishing between the relative performance of democracies. Secondly, for writers such as Altman and Pérez-Liñán (2002: 87) and Berg-Schlosser (2004: 248), the main ontological difference between studies emphasizing the quality of democracy rather than the level of democratization is that the former rely on a conception of democracy that is 'normatively more demanding' (Ibid.). Even if this is the case, measures of democratization, such as those that were identified in Chapter 3, are themselves based on normative choices about what does or does not constitute democracy. Indeed, this is one of the main reasons why all such measures are inherently problematic. Therefore, there is no a priori reason why measures of the quality of democracy are superior to measures of democratization. Again, therefore, the latter will be the focus of this chapter. Thirdly, even though cross-national time-series data exist for many indicators of performance, including narrow measures of economic performance (such as growth rates and unemployment) as well as broader indicators of well-being (such as the Human Development Index or the Gini coefficient), this book has provided a causal explanation for the link between institutions and democratic performance. There may be another link in this causal chain that would tie the particular subtypes of semi-presidential institutions to measures of economic performance and social well-being such as those mentioned above. However, such claims are not being made here. Therefore, in the context of this volume, the level of democracy is an entirely appropriate measure with which to judge the performance of semi-presidential democracies.

In Chapter 3, five measures of democracy were identified (Polity ≥+1, Polity ≥+6, FH F & PF, FH ED, and ACLP/DD). For the purposes of this chapter, only three of these measures are appropriate. This is because FH ED and ACLP/DD provide only a binary classification that distinguishes democracies from non-democracies. Therefore, they cannot be used to measure relative performance within the set of democracies themselves. By contrast, the other three measures can be used. Polity classifies countries on the basis of a twenty-one-point scale from −10 (full autocracy) to +10 (full democracy). As noted in Chapter 3, the threshold for democracy can be placed at a score of +1 or +6. In this chapter, as in Chapter 3, both thresholds are used. For its part, Freedom House provides a range of scores from 1 to 7. Countries with a score of 1 to 2.5 are classed as Free; those with a score from 3 to 5 are classed as Partly Free; and those with a score from 5.5 to 7 are classed as Not Free.[1] In this book, the threshold for democracy is taken as the boundary line between Partly Free and Not Free countries. Table 3.1 recorded the periods when countries with semi-presidential constitutions have been classed as democracies on the basis of the Polity ≥+1, Polity ≥+6, and the FH F & PF thresholds. These periods of democracy are the focus of this chapter. During these periods, to what extent, as the theory predicts, are premier-presidential countries associated with higher Polity scores within the range, first, +1 to +10 and, second, +6 to +10? Similarly, to what extent are premier-presidential countries associated with lower Freedom House scores within the range 1 (the best score for Free countries) to 5 (the worst score for Partly Free countries)?

THE PERFORMANCE OF DEMOCRACY UNDER PREMIER-PRESIDENTIALISM AND PRESIDENT-PARLIAMENTARISM – BASIC EMPIRICAL EVIDENCE

In this section, the basic performance of democracy is assessed in three different ways. The first takes a snapshot of the performance of semi-presidential countries in 2008/9. The second provides a cross-sectional analysis of all semi-presidential countries over time. The third pools all the data for all semi-presidential countries over time. For each of these three ways, summary statistics are provided and the results of a simple bivariate regression are reported. In addition, a basic test for the effect of the endogenous selection of semi-presidential subtype is undertaken.

The first way of assessing the performance of premier-presidential countries relative to president-parliamentary countries is to take a snapshot of the most recent Polity and Freedom House scores. For Polity, this book relies on the 2009 version of the Polity data set, which provides scores for the performance of countries up to and including 2008.[2] For Freedom House, the 2010 report provides details for their performance up to and including 2009.[3] For each indicator, the basic unit of analysis is a semi-presidential democracy. The explanatory variable is the subtype of semi-presidentialism and the dependent variable is the Polity or Freedom House score. Table 4.1 provides the summary statistics for each measure of democracy and Table 4.2 presents the results of a simple bivariate ordinary linear squares regression with heteroskedasticity-robust standard errors. The summary statistics are encouraging. For Polity ≥+1 and Polity ≥+6, the average score for premier-presidential democracies is higher than the average score for

TABLE 4.1 *Summary statistics for the performance of semi-presidential democracies – Polity2 scores for 2008, Freedom House scores for 2009*

	Premier-presidential	President-parliamentary
Polity ≥+1[a]		
Mean score	8.00	6.77
Standard deviation	2.17	2.09
Observations	24	13
Polity ≥+6[a]		
Mean score	8.75	7.36
Standard deviation	1.33	1.63
Observations	20	11
FH F & PF[b]		
Mean score	2.24	3.20
Standard deviation	1.30	1.32
Observations	25	15

Note: [a]Higher scores indicate better performance; [b]lower scores indicate better performance.

TABLE 4.2 *Results of bivariate OLS regressions of democracy score by form of semi-presidentialism – Polity2 scores for 2008, Freedom House scores for 2009*

	Outcome is democracy score		
	Polity ≥+1	Polity ≥+6	FH F & PF
Coefficient			
Premier-presidential	1.23	1.39	−0.96
Constant	6.77	7.36	3.20
Confidence interval (95%)			
Premier-presidential	(−0.24, 2.70)	(0.22, 2.55)	(−1.82, −0.10)
Constant	(5.61, 7.93)	(6.37, 8.35)	(2.51, 3.88)
Robust standard error			
Premier-presidential	0.72*	0.57**	0.43**
Constant	0.57***	0.48***	0.34**
R^2	0.07	0.18	0.12
N	37	31	40

Note: *Significant at $p < 0.1$, **significant at $p < 0.05$, ***significant at $p < 0.01$.

Polity scores for 2008; Freedom House scores for 2009.

Note also: positive signs on the coefficients for the Polity models correspond to an association with better performance; a negative sign on the coefficient for the Freedom House model corresponds to an association with better performance.

president-parliamentary democracies, suggesting that the former perform better. By the same token, the average Freedom House score for premier-presidential democracies is lower, again suggesting that they perform better. Indeed, the figures indicate that Freedom House would class the average premier-presidential democracy as Free, whereas the average president-parliamentary would be classed as Partly Free. The results of the bivariate regressions are also fairly encouraging. Using all three measures of democracy, the coefficients for the premier-presidential variable are in the predicted direction and they are fairly large: generally speaking, on a ten-point scale, democratic performance would be better by more than a point if a country were premier-presidential rather than president-parliamentary. Two models (Polity ≥+6 and FH F & PF) produce a result for the premier-presidential variable that is significant at the 5 per cent level and one (Polity ≥+1) at the 10 per cent level.

The second way of assessing the performance of semi-presidential democracies is based on a cross-sectional analysis of each country. Here, the basic unit of analysis is a continuous period of democracy in a country. For each period of democracy in a country, the mean Polity or Freedom House score is calculated. If there has been more than one period of democracy in a country (i.e. if democracy in a country collapsed, but the country was then reclassified as a democracy at a later point), then each episode of democracy is treated as a separate observation and the mean for each separate period of democracy is calculated. In addition, if a country has switched from one subtype of semi-presidentialism to another during a period of democracy, then each period under the particular subtype of semi-presidentialism is also treated as a separate observation and the mean Polity or Freedom House score is calculated for each period.[4] Table 4.3 provides the summary statistics for each measure of democracy identified in this way and Table 4.4 again presents the results of a bivariate ordinary linear squares regression with heteroskedasticity-robust standard errors. This time, the results are even more encouraging. The summary statistics provide essentially the same picture as for the 2008/9 snapshot results previously. This time, though, the results of the bivariate

TABLE 4.3 *Summary statistics for the performance of semi-presidential democracies – mean Polity2 and Freedom House scores for each period of democracy and subtype of semi-presidentialism*

	Premier-presidential	President-parliamentary
Polity ≥+1[a]		
Mean score	7.51	5.90
Standard deviation	1.92	1.77
Observations	30	29
Polity ≥+6[a]		
Mean score	8.34	7.13
Standard deviation	1.26	1.28
Observations	26	22
FH F & PF[b]		
Mean score	2.82	3.71
Standard deviation	1.26	1.12
Observations	33	39

Note: [a]Higher scores indicate better performance; [b]lower scores indicate better performance.

Note also: Polity scores 1919–2008 inclusive; Freedom House scores 1972–2009 inclusive.

TABLE 4.4 *Results of bivariate regressions of democracy score by form of semi-presidentialism – mean Polity2 and Freedom House scores for each period of democracy and subtype of semi-presidentialism*

	Outcome is democracy score		
	Polity ≥+1	Polity ≥+6	FH F & PF
Coefficient			
Premier-presidential	1.61	1.21	−0.90
Constant	5.90	7.13	3.71
Confidence interval (95%)			
Premier-presidential	(0.65, 2.58)	(0.47, 1.95)	(−1.46, −0.33)
Constant	(5.24, 6.56)	(6.58, 7.68)	(3.35, 4.07)
Robust standard error			
Premier-presidential	0.48*	0.37*	0.28*
Constant	0.33*	0.27*	0.18*
R^2	0.16	0.19	0.13
N	59	48	72

Note: *Significant at $p < 0.01$.

Polity scores 1919–2008 inclusive; Freedom House scores 1972–2009 inclusive.

Note also: positive signs on the coefficients for the Polity models correspond to an association with better performance; a negative sign on the coefficient for the Freedom House model corresponds to an association with better performance.

regressions are stronger. Using all three measures of democracy, the coefficients for the premier-presidential variable are in the hypothesized direction and for all three measures of democracy the premier-presidential variable is significant at the 1 per cent level.

The third way of assessing the performance of semi-presidential democracies treats each year of democracy as an observation and pools the data. Thus, the summary statistics simply provide the average score for all premier-presidential and president-parliamentary countries for every year when they have been classed as a democracy on the basis of the various Polity and Freedom House measures. This time, the bivariate statistical test is based on a pooled model with panel-corrected standard errors and implementing the Prais-Winsten transformation to account for AR(1) autocorrelation (Beck and Katz, 1995). The panels correspond to the same country-level democratic episodes and changes in semi-presidential subtype that were identified in the two previous models. Table 4.5 provides the summary statistics for each measure of democracy on the basis of the pooled data and Table 4.6 presents the results of the bivariate regression. Once again, the summary statistics show that premier-presidential democracies performed better in terms of the level of democratization than president-parliamentary democracies. In addition, the regressions again produce good results. For all three measures of democracy, the coefficients are in the expected direction. Moreover, all three models produce results that are significant at the 1 per cent level.

TABLE 4.5 *Summary statistics for the performance of semi-presidential democracies – all mean Polity2 and Freedom House scores for all periods of democracy*

	Premier-presidential	President-parliamentary
Polity ≥+1[a]		
Mean score	8.51	6.70
Standard deviation	1.90	2.36
Observations	462	314
Polity ≥+6[a]		
Mean score	9.02	7.85
Standard deviation	1.25	1.71
Observations	411	219
FH F & PF[b]		
Mean score	2.09	3.13
Standard deviation	1.10	1.34
Observations	417	425

Note: [a]Higher scores indicate better performance; [b]lower scores indicate better performance.
Polity scores 1919–2008 inclusive; Freedom House scores 1972–2009 inclusive.

TABLE 4.6 *Results of bivariate regressions of democracy score by form of semi-presidentialism – various measures of democracy, panel-corrected standard errors, and implementing the Prais-Winsten transformation for each period of democracy and subtype of semi-presidentialism*

	Outcome is democracy score		
	Polity ≥+1	Polity ≥+6	FH F & PF
Coefficient			
Premier-presidential	1.74	1.18	−0.97
Constant	5.98	7.25	3.58
Confidence interval (95%)			
Premier-presidential	(0.30, 3.18)	(0.66, 1.70)	(−1.36, −0.58)
Constant	(4.62, 7.35)	(6.97, 7.52)	(3.31, 3.86)
Standard error			
Premier-presidential	0.73*	0.27**	0.20**
Constant	0.70**	0.14**	0.14**
R^2	0.29	0.71	0.46
N	776	631	842
No. of units	59	48	72

Note: *Significant at $p < 0.05$, **significant at $p < 0.01$.

Polity scores 1919–2008 inclusive; Freedom House scores 1972–2009 inclusive.

Note also: positive signs on the coefficients for the Polity models correspond to an association with better performance; a negative sign on the coefficient for the Freedom House model corresponds to an association with better performance.

Finally, as in Chapter 3, a basic test for the endogenous selection of semi-presidential subtype is undertaken. As with the logic underlying the test in Chapter 3, it may be the case that the countries where there is likely to be poorer democratic performance are the ones that choose president-parliamentarism in the first place and those where there is likely to be better performance choose premier-presidentialism. If so, then the subtype of semi-presidentialism should not be associated with the differential level of performance. The difference should be associated with the circumstances behind the choice of subtype at the outset. As in Chapter 3, the proxy for the endogenous selection of institutions is the score won by the winning candidate at the first ballot (if there was more than one ballot) of the presidential election immediately prior to the selection of the semi-presidential subtype.[5] If no such election was held prior to the choice of semi-presidentialism, then the score at the first presidential election after the selection of semi-presidentialism is recorded if the election was held in the period soon after the choice of institutional subtype.[6] Table 4.7 reports the results of an ordinary linear squares regression with heteroskedasticity-robust standard errors and with two explanatory variables: semi-presidential subtype (a binary variable coded '1' for premier-presidentialism and '0' for president-parliamentarism) and the score for the winning candidate at the presidential election (a continuous variable bounded at 100). The units are the same

TABLE 4.7 *Results of logistic regressions of democratic performance by form of semi-presidentialism controlling for the endogenous selection of institutions*

	Outcome is democracy score		
	Polity ≥+1	Polity ≥+6	FH F & PF
Coefficient			
Premier-presidential	1.56	1.16	−0.86
Presidential election	0.01	−0.01	0.00
Constant	5.25	7.55	3.58
Confidence interval (95%)			
Premier-presidential	(0.58, 2.54)	(0.41, 1.91)	(−1.45, −0.28)
Presidential election	(−0.01, 0.03)	(−0.02, 0.01)	(−0.01, 0.01)
Constant	(4.04–6.47)	(6.37, 8.72)	(2.81, 4.34)
Robust standard error			
Premier-presidential	0.49*	0.37*	0.29*
Presidential election	0.01	0.01	0.01
Constant	0.60*	0.58*	0.38*
R^2	0.17	0.20	0.12
N	57	46	70

Note: *Significant at $p < 0.01$.

Polity scores 1919–2008 inclusive; Freedom House scores 1972–2009 inclusive.

Note also: positive signs on the coefficients for the Polity models correspond to an association with better performance; a negative sign on the coefficient for the Freedom House model corresponds to an association with better performance.

as those in Table 4.4, namely a period of continuous democracy under a particular subtype of semi-presidentialism. Thus, if the subtype changes during a continuous period of democracy, then a new observation is recorded. In this event, the score of the winning candidate at the election immediately prior to the change of subtype is recorded. The results clearly show that the impact of premier-presidentialism vs. president-parliamentarism is robust to the circumstances in which the choice of semi-presidential subtype was made. Indeed, while the results are not reported, when this exercise is repeated using the Beck and Katz (1995) method as in Table 4.6, the findings point to the same conclusion.

Overall, therefore, there is good *prima facie* evidence to suggest that the performance of democracy in premier-presidential countries is better than in president-parliamentary countries. This result stands when different measures of democracy are used, when a snapshot of current semi-presidential democracies is taken, when a cross-section of democracies over time is examined, and when all the data about semi-presidential democracies are pooled. The strength of the results varies slightly from one model to another and from one method to the next, but the general evidence strongly supports the hypothesis about the relative performance of the two subtypes of semi-presidentialism. That said, these results are no more than indicative. To provide a proper test of the relationship between the subtype of semi-presidentialism and the level of democratization, a full range of controls needs to be introduced. This exercise is the focus of the next section.

THE PERFORMANCE OF DEMOCRACY UNDER PREMIER-PRESIDENTIALISM AND PRESIDENT-PARLIAMENTARISM – CONTROLLED STATISTICAL ANALYSES

The models presented in this section are based on the Polity ≥+1, Polity ≥+6, and the FH F & PF measures of democracy. When a country has crossed the threshold for democracy on the basis of each of these measures, then it is included in the data set for that measure. The observations are annual. The Polity observations date from 1919 when the first countries with semi-presidential constitutions were identified. The Freedom House observations date from 1972, which was the first year when Free, Partly Free, and Not Free countries were recorded. For the Polity ≥+1, Polity ≥+6, and the FH F & PF data sets, there is a maximum of 776, 631, and 842 observations respectively. Table 4.8 identifies the distribution of the observations for each data set. The dependent variable is the Polity or Freedom House score for any given year when a semi-presidential country is included in a data set. The explanatory variable is the

TABLE 4.8 *Distribution of observations, various measures of democracy*

Polity ≥+1 score	Frequency	Per cent	Polity ≥+6 score	Frequency	Per cent	FH score	Frequency	Per cent
+1	8	1.03	+6	102	16.19	1	189	22.45
+2	6	0.77	+7	69	10.95	1.5	114	13.54
+3	24	3.09	+8	84	13.33	2	87	10.33
+4	23	2.96	+9	90	14.29	2.5	84	9.98
+5	85	10.95	+10	285	45.24	3	59	7.01
+6	102	13.14				3.5	92	10.93
+7	69	8.89				4	93	11.05
+8	84	10.82				4.5	68	8.08
+9	90	11.60				5	56	6.65
+10	285	36.73						
Total	776	100.00	Total	631	100.00	Total	842	100.00

subtype of semi-presidentialism. This is a binary variable coded '1' for premier-presidentialism and '0' for president-parliamentarism.

The models include a number of control variables. There are two economic control variables. The first is overall economic development. The expectation is that countries with higher levels of GDP per capita will have higher democracy scores. Therefore, a variable recording the natural log of GDP per capita is included in all the models. In addition, the level of economic growth is also recorded. The expectation here is that countries with lower levels of growth, including negative growth, will have lower democracy scores. For the two Polity data sets, the main source of the data for both economic variables is the Angus Maddison Statistics on World Population, GDP and Per Capita GDP, 1–2008 AD data set. This source is used because of the long historical time series available. For the Freedom House data set, the Economic Research Service International Macroeconomic Data Set is used. This data set provides up-to-date figures for both GDP per capita in US$2005 and economic growth for every country in the Freedom House data set.

There are also two basic social control variables. The first is the level of ethnic fragmentation as measured by Alesina et al. (2003). The simple assumption here is that countries with higher levels of ethnic fragmentation are more difficult to manage than more homogeneous countries. Therefore, the expectation is that countries with higher levels of ethnic fragmentation will have worse democracy scores. The second social variable is the effective number of political parties. The logic underlying the inclusion of this variable is the same as for ethnic fragmentation. The higher the effective number of parliamentary parties, the more actors there are to be accommodated in political deals. Whereas ethnic fragmentation records the heterogeneity of social structures, the effective number of parliamentary parties may also reflect ideological divisions within society. In other words, ethnically homogeneous countries may still have a high effective number of parliamentary parties. The main source for the effective number of parliamentary parties is Michael Gallagher's data set with additional calculations where a country is not recorded there.[7]

There are three cultural and/or contextual control variables. The first captures whether or not a country has experienced colonization at any point after 1918. This is a binary variable that is coded '0' if the country has not experienced colonization since this time and '1' if it has. The assumption is that former colonies will have had less opportunities to embed an independent democratic tradition. Therefore, they are likely to have lower democracy scores. For the purposes of this chapter, countries in the former USSR and the former Yugoslavia are classed as having experienced colonization. The second variable captures whether or not a country is in the general European geographical space. This is also a binary variable that is coded '0' if the country is not in the European space and '1' if it is. The logic is that Europe contains many long-standing democracies. Moreover, in recent times the European Union has taken considerable efforts to support the democratization process in the European geographical space. Therefore, countries in this space are more likely to exhibit higher democracy scores. In the models that follow, the European geographical space is coded to include both Russia and the Caucasus. The third variable captures political events after the end of the Cold War. From the beginning of the 1990s, there was a wave of democratization that shifted established patterns of political competition. All else equal, countries are likely to have higher democracy scores after 1990 than before. A binary variable captures this intuition. It is coded '1' from 1990 onwards and '0' for any year beforehand.

Finally, there are four political control variables. Both cohabitation and a divided executive are included as a control variable. The assumption is that they both make governing more difficult. Therefore, they are likely to be associated with lower democracy scores. Both are coded as dummy variables with a score of '1' if they are present for more than six months of a given year and '0' otherwise. Minority government is also included as a control variable. The assumption is that governance is more difficult under minority government. For that reason, minority government should be associated with lower democracy scores. This variable is coded '1' if a country experienced minority government for more than six months in any given calendar year and '0' if not. The final political variable captures presidential power. Presidents with considerable constitutional powers may have the ability and/or the temptation to flout the rule of law. This leads to the expectation that strong presidencies should be associated with lower democracy scores. Moreover, there is also perhaps a separate concern that premier-presidentialism and president-parliamentarism are themselves merely reflecting the general powers of presidents with premier-presidential countries having weaker presidents than president-parliamentary countries. Therefore, including presidential power as a separate control variable allows the independent effect of the semi-presidential subtype to be isolated. To capture the strength of the presidency, Siaroff's index (2003) of presidential power is used. The correlation between the binary premier-presidential/president-parliamentary variable and the Siaroff scores across the three data sets is −0.22, −0.14, and −0.22 for the Polity ≥+1, Polity ≥+6, and the FH F & PF measures of democracy respectively, so there is no danger of multicollinearity.[8]

To test for the effect of premier-presidentialism relative to president-parliamentarism on the level of democracy and controlling for a variety of economic, social, contextual, and political factors, various estimation techniques are used. The list of such techniques that could be used is almost endless and there are always alternatives to the choice that is eventually made. Generally, though, over the course of this book, the aim is to test the basic hypothesis about premier-presidentialism vs. president-parliamentarism in various ways, for example using competing measures of democracy, using quantitative and qualitative analysis, and so on. Consistent with this logic, this section employs various estimation techniques. Needless to say, the estimation techniques are not chosen idiosyncratically. They are all externally validated. Together, though, they are quite different from each other. They include pooled models and cross-sectional models. They include ordinary linear regressions and logistic regressions. They include models that treat the dependent variable as a continuous measure and those that treat it as a binary measure. In general terms, the aim behind the choice of models in this section is to set the evidential bar very high. In this context, if the hypothesis about the effects of different subtypes of semi-presidentialism is robust to very different types of model specification, then it is reasonable to place more confidence in the findings. To this end, five different estimation techniques are used. Each of the five techniques is applied to the three different Polity and Freedom House data sets, thus generating fifteen separate models. It would be highly surprising if every variable produced exactly the same result for every model. However, if a particular variable generates the same basic result across all or most of the models, then this would suggest that there is good general evidence to support the finding about that variable.

The first two estimation techniques use a time-series cross-sectional (TSCS) approach. This is a common estimation strategy when countries are being compared. In this context, the first estimation technique is a fixed-effects vector decomposition (FEVD) model (Plümper and Troeger, 2007).[9] This model is appropriate when units (i.e. countries) exhibit a combination of time-invariant variables or at least variables that change only rarely over time, as well as time-varying variables, such as GDP per capita. For example, this model is particularly appropriate when the effect of cross-national institutions is being estimated. This is because institutions are 'sticky'. Therefore, while there may be institutional variation across units, there is usually little variation over time within units. The combination of time-invariant and time-varying variables neatly captures the set of variables to be tested here. In all three data sets, while there are time-varying variables, many of the unit variables are time-invariant, for example ethnic fractionalization, geographical location, and colonial status, or at least change very rarely, for instance Siaroff scores. Therefore, an FEVD model with heteroskedasticity-robust standard errors and implementing the Prais-Winsten transformation to account for autocorrelation provides a useful way of combining a fixed-effects model with a combination of time-invariant and time-varying variables.

The second estimation technique also pools the data. Here, Beck and Katz (1995) have shown that a model employing panel-corrected standard errors (PCSE) with the Prais-Winsten transformation is an appropriate way of accounting for contemporaneously correlated panels. As with the FEVD model, a panel comprises a continuous period of democracy with a given semi-presidential subtype. So, a new period of democracy generates a new panel even if the semi-presidential subtype has remained the same. Similarly, a change of semi-presidential subtype generates a new panel even within a continuous period of democracy. Thus, the second model follows the Beck and Katz method and employs a TSCS model with PCSE and the Prais-Winsten transformation.

The third estimation technique is based on Elgie and McMenamin (2008), which uses Newey-West standard errors to correct for heteroskedasticity and autocorrelation. Both the FEVD and the PCSE models operationalize the dependent variable as an interval measure. While plenty of studies have treated Freedom House and Polity scores as in this way (e.g. Desai et al., 2003; Kono, 2006), arguably it is not appropriate to do so. Indeed, this is particularly the case for Polity scores, which are best treated as an ordinal measure.[10] For this reason, the third model transforms the Freedom House and Polity scores into a binary variable and performs a logistic regression. For the Polity ≥+1 data set, worse democratic units are those that score between +1 and +5 inclusive and are coded 0, whereas better democratic units are those that score +6 or more and are coded 1. For the Polity ≥+6 data set, worse democratic units are those that score +6 or +7 and are coded 0, while better democratic units are those that score +8 or more and are coded 1. For the FH F & PF data set, better democratic units are those classed as Free and are coded 1, while worse democratic units are those classed as Partly Free and are coded 0. On this basis, a logistic regression with Newey-West standard errors tests whether there is an association between premier-presidentialism and better democratic units.

Whereas the first three estimation strategies pool the data, the final two techniques are based on a cross-sectional approach. In a pooled model, the time dimension is not relevant for time-invariant variables such as institutions. The FEVD approach is one way of dealing with this issue and, as noted above, this is the main reason why this particular estimation strategy will be used. Another way of accounting for time-invariant variables is to adopt a cross-sectional strategy and to time-average all of the variables. This strategy has recently been used by Keefer (2007) to test for the impact of young democracies relative to older democracies on policy choices. As in the first two models, the units in Models 4 and 5 are continuous periods of democracy in a country plus continuous periods of semi-presidential subtype. Thus, a new period of democracy in a country automatically generates a new case. Equally, a change of semi-presidential subtype also generates a new case. In total, there are sixty observations for the Polity ≥+1 data set, forty-nine observations for the Polity ≥+6 data set, and seventy observations for the FH F & PF data set. For each observation, the mean score for the dependent variable and each of the control variables is calculated with the exception of the Cold War control variable, which it is not appropriate to calculate in this way as there would be no variation across countries. On this basis, Model 4 is a linear regression with robust standard errors. Thus, this model treats the dependent variable as an interval measure. By contrast, Model 5 is an ordered probit model with robust standard errors. This model treats the dependent variable as an ordinal measure.

On the basis of three different measures of democratic performance and five different estimation techniques, what are the findings? (see Tables 4.9–4.13). In terms of the main explanatory variable, the findings are very consistent. In eleven of the fifteen models, premier-presidentialism was associated with a better democratic performance than president-parliamentarism at the 10 per cent level or better. Indeed, in the remaining models, the result only marginally exceeded conventional levels of significance and was in the expected direction. In nine models, the level of significance was at the 1 per cent level and in the remaining two models it was at the 5 per cent level. Moreover, in all of the models that produced a significant result, the coefficient was of a reasonable magnitude. For example, the results of the TSCS PCSE model for the Polity ≥+1 measure of democracy (Table 4.10, Model 4) suggested that on a ten-point scale, a shift from president-parliamentarism to premier-presidentialism would, all else equal, result in a one-point gain in democratic performance. These results are encouraging not merely in themselves but also in the context where a presidential power variable was included in all the equations. In other words, even controlling for presidential power, the subtype of semi-presidentialism had considerable explanatory power in all but one of the models. Needless to say, the results were subject to a number of robustness tests. For example, the findings were found to be almost identical when the full Siaroff score for presidential power was replaced by a more restricted measure that counted solely the president's legislative powers. In addition, for every model, each state was removed one by one and the model was re-estimated to determine whether the results were sensitive to the inclusion of particular countries. This exercise demonstrated that the findings were entirely robust to the exclusion of countries on a case-by-case basis within the conventional levels of significance.

In terms of the control variables, the clearest finding is a strong and consistently negative association between presidential power and democratic performance. In twelve of the fifteen models, presidential power was significant in this way at the 1 per cent level and in the remaining three models it was significant at

TABLE 4.9 *Fixed-effects vector decomposition model, various measures of democracy*

	Outcome is democracy score		
	Model 1 Polity ≥+1	Model 2 Polity ≥+6	Model 3 FH F & PF
Premier-presidentialism	1.148	0.888	−0.596
	(0.024)***	(0.005)***	(0.004)***
Cohabitation	0.050	0.079	−0.380
	(0.010)***	(0.004)***	(0.004)***
Divided executive	−0.020	0.133	−0.304
	(0.032)	(0.001)***	(0.002)***
Minority government	0.131	0.119	−0.071
	(0.037)***	(0.003)***	(0.006)***
Presidential power	−0.351	−0.317	0.153
	(0.003)***	(0.000)***	(0.001)***
Log GDP per capita	0.393	0.183	−0.462
	(0.314)	(0.048)***	(0.138)***
Growth GDP per capita	−0.003	0.001	0.001
	(0.001)**	(0.000)***	(0.001)*
Effective no. of parliamentary parties	−0.054	−0.011	0.003
	(0.006)***	(0.001)***	(0.013)***
Ethnic fragmentation	0.710	−1.715	0.064
	(0.136)***	(0.031)***	(0.017)***
Former colony	0.981	0.581	(0.030)
	(0.025)***	(0.001)***	–
European area	0.294	−0.695	0.436
	(0.028)***	(0.004)***	(0.003)***
Post-1990	−0.005	−0.063	0.178
	(0.141)	(0.223)***	(0.035)***
Constant	4.516	8.622	5.441
	(0.048)***	(0.004)***	(0.012)***
N	653	529	693
Adjusted R^2	0.48	0.83	0.90
Durbin-Watson statistic (original)	0.18	0.22	0.45
Durbin-Watson statistic (transformed)	1.44	1.59	1.53

Note: Standard errors in parentheses.
*Significant at $p < 0.1$, **significant at $p < 0.05$, ***significant at $p < 0.01$.

For premier-presidentialism, positive signs on the coefficients for Models 1 and 2 correspond to an association with better performance, whereas negative signs on the coefficients for Model 3 correspond to an association with better performance.

the 5 per cent level. This finding is interesting not only because it is so unequivocal but also because in Chapter 3 presidential power was shown to have little or no independent effect on the survival of semi-presidential democracies over and above the effect of the subtype of semi-presidentialism in that country. Here, though, both the president-parliamentarism and presidential power

TABLE 4.10 *Time-series cross-section model with panel-corrected standard errors, various measures of democracy*

	Outcome is democracy score		
	Model 4 Polity ≥+1	Model 5 Polity ≥+6	Model 6 FH F & PF
Premier-presidentialism	1.005 (0.351)***	0.931 (0.107)***	−0.565 (0.113)***
Cohabitation	0.034 (0.071)	0.033 (0.043)	−0.056 (0.038)
Divided executive	−0.020 (0.099)	0.028 (0.058)	−1.110 (0.059)*
Minority government	0.097 (0.087)	0.036 (0.044)	−0.026 (0.048)
Presidential power	−0.423 (0.066)***	−0.221 (0.026)***	0.131 (0.025)***
Log GDP per capita	−0.092 (0.044)**	0.456 (0.101)***	−0.487 (0.047)***
Growth GDP per capita	0.010 (0.004)**	0.000 (0.003)	−0.001 (0.003)
Effective no. of parliamentary parties	−0.027 (0.040)	0.007 (0.023)	0.003 (0.004)
Ethnic fragmentation	0.413 (0.573)	−0.749 (0.524)	−0.364 (0.278)
Former colony	0.918 (0.254)***	0.675 (0.186)***	−0.252 (0.119)**
European area	0.840 (0.392)**	−0.607 (0.245)**	0.215 (0.137)
Post-1990	0.010 (0.214)	0.040 (0.086)	0.072 (0.092)
Constant	8.111 (0.446)***	5.256 (0.903)***	6.277 (0.520)***
N	768	623	831
No. of panels	59	48	69
R^2	0.47	0.85	0.67

Note: Standard errors in parentheses.
*Significant at $p < 0.1$, **significant at $p < 0.05$, ***significant at $p < 0.01$.

For premier-presidentialism, positive signs on the coefficients for Models 4 and 5 correspond to an association with better performance, whereas negative signs on the coefficients for Model 6 correspond to an association with better performance.

variables are independently shown to be strongly and negatively correlated with democratic performance. This finding suggests that if a country does decide to choose a president-parliamentary form of semi-presidentialism, then to maximize its democratic credentials it would be advised to provide the president with few independent powers. Various cases are instructive in this regard. For example, Austria and Iceland are president-parliamentary, but in practice the president has

TABLE 4.11 *Logistic regression with Newey-West standard errors, various measures of democracy*

	Outcome is democracy score		
	Model 7 Polity ≥+1	Model 8 Polity ≥+6	Model 9 FH F & PF
Premier-presidentialism	0.851	2.615	−1.986
	(0.251)***	(0.452)***	(0.297)***
Cohabitation	2.210	2.063	−2.281
	(1.020)**	(0.831)**	(0.842)***
Divided executive	−0.690	1.652	−1.947
	(0.373)*	(0.694)**	(0.465)***
Minority government	0.427	0.635	−1.426
	(0.283)	(0.375)*	(0.325)***
Presidential power	−0.542	−0.686	0.210
	(0.078)***	(0.100)***	(0.073)***
Log GDP per capita	0.739	1.797	−1.380
	(0.175)***	(0.241)***	(0.135)***
Growth GDP per capita	−0.004	0.014	−0.046
	(0.019)	(0.018)	(0.022)**
Effective no. of parliamentary parties	−0.179	−0.128	0.205
	(0.064)***	(0.125)	(0.070)***
Ethnic fragmentation	3.546	−0.654	1.079
	(0.853)***	(1.266)	(0.620)*
Former colony	0.399	1.426	−0.845
	(0.350)	(0.384)***	(0.269)***
European area	1.076	−2.397	2.232
	(0.452)**	(0.522)***	(0.369)***
Post-1990	0.257	−0.312	1.049
	(0.321)	(0.415)	(0.418)**
Constant	−3.589	−10.587	8.069
	(1.458)**	(1.993)***	(1.141)***
N	768	623	831
Chi^2	184.95	110.57	297.78

Note: Standard errors in parentheses.
*Significant at $p < 0.1$, **significant at $p < 0.05$, ***significant at $p < 0.01$.

For premier-presidentialism, positive signs on the coefficients for Models 7 and 8 correspond to an association with better performance, whereas negative signs on the coefficients for Model 9 correspond to an association with better performance.

few powers (see Chapter 7). Arguably, the weakness of the president in these two countries has offset the potential problems of president-parliamentarism and has helped to generate a better democratic performance. By contrast, Mali has been democratic since the early 1990s, but it has failed to register a Polity score greater than +7 at any time during this period. Democracy has survived, but on the basis of the Polity ≥+6 measure of democracy the performance of democracy has been relatively poor. In short, it has been a quasi-democracy (Diamond, 1996).

TABLE 4.12 *Cross-sectional models, ordinary linear regression, various measures of democracy*

	Outcome is democracy score		
	Model 10 Polity ≥+1	Model 11 Polity ≥+6	Model 12 FH F & PF
Premier-presidentialism	0.613	0.869	−0.332
	(0.435)	(0.405)**	(0.265)
Cohabitation	3.080	0.810	−2.752
	(1.056)***	(1.100)	(0.888)***
Divided executive	1.205	0.804	−0.370
	(0.707)*	(0.603)	(0.390)
Minority government	0.875	0.485	−0.509
	(0.680)	(0.509)	(0.403)
Presidential power	−0.399	−0.224	0.123
	(0.147)***	(0.095)**	(0.061)**
Log GDP per capita	0.406	0.529	−0.482
	(0.381)	(0.238)**	(0.134)***
Growth GDP per capita	−0.083	−0.016	−0.026
	(0.040)**	(0.031)	(0.042)
Effective no. of parliamentary parties	−0.209	−0.016	0.000
	(0.087)**	(0.107)	(0.002)
Ethnic fragmentation	0.949	−0.135	−0.813
	(0.778)	(1.017)	(0.512)
Former colony	0.682	0.689	−0.103
	(0.529)	(0.465)	(0.281)
European area	0.288	−0.675	0.410
	(0.879)	(0.487)	(0.334)
Constant	4.911	4.129	6.807
	(2.467)*	(2.036)**	(1.027)***
N	59	48	69
R^2	0.60	0.57	0.65

Note: Standard errors in parentheses.
*Significant at $p < 0.1$, **significant at $p < 0.05$, ***significant at $p < 0.01$.

For premier-presidentialism, positive signs on the coefficients for Models 10 and 11 correspond to an association with better performance, whereas negative signs on the coefficients for Model 12 correspond to an association with better performance.

Mali has a premier-presidential constitution, but it also has a president with considerable constitutional powers. While the evidence suggests that the performance of democracy in countries with a premier-presidential constitution and a weak president has generally been good, the strength of the presidency in Mali may have hindered the performance of democracy there, even if democracy survived. While there are always dangers in going from observations about the general characteristics of a particular group to observations about particular members of that group, these examples suggest that the power of the president needs to be

TABLE 4.13 *Cross-sectional models, ordered probit, various measures of democracy*

	Outcome is democracy score		
	Model 13 Polity ≥+1	Model 14 Polity ≥+6	Model 15 FH F & PF
Premier-presidentialism	0.522 (0.322)	0.976 (0.429)**	−0.279 (0.340)
Cohabitation	3.052 (0.911)***	0.880 (1.115)	−3.829 (1.136)***
Divided executive	0.767 (0.548)	0.994 (0.599)*	−0.685 (0.520)
Minority government	0.709 (0.482)	0.602 (0.517)	−0.506 (0.476)
Presidential power	−0.365 (0.122)***	−0.272 (0.109)**	0.245 (0.088)***
Log GDP per capita	0.481 (0.283)*	0.618 (0.251)**	−0.741 (0.208)***
Growth GDP per capita	−0.070 (0.030)**	−0.043 (0.036)	−0.021 (0.057)
Effective no. of parliamentary parties	−0.144 (0.070)**	−0.065 (0.122)	−0.000 (0.003)
Ethnic fragmentation	0.721 (0.594)	−0.136 (1.008)	−1.040 (0.730)
Former colony	0.405 (0.380)	0.686 (0.468)	0.006 (0.343)
European area	−0.115 (0.638)	−0.679 (0.513)	0.689 (0.460)
N	59	48	69
Wald Chi^2	65.70	37.65	145.05

Note: Standard errors in parentheses.
*Significant at $p < 0.1$, **significant at $p < 0.05$, ***significant at $p < 0.01$.

For premier-presidentialism, positive signs on the coefficients for Models 13 and 14 correspond to an association with better performance, whereas negative signs on the coefficients for Model 15 correspond to an association with better performance.

considered in the in-depth case studies of semi-presidentialism and democratic performance that follow.

As regards the other control variables, there is good evidence to suggest that, as expected, economic performance is positively correlated with democratic performance. In twelve of the fifteen models, economic performance was significant in this way at the 10 per cent level or better and in eight of these ten models it was significant at the 1 per cent level. However, in one model a significant negative association was observed and in the three remaining models there was no association at conventional levels of significance. Generally, though, the effect of economic performance was in line with expectations. For the other control variables, the results were either significant in the expected direction in only a small number of models or the evidence was mixed. For instance, the effective number of parliamentary parties was, as expected, negatively associated with democratic performance in six models, though in three of these models the coefficient was very small. Similarly, ethnic fragmentation was, as expected, negatively associated with democratic performance in three models, but it was also positively associated with it in five models. Overall, what can be said about the control variables is that across the range of estimation techniques and specific models they did not produce results that were completely out of line with each other. Therefore, it is reasonable to suggest that an appropriate set of controls was included in these models, thus increasing the validity of the findings relating to the explanatory variable.

TABLE 4.14 *Reduced model, fixed-effects vector decomposition, various measures of democracy*

	Outcome is democracy score		
	Model 16 Polity ≥+1	Model 17 Polity ≥+6	Model 18 FH F & PF
Premier-presidentialism	1.150 (0.012)***	0.697 (0.002)***	−0.546 (0.001)***
Presidential power	−0.354 (0.006)***	−0.259 (0.001)***	0.144 (0.001)***
Log GDP per capita	0.476 (0.247)*	0.268 (0.036)***	−0.386 (0.104)***
Growth GDP per capita		0.001 (0.000)***	
Effective no. of parliamentary parties	−0.053 (0.007)***	−0.062 (0.001)**	0.004 (0.000)***
Ethnic fragmentation		−1.708 (0.004)***	0.139 (0.003)***
European area	0.166 (0.020)***		
Constant	4.612 (0.026)***	7.748 (0.001)***	5.113 (0.004)***
N	653	529	694
Adjusted R^2	0.45	0.82	0.90
t (eta)	34.09	1235.99	1215.15
Durbin-Watson statistic (original)	0.15	0.20	0.41
Durbin-Watson statistic (transformed)	1.44	1.57	1.51

Note: Standard errors in parentheses.
*Significant at $p < 0.1$, **significant at $p < 0.05$, ***significant at $p < 0.01$.

For premier-presidentialism, positive signs on the coefficients for Models 1 and 2 correspond to an association with better performance, whereas negative signs on the coefficients for Model 3 correspond to an association with better performance.

TABLE 4.15 *Reduced model, time-series cross-section with panel-corrected standard errors, various measures of democracy*

	Outcome is democracy score		
	Model 19 Polity ≥+1	Model 20 Polity ≥+6	Model 21 FH F & PF
Premier-presidentialism	1.158	0.982	−0.563
	(0.510)*	(0.192)**	(0.161)**
Presidential power	−0.360	−0.127	0.109
	(0.088)**	(0.033)**	(0.035)**
Log GDP per capita	0.593	0.466	−0.466
	(0.170)**	(0.094)**	(0.043)**
Growth GDP per capita	0.008		
	(0.004)*		
European area	−0.009		
	(0.573)		
Constant	3.535	4.242	6.209
	(1.267)**	(0.828)**	(0.495)**
N	768	624	834
No. of panels	59	48	70
R^2	0.42	0.79	0.61

Note: Standard errors in parentheses.
*Significant at $p < 0.05$, **significant at $p < 0.01$.

For premier-presidentialism, positive signs on the coefficients for Models 4 and 5 correspond to an association with better performance, whereas negative signs on the coefficients for Model 6 correspond to an association with better performance.

The final battery of tests takes the form of a set of reduced models (see Tables 4.14–4.18). Each of Models 1–15 was re-estimated, including only those variables that were originally found both to be in the expected direction and significant at the 10 per cent level or better, except for the premier-presidential and economic performance variables (log GDP per capita), which are included in all of the reduced models. The latter variable is included in the reduced models on the assumption that it is the standard control variable that should be included in any estimation of democratic performance. Again, the results are reassuring. The premier-presidential variable is significant at the 10 per cent level or better in fourteen of the fifteen reduced models. In addition, the economic performance control is now significant at the 10 per cent level or better in all of the fifteen reduced models. The control for presidential power is slightly weakened, now being significant at the 10 per cent level or better in fourteen of the fifteen reduced models. The results for all three variables remain in the expected direction. There is also some support for the negative effects of ethnic fragmentation and the effective number of parliamentary parties on democratic

TABLE 4.16 *Reduced model, logistic regression with Newey-West standard errors, various measures of democracy*

	Outcome is democracy score		
	Model 22 Polity ≥+1	Model 23 Polity ≥+6	Model 24 FH F & PF
Premier-presidentialism	0.764 (0.234)**	1.983 (0.271)**	−1.531 (0.221)**
Divided executive	−0.663 (0.331)*		
Presidential power	−0.470 (0.072)**	−0.549 (0.062)**	0.044 (0.069)
Log GDP per capita	0.544 (0.133)**	1.392 (0.135)**	−1.046 (0.088)**
Growth GDP per capita			−0.051 (0.019)**
Effective no. of parliamentary parties	−0.152 (0.055)**		0.236 (0.056)**
Ethnic fragmentation			1.402 (0.558)*
European area	0.172 (0.376)		
Constant	−0.127 (1.133)	−8.820 (1.099)**	7.001 (0.922)**
N	768	624	831
Chi^2	211.34	146.53	413.23

Note: Standard errors in parentheses.
*Significant at $p < 0.05$, **significant at $p < 0.01$.

For premier-presidentialism, positive signs on the coefficients for Models 7 and 8 correspond to an association with better performance, whereas negative signs on the coefficients for Model 9 correspond to an association with better performance.

performance. Where they are included, both variables are significant in the expected direction at the 10 per cent level or better.

Taken as a whole, the hypothesis that premier-presidential countries are associated with a better democratic performance than president-parliamentary countries finds strong and robust support. Controlling for a range of economic, social, cultural, and political factors, the overall results of both the full models and the reduced models showed that if a democracy were to switch from a president-parliamentary form of semi-presidentialism to a premier-presidential form, then it would register a significantly better score for democratic performance. By itself, such a switch would constitute a relatively minor constitutional reform. The evidence strongly suggests that president-parliamentary countries in quasi-democracies should be encouraged to adopt it.

TABLE 4.17 *Reduced model, cross-sectional models, ordinary linear regression, various measures of democracy*

	Outcome is democracy score		
	Model 25 Polity ≥+1	Model 26 Polity ≥+6	Model 27 FH F & PF
Premier-presidentialism	0.967	0.935	−0.515
	(0.465)*	(0.343)**	(0.235)*
Presidential power	−0.496	−0.192	0.146
	(0.139)**	(0.096)**	(0.068)*
Log GDP per capita	0.428	0.494	−0.417
	(0.187)*	(0.156)**	(0.070)**
Effective no. of parliamentary parties	−0.179		
	(0.076)*		
Constant	6.205	4.280	5.670
	(2.000)**	(1.517)*	(0.747)**
N	59	48	70
R^2	0.48	0.44	0.50

Note: Standard errors in parentheses.
*Significant at $p < 0.05$, **significant at $p < 0.01$.

For premier-presidentialism, positive signs on the coefficients for Models 10 and 11 correspond to an association with better performance, whereas negative signs on the coefficients for Model 12 correspond to an association with better performance.

TABLE 4.18 *Reduced model, cross-sectional models, ordered probit, various measures of democracy*

	Outcome is democracy score		
	Model 28 Polity ≥+1	Model 29 Polity ≥+6	Model 30 FH F & PF
Premier-presidentialism	0.707	0. 900	−0.431
	(0.312)*	(0.345)**	(0.281)
Presidential power	−0.371	−0.211	0.227
	(0.093)**	(0.103)*	(0.088)**
Log GDP per capita	0.342	0.470	−0.478
	(0.140)*	(0.165)**	(0.101)**
Effective no. of parliamentary parties	−0.123		
	(0.056)*		
N	59	48	70
Wald Chi^2	47.55	31.43	38.53

Note: Standard errors in parentheses.
*Significant at $p < 0.05$, **significant at $p < 0.01$.

For premier-presidentialism, positive signs on the coefficients for Models 13 and 14 correspond to an association with better performance, whereas negative signs on the coefficients for Model 15 correspond to an association with better performance.

CONCLUSION

In Chapter 3, there was strong evidence to suggest that democracy in countries with a president-parliamentary form of semi-presidentialism was likely to last less long than in those with a premier-presidentialism form. In this chapter, there is equally strong evidence to suggest that democratic performance is worse in president-parliamentary democracies than in premier-presidential democracies. Given that since the 1990s semi-presidentialism has emerged as the dominant constitutional choice in most parts of the world, these findings produce a very strong general policy recommendation. If a country chooses to have both a directly elected president and a prime minister and cabinet that are collectively accountable to the legislature, then for the sake of its democratic credentials that country is strongly advised to ensure that the prime minister and cabinet are responsible solely to the legislature and not to the president as well. That said, all of the evidence presented so far has been based on large-n statistical analyses. Very different types of statistical analysis have been used, ranging from the very simple to the more sophisticated. Moreover, whatever the type of analysis, the tests have been carried out using various measures of democracy, thus ensuring that the results are not merely a function of a single case-selection procedure. All the same, there are those who reject the applicability of this sort of analysis in the study of comparative politics. In addition, even though various measures of democracy have been operationalized, it is possible that some or other methodological flaw is common to all of the measures. Therefore, it is necessary to explore the hypothesized effects of premier-presidentialism vs. president-parliamentarism in a different way. To this end, Chapters 5 and 6 contain four in-depth case studies – two relating to democratic collapse/survival and two regarding democratic performance. Given the very different nature of the analysis in Chapters 5 and 6, if the hypothesized effects concerning the two forms of semi-presidentialism can be observed in these cases as well, then the evidence in favour of the hypothesis presented in Chapter 2 will be even more compelling.

NOTES

1. Until 2003, Freedom House classified countries with a score of 5.5 as Partly Free. However, in this book, 5 is taken as the threshold for a Partly Free country, even for scores prior to 2003.
2. Available at: http://www.systemicpeace.org/polity/polity4.htm (accessed 17 June 2010).
3. Available at: http://www.freedomhouse.org/template.cfm?page=505 (accessed 17 June 2010).

4. For example, using the Polity ≥+1 measure, there are three observations for Armenia: (*a*) 1991–5, after which point democracy collapsed and Armenia exits this data set; (*b*) 1998–2005, from the point when Armenia was reclassified as a democracy and re-enters the data set, until it amended its constitution and switched from a president-parliamentary to a premier-presidential form of semi-presidentialism; and (*c*) 2006–8 when it was a democracy with a premier-presidential form of semi-presidentialism.
5. This may be a direct presidential election, or it may be an indirect election by parliament.
6. Mongolia and Macedonia are omitted for this reason. Data is not available for the election of the president prior to the choice of semi-presidentialism, and the first presidential election under semi-presidential was held up to three years after the choice of institutions.
7. Available at: www.tcd.ie/Political_Science/staff/michael_gallagher/ElSystems/index.php (accessed 15 March 2010).
8. The VIF tests show that there is no problem of collinearity among the variables in any of the three data sets. The highest VIF figures were 3.57 (mean 1.78), 4.88 (mean 1.93), and 3.53 (mean 1.70) for Polity ≥+1, Polity ≥+6, and the FH F & PF respectively. The lowest Tolerance figures were 0.28, 0.20, and 0.28 respectively. The VIF/Tolerance figures for the premier-presidential and presidential power variables were 1.05/0.95, 1.02/0.98, and 1.05/0.95 respectively.
9. Hausman tests rejected the Random Effects model in favour of Fixed Effects.
10. Personal communication from Monty G. Marshall, Director, Polity IV and Armed Conflict and Intervention Projects.

5

Semi-Presidentialism and Democratic Survival and Collapse – Country Narratives

Chapters 3 and 4 provided statistical evidence to suggest that there was a link between the form of semi-presidentialism and democratic performance. Democracies with a president-parliamentary form of semi-presidentialism were shown to be much more likely to collapse than those with a premier-presidential form. Also, even when they did not collapse, the level of democracy was shown to be much lower under president-parliamentarism than under premier-presidentialism. In this chapter and in Chapter 6, the focus shifts to the in-depth studies of individual cases. In Chapter 2, the causal process explaining why president-parliamentarism was likely to lead to a worse democratic performance than premier-presidentialism was outlined. While Chapters 3 and 4 provided general evidence to link the type of semi-presidentialism with the performance of democracy, they did not confirm any causal link. This chapter examines whether the causal process outlined in Chapter 2 can be identified in the context of the collapse and survival of semi-presidential democracies. If it can, then it would suggest that the statistical association identified in Chapter 3 accurately reflected the hypothesized causal process. If it cannot, then it would suggest that the statistical link between the type of semi-presidentialism and performance of democracy was purely spurious.

To this end, this chapter compares the case of Guinea-Bissau, where democracy collapsed under president-parliamentarism, with the case of Mali, where it has survived under premier-presidentialism. These countries differ in various respects. For example, they were ruled by different colonial powers. Guinea-Bissau was a colony of Portugal, whereas France ruled Mali. Moreover, they gained independence at different times and in different contexts. Mali obtained independence relatively peacefully in 1960. By contrast, Guinea-Bissau achieved independence only in 1974 following a long-standing guerrilla war and the collapse of the authoritarian regime in Portugal that ended the country's colonial ambitions. At the same time, though, the two countries share similar characteristics. They were both ruled by colonial powers for a considerable period of time. Following independence, they were then both ruled by one-party authoritarian regimes. Both democratized in the early 1990s when there was a wave of democratization globally. Crucially, both are extremely poor countries and both are also highly divided along ethnic lines. In short, while semi-presidentialism has operated in the context of, necessarily, different historical and cultural circumstances in Guinea-Bissau and Mali, it has also operated in contexts that are similar in a number of key respects. Therefore, the case can be made that like is being compared with like. Given that the form of semi-presidentialism varies across the two countries and that both have experienced different democratic outcomes, then it is reasonable to explore whether the particular form of semi-presidentialism in each country was causally associated with the performance of democracy there.

The two cases are examined separately. However, each study is organized along similar lines. Each case begins with a brief overview of the country's democratic record. It then sketches the economic, social, and cultural context in which democracy has operated. The founding circumstances of semi-presidentialism are then discussed and the salient features of the country's constitution are identified. The bulk of the case study then comprises a narrative of key events since democratization, focusing primarily on the relationship between the president, the legislature, and the government. If president-parliamentarism is causally responsible at least in part for the collapse of democracy, then there is likely to be instability in the political process. There are few incentives for the president and the legislature to reach a general political agreement. Therefore, there is likely to be ongoing conflict between the two institutions. The president may try to force presidential governments on a reluctant legislature. The legislature may try to dismiss the prime minister and ministers considered close to the president. The president may resort to rule by decree as a way of bypassing a recalcitrant legislature. The legislature may start impeachment proceedings as a way of trying to dismiss the president. The result is likely to be an unstable situation in which one actor or institution tries to act unilaterally, thereby threatening the rule of law and the system of democracy as a whole. Alternatively, the military may intervene in order to restore some sort of equilibrium, but again at the expense of democracy. By contrast, if premier-presidentialism is causally responsible, again at least in part, for the collapse of democracy, then there is likely to be a different dynamic. The relations between the president, the government, and legislature are likely to be more accommodating. This is because the president is aware that the only way to govern is with the legislature's consent. Governments are likely to be more broadly based. The legislature is likely to try to vote down the government only in extremis. The president is likely to veto legislation only rarely. When crises occur, there is likely to be dialogue with a view to reaching an agreement that is acceptable to all parties. Overall, there is no reason to expect that relations under president-parliamentarism will always be fractious or that under premier-presidentialism they will always be harmonious. However, there should be observable differences between the two cases that are broadly consistent with the expectations outlined above. The chapter begins with the case of Guinea-Bissau and the collapse of democracy there.

PRESIDENT-PARLIAMENTARISM AND DEMOCRATIC COLLAPSE: THE CASE OF GUINEA-BISSAU

Portuguese rule in West Africa dates back to the fifteenth century. In 1886, the Franco-Portuguese Convention defined the borders of modern-day Guinea-Bissau. In 1974, Guinea-Bissau gained independence from Portugal. For the next decade, the African Party for the Independence of Guinea and Cape Verde (*Partido africano da independência da Guiné e Cabo Verde* – PAIGC) governed the country on the basis of an authoritarian Marxist-inspired regime in which the PAIGC was the only party that was allowed to operate. In the early 1990s, in line with the general wave of democratization at the time, Guinea-Bissau underwent a process of political liberalization. In 1991, multiparty competition was legalized. Then, in 1994, the first multiparty elections were held. At this point, some observers believe that Guinea-Bissau crossed the threshold between autocracy and democracy. Thus, in 1994, Freedom House classed the country as Partly Free for the first time.[1] In the same year, Freedom House classed Guinea-Bissau as an Electoral Democracy. The country also crossed the Polity ≥+1 threshold in 1994 registering a score of +5 on the scale from 10 (complete autocracy) to +10 (full democracy). However, other observers record a later starting point. For Alvarez, Cheibub, Limongi, Przeworski (ACLP/DD), democracy begins with the first alternation in power in 2000, while Polity ≥+6 classes Guinea-Bissau as a democracy only from 2005 onwards. In terms of the collapse of democracy, Polity ≥+1, FH ED, and ACLP/DD all record a collapse in 2003. However, Polity ≥+1 also records an additional collapse in 1998 with a quick return to democracy in 1999, while Freedom House as Free and Partly Free (FH F & PF) has classed Guinea-Bissau as Partly Free continuously since 1994 and Polity ≥+6, which records democracy as beginning only in 2005, has also not yet recorded a collapse. In short, there is no unanimity as to when Guinea-Bissau should be classed as a democracy and when a collapse occurred. That said, four of the five measures record Guinea-Bissau as a democracy in the period 2000–2 inclusive, and three of those four measures also record a collapse in 2003. Therefore, for the purposes of this chapter, the focus will primarily be on events in the period 2000–3 inclusive.

In this period, Guinea-Bissau experienced economic and social conditions that are often associated with the collapse of democracy. For example, measured in constant 2000-US$, Guinea-Bissau's average GDP per capita in the period 2000–2 inclusive was $158.[2] By contrast, the average for OECD countries in the same period was $26,996, while the average for sub-Saharan African countries generally was $514. Therefore, even when compared with only its peer-group countries, Guinea-Bissau was very undeveloped economically. Given Chapter 3 demonstrated that there is a strong link between economic development and democratic performance, it is clear that democracy was operating in a very hostile economic environment. Indeed, the non-payment of civil servants' wages was a major cause of social unrest in 2002. Guinea-Bissau was also highly divided along ethnic lines. Using Alesina et al.'s measures (2003) of fractionalization, which calculate the diversity of countries on a scale from 0 (completely homogenous) to 1 (completely fractionalized), Guinea-Bissau scores 0.8 for both ethnic and linguistic fractionalization and 0.6 for religious fractionalization. The model in Chapter 3 provided ambiguous results about the effects of fragmentation on democratic survival. In the case of Guinea-Bissau, though, it is reasonable to suggest that the highly fractionalized nature of society increased the likelihood of democratic collapse. Certainly, the so-called 'balantization' of political offices during the 2000–3 period, meaning the appointment of members of President Yalá's Balanta ethnic group, has been proposed as one of the sources of the country's political crisis during this period (Augel and Meyns, 2002: 26–7). The country experienced other difficulties too. For example, there were international factors that affected domestic politics. The conflict between Senegal and Casamance separatist fighters has sometimes spilled over into Guinea-Bissau. Indeed, the Casamance conflict provided the background to the 'civil war' in Guinea-Bissau in 1998, the year when Polity ≥+1 recorded the first collapse of democracy. Moreover, Guinea-Bissau was operating in a regional context where the roots of democracy were very shallow. Guinea-Bissau is bordered by Senegal, where there is a consensus that democracy began only in 2000,[3] and Guinea, which has never been classed as a democracy at all. There is little doubt that all of these factors affected the collapse of democracy in Guinea-Bissau. The aim of this book is to avoid a monocausal, institutionally deterministic argument and to acknowledge that economic, social, cultural, and international factors often play a major role in the performance of democracies. However, the aim is also to suggest that institutions can and often do matter. Thus, while acknowledging the undoubted importance of all the factors identified above, the focus here is on the ways in which Guinea-Bissau's president-parliamentary system contributed to the collapse of democracy in 2003.

In contrast to the situation in Mali, the choice of president-parliamentarism in Guinea-Bissau was a gradual process (Silva, 2006/2007). In May 1984, a new Constitution was adopted. This document reiterated the single-party, Marxist-inspired nature of the regime.[4] The text of this document stated that the government was responsible both to the legislature (the *Assembleia Nacional Popular* (ANP) – National People's Assembly) and to the Council of State (Art. 75). However, there was no position of prime minister and the head of state was the President of the Council of State who was elected by the ANP. In May 1991, a constitutional amendment introduced multiparty competition. In December 1991, another constitutional amendment created the position of prime minister (Art. 70) without altering the text of Art. 75. In February 1993, there were major changes to the constitution with the result that even though the 1984 constitution was still legally extant, there was in effect a 'materially new' constitution (Ibid.: 71).[5] The

1993 amendments included provision for the direct election of the head of state, who was now termed the President of the Republic. Moreover, Art. 103 (the new version of Art. 75) stated that the prime minister was responsible both to the president and to the ANP. Thus, by February 1993, by way of a series of amendments, Guinea-Bissau had come to adopt a semi-presidential constitution with a president-parliamentary form of semi-presidentialism.

To what extent are events that may subsequently be attributed to president-parliamentarism endogenous to the circumstances in which this form of semi-presidentialism was chosen? In 1980, João Bernardo (Nino) Vieira seized power in a coup. He then served as head of state from that time until he was forced out of office in May 1999. In this way, even though president-parliamentarism emerged as a function of a series of incremental constitutional changes from 1984 to 1993, the same person was effectively in charge of the political system from the beginning to the end of this time. Moreover, that person was then the first directly elected president during the transition to democracy under president-parliamentarism, and he was still in charge in 1998 when Polity $\geq$+1 recorded the first collapse of democracy. Thus, arguably, there was an endogeneity problem in the period 1994–8.[6] Even if this is the case, thereafter any such problem was mitigated by a number of factors. Following defeat in the 1998–9 civil war, Vieira went into exile in June 1999. Indeed, he was expelled from the PAIGC in that year. Therefore, in the period 2000–3, which is the focus of this case study, Vieira played no part in events. Moreover, during this time, the president was Kumba Yalá, who had been Vieira's main opponent at the 1994 presidential election, and the PAIGC was in opposition. Thus, even if the institutions were tailored at least in part for Vieira and the PAIGC, they were certainly not tailored for his main opponent and the opposition party. In sum, the endogeneity problem is at its most severe where an incumbent leader oversees the writing of a constitution that reflects his/her institutional preferences safe in the knowledge that the first elections under the new constitution will return the incumbent and his/her party to power. Even if there are some grounds for thinking that the Polity $\geq$+1 collapse in 1998 may be tainted by an endogeneity problem, such a concern is much less relevant to the period from 2000 to 2003.

As noted above, Guinea-Bissau operates under a constitution that dates back to 1984 but that has been amended on a number of occasions since, most recently in December 1996. The Constitution allows for a directly elected (Art. 63–1), five-year fixed-term president (Arts. 66, 71, and 72), a prime minister who is head of government (Art. 97–1), and a government that is explicitly responsible to both the president and the legislature (Art. 103). Thus, the constitution unequivocally establishes a president-parliamentary form of semi-presidentialism. In addition, the president enjoys quite considerable constitutional powers (Arts. 68, 69, and 70), including the power to appoint the prime minister following consultation with the political forces in the ANP (Arts. 68-g and 98–1), and to veto legislation, although the ANP may override the veto with a two-thirds majority (Art. 69–2).

The government leads the general policy of the country (Art. 96–2), while the prime minister directs and coordinates the government (Art. 97–2). There is no explicit mention of an investiture vote for either the prime minister or the government, but Art. 96–2 states that the government leads the country on the basis of a programme that has been approved by the ANP. Moreover, Art. 104-b states that if the ANP rejects the government's programme for a second time, then the government has to resign. Thus, while it is not explicitly stated, there is the implicit assumption that a new government will require the support of the legislature. The ANP may lodge a motion of no-confidence in the government at the request of one-third of deputies (Art. 85–4) and if the motion is approved by an absolute majority of deputies, then the government is brought down (Art. 85–5). Overall, while the president is placed in a powerful position, there is, on paper at least, a system of checks and balances both within the executive and between the executive and the legislature.[7] In this context, what is the evidence that events in the period 2000–3 are consistent with a president-parliament reading of the political process as outlined in Chapter 2 and again at the beginning of this chapter? To begin, it is necessary to sketch very briefly the events leading up to this point.

In July 1994, at the first elections since democratization, the PAIGC was returned with a large parliamentary majority winning 62 of the then 100 seats in the legislature. At the same time, João Bernardo (Nino) Vieira of the PAIGC won 46.2 per cent of the vote at the first ballot of the presidential election, while his nearest rival, Kumba Yalá from the Social Renewal Party (*Partido da renovação social* – PRS), won only 21.9 per cent. However, in August, Vieira was elected at the second ballot with only 52 per cent of the vote, with Yalá managing to pick up most of the anti-PAIGC electorate. By 1997, the economic situation was extremely difficult and there was social unrest. In May 1997, in an attempt to 'deflect criticism' (Forrest, 2002: 254), President Vieira dismissed the prime minister, Manuel Saturnino da Costa, citing 'a serious political crisis' that threatened 'the normal functioning of the republic'.[8] The strategy failed. Throughout 1998, the political and economic situation worsened. Legislative elections were due in June 1998, but were delayed. President Vieira was unpopular and the opposition parties felt that they would make gains at the upcoming election (Azevedo and Nijzink, 2007: 147). Indeed, there was a real possibility that President Vieira would have to cohabit with an opposition legislature if elections were held as scheduled. However, elections did not take place. In June 1998, there was an army mutiny. The rebellion followed President Vieira's decision in February to suspend the army chief of staff, General Ansumane Mané. He was accused of selling arms to the rebels in the Casamance region of Senegal who were fighting for independence. The legislature established a special committee to investigate the claim. The committee's report concluded that the accusations against Mané were unjustified and that people close to the president had conducted the trafficking (Azevedo and Nijzink, 2007: 148). In advance of the publication of the report, on 6 June, President Vieira appointed a replacement for General Mané. This decision precipitated the former chief of staff to go into rebellion, and there was a low-level civil war between his supporters and those of President Vieira. In effect, this marked the first collapse of democracy, although Vieira was finally overthrown only in May 1999. At this point, General Mané assumed power at the head of a military junta. However, power was quickly handed over, at least nominally, to an interim president, Malan Bacai Sanhá, of the PAIGC and the transition back to democracy began. On 28 November 1999, elections for the ANP were held. They produced a divided legislature in which the PRS was the largest party with 38/102 seats in the Assembly (see Table 5.1). At the same time, the first round of the presidential election was held. At this election, Kumba Yalá, the PRS's presidential candidate, headed the poll with 38.8 per cent of the vote ahead of Malan Bacai Sanhá of the PAIGC who won 23.4 per cent. On 16 January 2000, Yalá was overwhelmingly elected winning 72.0 per cent of the vote. On 17 February, he was sworn in as president.

President Yalá assumed power as an 'immensely popular politician' (Forrest, 2005: 259) but in very difficult circumstances. The economic situation was extremely poor and the country was reliant on the international financial community for assistance. In addition, while the armed rebellion was over, General Mané had not left power. Indeed, initially, he occupied an office opposite the president's with a sign announcing himself as the 'Military Junta's Highest Commander, *Co-Presidente*' (Rudebeck, 2001: 66), thus challenging the president's authority. However, Yalá quickly set to work. Immediately following his election and before his swearing-in, he named Caetano N'Tchama from the PRS as prime minister. In February, he announced a coalition government, mainly comprising the PRS and the second party in the legislature, the *Resistência Guiné-Bissau/Movimento Bafatá* (Resistance of Guinea-Bissau-Bafatá Movement – RGB-MB), but also including a number of independents and defeated presidential candidates from small parties. The government also included a close colleague of General Mané as

TABLE 5.1 *The November 1999 election to the* Assembleia Nacional Popular *(ANP), Guinea-Bissau*

Party	Seats
Social Renewal Party (PRS)	38
Resistance of Guinea-Bissau-Bafatá Movement (RGB-MB)	29
African Party for the Independence of Guinea and Cape Verde (PAIGC)	24
Democratic Alliance (AD)	3
Union for Change (UM)	3
Social Democratic Party (PSD)	3
Democratic Social Front (FDS)	1
National Union for Democracy and Progress (UNDP)	1
Total	102

Source: http://africanelections.tripod.com/gw.html (accessed 28 April 2010).

Minister for Defence. Indeed, in March, in an attempt to address the security situation and following mediation by the Foreign Minister of Gambia, Yalá appointed all sixteen members of the former junta to the government as Ministers of State. That said, their status was tenuous and in May the Foreign Minister, Mamadú Iaia Djaló, explained that they were not really ministers (quoted in Rudebeck, 2001: 69). Thus, the security situation remained tense.

The beginning of the Yalá presidency seems to mark a period of consensus government. Indeed, the N'Tchama administration was labelled a government of 'national unity' by sources close to the PRS.[9] However, from the start there were signs that the consensus was merely a veneer. For example, even though the PRS's ruling body approved the choice of N'Tchama as prime minister by forty-six votes to six,[10] there are reports that Yalá imposed his preferred candidate on the party (Novais, 2007: 125). In any case, the constitution states that the president has to consult with the parties in parliament before appointing the prime minister and Yalá had failed to do so, leading to the headline 'The PRS government's first unconstitutional blunder' (quoted in Rudebeck, 2001: 65). Moreover, immediately after the coalition with the RGB-MB had been formed, there were tensions between the two parties. They could not agree whose representative should be elected to the post of Speaker of the ANP. In this context, the PRS 'allowed their candidate . . . to be elected with the support of PAIGC's votes in an open contest against Hélder Vaz, the leader of RGB/MB' (Rudebeck, 2001: 66). While it is certainly the case that parties in Guinea-Bissau lack ideological bases and are often organized on the basis of highly personalized factions (Nóbrega, 2003: 15–17), the speed with which relations deteriorated between the PRS and RGB-MB is exceptional.

In general, the relations between the President Yalá and the PRS, on the one hand, and the RGB-MB, on the other, were extremely poor. There is little doubt that this was in part due to President Yalá, who was a highly interventionist president. One observer noted that his 'lack of consultation with the relevant government ministers before taking decisions created extreme friction within the government, particularly in the RGB-MB' (Ostheimer, 2001: 2), citing examples that impinged on Vaz's responsibilities as Minister for the Economy and Regional Development. In September 2000, the RGB-MB leader wrote to Prime Minister N'Tchama criticizing the criteria by which ambassadors were being appointed.[11] In return, on 5 September, Yalá dismissed the five RGB-MB ministers from the government by presidential decree. However, on 14 September, President Yalá cancelled the decree when it became clear that the government would not be able to command a majority in the legislature. The reinstatement of the coalition, though, was merely temporary. On 23 November 2000, General Mané again went into rebellion, only to be killed a week later in a shoot-out with government forces. The stabilization of the security situation seemed to embolden Yalá. On 23 January 2001, a government reshuffle was announced in which the number of PRS ministers was increased at the expense of the RGB-MB[12] and apparently without any consultation.[13] There were negotiations between the PRS and the RGB-MB the next day,[14] but they came to nothing and the RGB-MB withdrew from the government. On 25 January, Prime Minister N'Tchama was reappointed, but this time at the head of essentially a single-party PRS government with the addition of a small number of other figures. Overall, the coalition between the PRS and the RGB-MB had lasted less than a year with, in the end, President Yalá preferring to rely on a minority PRS government than engage with a coalition partner.

The new government lasted only a short time. In March, the executive committee of the PRS ruled that Prime Minister N'Tchama should resign,[15] though there is certainly a sense that President Yalá was behind the decision (Novais, 2007: 126). While Yalá and the PRS agreed on the need for a new prime minister, they disagreed as to who his replacement should be.[16] The PRS's executive committee recommended that the Minister of the Interior, Artur Sanha, should be the new prime minister,[17] but, instead, on 19 March, Yalá chose to appoint an independent, Faustino Fudut Imbali. President Yalá calculated that a non-partisan figure might be able to construct a parliamentary majority without the need for a formal coalition (Azevedo, 2009: 164). The new government was dominated by the PRS, though there were representatives from a number of other, very small parties and also from both the RGB-MB and the PAIGC, though ministers from the latter two parties were appointed in an 'individual capacity' rather than as official representatives of their party.[18] Overall, even though the prime minister was non-partisan and a number of parties were represented in the government, and even though from this point on opposition parties became increasingly split into pro-Yalá and anti-Yalá camps,[19] the government still lacked a parliamentary majority.

The beginning of the Imbali government was very difficult. The government required approval for its general programme, whereas the opposition wished to lodge a motion of no-confidence. In April 2001, there was a battle of procedure within parliament, with the opposition trying to force an extraordinary session of the ANP so that it could vote on the censure motion and with the PRS Speaker being forced to concede the extraordinary session but ruling that votes on such motions could not be taken during such a session.[20] For his part, President Yalá threatened to dissolve the ANP if a motion of no-confidence was passed.[21] There was certainly pressure from civil society and from international organizations to resolve the impasse, and it is quite possible that President Yalá's threat had the intended effect, but in early May the opposition dropped the motion of confidence. On 17 May, the ANP approved the programme of government by fifty-six votes to forty-three and on 30 May the budget was approved also by fifty-six votes in favour and with thirty-nine abstentions.[22] While these votes allowed the government to proceed with its business, they did not mark the formation of a new majority. For example, on 5 April 2001, the ANP passed a new constitution that included articles aimed at reducing the powers of the president. However, on 23 May, President Yalá announced that he was not promulgating the law, sending it back to ANP with various recommendations for increasing the president's powers (Azevedo, 2009: 144). Even though subsequently the ANP tried to persuade the president to sign the constitution into law, Yalá simply ignored the requests.

On 10 September 2001, a new crisis erupted. The Supreme Court ruled that a presidential decision to expel the Ahmadiyya Muslim group from the country was unconstitutional.[23] In return, President Yalá sacked three judges from the Court and, a week later, appointed three new ones. There were reports that the government was not fully behind the president's decision[24] and it precipitated a strike by the country's magistrates that paralysed all court sittings for a month.[25] Meanwhile, in the ANP another battle of procedure resulted. The Speaker indefinitely postponed the parliamentary session that was due to start at the beginning of October,[26] but the opposition managed to force an extraordinary two-day session three weeks later. During the session, a vote of no confidence in President Yalá was taken. It was supported by fifty-six votes in favour, with thirty-four votes against (primarily from the PRS) and four abstentions.[27] The vote had no constitutional foundation, but it was a sign not only that President Yalá was no longer able to command majority support in the ANP but also that there was now a majority hostile to him there. Generally, the country was described as being in a state of 'institutional uprising'[28] with large demonstrations against the head of state. In this context, on 9 December 2001, President Yalá sacked Prime Minister Imbali, stating that he had failed in his job.[29]

The new Prime Minister, Alamara Ntchina Nhassè, had been a minister in the previous government and was a high-ranking figure in the PRS. He took office amid rumours of a coup that was supposedly being orchestrated by officers loyal to the late General Mané. However, there was a strong belief among opposition forces that the rumours were being fabricated in an attempt to justify a crackdown on the media and civil society.[30] While, initially, the change of prime minister stabilized the political situation somewhat, by August 2002 the relations between the president and prime minister had deteriorated. The president had dismissed a number of government ministers and Prime Minister Nhassè accused President Yalá of abusing his power.[31] Moreover, at the beginning of October, the PAIGC and RGB-MB in conjunction with the smaller *Aliança Democrática* (Democratic Alliance – AD) and the *Frente Democrática e Social* (Democratic and Social Front – FDS) signed a motion calling for President Yalá to resign, labelling him the principal obstacle to peace and development in the country.[32] With the government unable to pass legislation in parliament, on 14 November 2002, President Yalá officially dissolved the ANP, accusing it of acting 'subversively'.[33] Then, on 17 November the president dismissed Prime Minister Nhassè. Again, the government had lasted less than a year.

The new Prime Minister, Mário Pires, from the PRS, headed a government of 'presidential initiative' (Novais, 2007: 127), indicating very clearly that President Yalá intended to take charge of government affairs. While the opposition parties were angry at Yalá's snap decision to dissolve the ANP, they were content that an election would clarify the political situation.[34] However, they also condemned the appointment of a new prime minister following the decision to dissolve the ANP (Azevedo, 2009: 165). There is little doubt that Yalá sequenced the events deliberately in this way, so that the new prime minister would not have to face a vote on the government's programme, a vote that the government would almost certainly have lost. In the end, the downfall of the Yalá regime mirrored that of President Vieira four years earlier. While the president promised elections, they were never forthcoming. The election date was postponed from February to April 2003, and then from July to August 2003. President Yalá was very well aware that the opposition would in all likelihood win the election and that he would be forced to cohabit with an opposition prime minister. Finally, on 14 September 2003, following an announcement that the election was being postponed once again, the military intervened and ousted President Yalá. So authoritarian had Yalá become that, for one writer, the military acted to restore democracy rather than to end it (Forrest, 2005: 263).

The collapse of democracy in Guinea-Bissau in 2003 illustrates the problems of president-parliamentarism very well. President Yalá had begun as an immensely popular politician, but his actions soon drifted into 'bonapartism, zero-sum politics, and authoritarian behavior' (Forrest, 2005: 259). He did not attempt to construct a cohesive majority with legislative backing. Indeed, immediately after forming his first coalition government, he undermined the position of his coalition partner in the Assembly. He appointed prime ministers in the knowledge that they did not have majority support. He preferred to try to cobble together a working majority by appointing an independent prime minister and by encouraging opposition party dissidents to enter the government rather than by working with a coalition partner on the basis of a stable majority. When it became clear that the legislature would no longer tolerate a PRS-dominated government, Yalá dissolved parliament and formed a government of 'presidential initiative', ruling by decree rather than through the legislature. Generally, President Yalá appeared to work against the legislature. He did not systematically veto laws (Novais, 2007: 138), but he did use a 'pocket veto' to avoid promulgating the constitution that had been duly passed by the legislature. His party used procedural rules in the ANP to try to forestall debate when it was clear that the majority was hostile to the government. Within the executive, President Yalá was highly interventionist, serially dismissing ministers and prime ministers as a way of trying to resolve political problems. When it was clear that elections would return an opposition majority, Yalá delayed them. Indeed, Guinea-Bissau is an excellent example of why cohabitation is very rare in president-parliamentary systems. Had the political process been allowed to operate normally, then there would have been elections and cohabitation would almost certainly have ensued (Elgie, 2010*b*). However, the dynamics of president-parliamentarism meant that the president preferred to rule against the legislature, thus never allowing cohabitation to manifest itself. Overall, while Guinea-Bissau faced a parlous economic situation, a partly constitutional military, and increasing ethnic tensions during the period 2000–3, the instability provoked by the president-parliamentary form of semi-presidentialism did not help to foster democratic stability.

PREMIER-PRESIDENTIALISM AND THE SURVIVAL OF DEMOCRACY: THE CASE OF MALI

French rule in the area that is now Mali began in the late nineteenth century. In 1959, with the granting of increased autonomy, the Sudanese Republic, as the area was then known, formed a confederation with Senegal. This was known as the Federation of Mali. In June 1960, the Federation of Mali achieved independence from France. However, in August 1960, Senegal withdrew from the Federation. A month later, the Sudanese Republic adopted a new constitution and the country was renamed Mali. In theory, the Malian constitution allowed for pluralist political competition, but in practice the *Union Soudanaise-Rassemblement Démocratique Africain* (Sudanese Union-African Democratic Rally – US-RDA) led by the head of state, Modibo Keïta, soon became the dominant party. In 1968, Keïta was overthrown in a coup led by Lieutenant Moussa Traoré, who suspended the constitution. In 1974, a new constitution was passed. This established a single-party regime with Traoré as both head of state and the leader of the ruling party, the *Union Démocratique du Peuple Malien* (Democratic Union of the Malian People – UDPM). The Traoré regime lasted until 1991. In March of that year, in response to government repression of student demonstrations, Lieutenant Colonel Amadou Toumani Touré staged a coup that ended the UDPM regime. In conjunction with civilian leaders in the so-called *Comité de transition pour le salut du peuple* (Transition Committee for the Salvation of the People – CTSP), a new constitution was soon drafted. The document was adopted by a national conference in August 1991 and was overwhelmingly approved in a referendum in January 1992. In February and March, elections to the *Assemblée nationale* (National Assembly) were held and in April 1992 the first presidential election under the new constitution took place. The *Alliance pour la Démocratie en Mali* (Alliance for Democracy in Mali – ADEMA) won a majority of seats at the legislative election and Alpha Oumar Konaré of ADEMA won the presidential election.

There is general agreement that in Mali democracy began in 1992. As noted in Table 3.1, all five of the measures of democracy referred to in this book record an ongoing period of democracy since that time. There is some variation in the Polity and Freedom House scores after 1992. For Polity, Mali records a score of +7 from 1992 to 1996 inclusive, a score of +6 from 1997 to 2001 inclusive, and a score of +7 thereafter. For Freedom House, Mali was classed as Free with a score of 2.5

from 1992 to 1993 inclusive, Partly Free with a score of 3 in 1993, and Free thereafter with a score ranging from 2 to 3.[35] In general, though, the classification of Mali as a democracy is consistent across the set of measures and, where scores are recorded, they too have been remarkably stable. It must be noted that Mali is not a consolidated democracy on the basis of these figures. In Mali, democracy is still relatively fragile. However, all of the measures indicate that democracy has survived since 1992. Therefore, while the performance of democracy in Mali has room to improve, it can be taken as an example of a country where a fledgling democracy has survived.

To what extent does Mali's premier-presidential system account for the survival of democracy since 1992? The first point to note in this regard is that, like Guinea-Bissau, the level of economic development in Mali is very low. From 2002 to 2007 inclusive the average GDP per capita measured in constant 2000-US$ was $275 in Mali, compared with $556 in sub-Saharan Africa as a whole, and $28,448 in OECD countries during the same period.[36] Thus, levels of relative economic development cannot account for why democracy in Guinea-Bissau collapsed, yet in Mali it survived. In Mali, democracy survived despite the low level of economic development. Similarly, using Alesina et al.'s measures (2003), Mali scores 0.7 for ethnic fractionalization, 0.8 for linguistic fractionalization, and 0.2 for religious fractionalization. These figures are comparable to those in Guinea-Bissau, suggesting that this factor does not account for the difference in the democratic fortunes of the two countries. Instead, by and large, those who try to explain the apparent success of democracy in Mali tend to privilege historical and cultural explanations. For example, while acknowledging the geopolitical significance of the end of the Cold War and the importance of President Konaré's leadership after 1992, Docking (1997) states: 'I maintain that a major factor that must be taken into consideration when looking at the Malian case is the nature of political culture that has pervaded society in this part of the Western Sahel for centuries' (Ibid.: 201), namely a 'rich network of social organizations and associational groups' (Ibid.: 205) that encourages popular participation and political accountability (Ibid.). Pringle (2006: 33) makes a similar argument but does so somewhat more colourfully: 'When I asked Malians to explain their aptitude for democracy, their answers boiled down to "It's the history, stupid," of course expressed more politely'. Similarly, Smith (2001: 76) notes the importance of a number of factors, but states specifically that 'Many aspects of Malian traditional society encourage norms consistent with democratic citizenship, including tolerance, trust, pluralism, the separation of powers, and the accountability of the leader to the governed'. So, even though Moestrup (1999) adopts an institutionalist explanation of the survival of democracy in Mali, it must be acknowledged that most observers have tended to prioritize cultural accounts of democracy's success there. This book does not aim to test the validity of such arguments. The aim is to demonstrate that political institutions can affect the prospects for the survival of democracy, specifically the form of semi-presidential institutions in a country, while acknowledging that other factors always matter too. In the case of Mali, it is merely noted that other writers tend to focus on cultural factors in this regard.

To what extent is the success of democratization in Mali endogenous to the choice of premier-presidentialism? To put it another way, to what extent is any consensual and accommodative behaviour since 1992 a function of the circumstances surrounding the choice of this form of semi-presidentialism in 1991? Various scholars have singled out the national conference in that year as being an important moment in the story of Mali's democracy, with some writers stressing the importance of the particularities of the Malian conference (Clark, 1995; Wing, 2008: 36) and others emphasizing the importance of such conferences in general (Nzouankeu, 1993). In Mali, the national conference was held from 29 July to 12 August 1991 (Diarra, 2010: 153–72). The composition of the conference was extremely heterogenous with over 1,800 people attending (Diarra, 1995: 253) and with representation from groups ranging from the military to the artistic community. The conference had limited sovereignty, meaning that it worked within the framework established by the CTSP and that it focused on a number of specific issues. One of these issues was the constitution, which was approved by the conference. Arguably, the inclusive nature of the conference meant that subsequently the constitution itself was not a focus of contestation, thus anchoring the political system. According to this logic, premier-presidentialism was the result of consensus, it has not generated consensus. However, it should be noted that the constitution was not the product of the conference. The conference merely legitimized the text that had been drafted beforehand by the CTSP. In this regard, what is noticeable is that the leader of the CTSP, Amadou Toumani Touré, did not stand for election in 1992. Therefore, it is difficult to argue that the constitution reflected the interests of the first president of the new regime. In fact, the first president, Alpha Oumar Konaré, was only one actor in the drafting process. Equally, even though Touré did decide to stand for election in 2002, he had not been an active participant in the domestic political life of the country in the decade prior to his election. So, again, it is scarcely convincing to argue that the operation of the constitution was endogenous to the preferences of the president after 2002. Generally, there is little to suggest that a premier-presidential reading of the survival of democracy in Mali suffers fatally from an endogeneity problem.

To date, the text of the 1992 constitution has remained unchanged.[37] The text was 'inspired by' (Ibid.: 155) the 1958 French constitution. Indeed, an insider account identifies by name two senior French constitutional experts who were called upon to advise the committee that was responsible for drafting the constitution (Massicotte, 2009). The constitution provides for a premier-presidential form of semi-presidentialism with a balance of power between the president and the prime minister.[38] Art. 30 states that the president is elected for five years by universal suffrage. Art. 38 indicates that the president names the prime minister and terminates the prime minister's functions when presented with the government's resignation. The president also has the right to return a bill to the National

Assembly for a second reading (Art. 40), to dissolve the Assembly (Art. 42), and to assume emergency powers when there is a grave and immediate threat to the country (Art. 50). Art. 55 identifies the prime minister as the head of government, specifying that the prime minister directs and coordinates the work of the government. Art. 53 states that the government determines and leads the policy of the nation and Art. 54 specifies that the government is responsible to the National Assembly. There is no mention of the government or the prime minister being responsible to the president and the circumstances in which the government is responsible to the legislature are set out in Arts. 78 and 79. The Assembly may lodge a motion of no-confidence in the government. If the motion receives the support of two-thirds of the members of the Assembly, then the government must resign. In addition, the government may make a text a matter of confidence, in which case the text is considered to be passed unless the Assembly successfully lodges and passes a motion of no-confidence. While the supermajority requirement for a motion of no-confidence is unusual and does not follow the French example, the fact that the prime minister and government are responsible solely to the legislature means that Mali is an example of premier-presidentialism.

While the general level of democracy in Mali has remained more or less stable since 1992 and while the constitution has remained unchanged, the political situation within the country has varied considerably. At the 1992 National Assembly election, ADEMA won 76 of the then 116 seats in the legislature. A month later, Alpha Oumar Konaré of ADEMA won the presidential election, recording 69.0 per cent of the vote at the second ballot. In 1997, the main opposition parties boycotted the presidential and legislative elections, meaning that President Konaré was re-elected with 95.9 per cent of the vote and that ADEMA won 128/147 seats in the National Assembly. In 2002, however, the situation changed. In April/May of that year, Amadou Toumani Touré, standing as an independent candidate, won the presidential election, gaining 28.7 per cent of the vote at the first ballot and 64.4 per cent in a contest against his ADEMA opponent at the second ballot. The July 2002 elections to the National Assembly failed to return a clear majority (see Table 5.2). The largest group of parties, *Espoir 2002* (Hope 2002), supported the newly elected President but enjoyed only a relative majority in the legislature, while ADEMA was the largest party.[39] In 2007, President Touré stood for re-election under the banner of the *Alliance pour la démocratie et le progrès* (Alliance for Democracy and Progress – ADP), which, this time, included ADEMA. The ADP won 113/147 seats in the legislature and ADEMA was returned as the largest party with fifty-one seats. Thus, for the first decade of democracy, ADEMA was the dominant party in the system. Indeed, there was scarcely any parliamentary opposition to ADEMA at all during this time. By contrast, from 2002 to 2007 the president was an explicitly non-partisan figure and no single party or coalition enjoyed majority support in the National Assembly. After 2007, the president cultivated a Gaullist aloofness from political parties, but

TABLE 5.2 *The July 2002 election to the* Assemblée nationale *of Mali*

Party	Seats
Hope 2002 Coalition	66
Rally for Mali (RPM) – 46 seats	
National Congress for Democratic Initiative (CNID) – 13 seats	
Patriotic Movement for Renewal (MPR) – 5 seats	
Rally for Democracy and Labor (RDT) – 1 seat	
Alliance for the Republic and Democracy (ARD)	59
Alliance for Democracy in Mali (ADEMA) – 53 seats	
Others – 6 seats	
Convergence for Alternation and Change (ACC)	10
African Solidarity for Democracy and Independence (SADI)	6
Independents	6
Total	147

Note: Figures record seats following the October 2002 by-elections.
Source: http://africanelections.tripod.com/ml.html (accessed 11 May 2010).

he was able to rely on the support of a group of parties that had a very clear parliamentary majority.

In this context, the focus in this section will be on events in Mali from 2002 to 2007. This period maximizes the opportunity for comparison with Guinea-Bissau from 2000 to 2003. In Mali, as in Guinea-Bissau, there was a newly elected president and no clear majority for any party in the legislature. At the time, one observer (Lissouck, 2004: 35) outlined the difficulties that the absence of a presidential majority was likely to cause in Mali, particularly in the context of a system where parties had an incentive to 'outbid' each other, predicting that the country might experience a period of governmental instability (Ibid.: 40). The prediction was incorrect. In Mali, the period from 2002 to 2007 was a period of governmental consensus and political stability. So, whereas in Guinea-Bissau democracy collapsed in a way that was broadly consistent with the hypothesized effects of a president-parliamentary form of semi-presidentialism, in Mali, by contrast, democracy survived. To what extent was the survival of democracy in Mali consistent with a premier-presidential reading of events?

Even prior to his election in May 2002, Amadou Toumani Touré was a very well-known figure, having led the coup against the repressive regime of Moussa Traoré in March 1991, having gained plaudits for deciding not to contest the 1992 presidential election, and having engaged in a number of high-profile humanitarian projects since that time. However, his election was by no means guaranteed. In 2002, he stood for election without the backing of a political party or alliance. Equally, he was not seen as the candidate of a particular ethnic group. There was a perception that he had the tacit support of the outgoing president, Alpha Oumar Konaré, even though there was a candidate from the president's own ADEMA party (Boilley, 2002: 181). Even so, President Konaré did not openly express support for Touré. At the first round of the election, he was ahead of his nearest rival, but he won less than 30 per cent of the votes cast. At the second round he was elected easily, but as much for the fact that he was able to rally the anti-ADEMA vote as because he enjoyed overwhelming personal support. Similarly, once elected, Touré was able to transform his popularity into a certain political capital, but he was by no means dominant. At the July National Assembly election, President Touré did not openly support any political alliance, though he was closest to the parties in the *Convergence pour l'alternance et le changement* (Convergence for Alternation and Change – ACC) that returned ten deputies to the legislature. In addition, the anti-ADEMA parties in the *Espoir 2002* (Hope 2002) coalition also pledged their support for him. However, the election failed to produce a majority for any party or coalition. Moreover, following the election the component parts of the different electoral coalitions dispersed into eight separate parliamentary groups (Diarra, 2010: 216). Thus, in 2002 the newly elected president was faced with the situation where, like President Yalá immediately following his election, he was an extremely popular, indeed charismatic, figure (Villalón and Idrissa, 2005: 68–72), but where, also like President Yalá, he lacked the support of a parliamentary majority.

Faced with this situation, President Touré adopted a strategy of consensus. As prime minister, he appointed Ahmed Mohamed Ag Hamani, who had previously been a minister under the regime of Moussa Traoré, but who was not discredited by his association with the regime. Prime Minister Hamani was not affiliated to any political party. The first Hamani government was formed shortly prior to the legislative election and was a '*gouvernement de mission*' (a technical government), comprising mainly independent figures, but also including a broad range of party representatives. In October 2002, following the legislative election, President Touré reappointed Prime Minister Hamani. Crucially, while the second Hamani government contained both a large number of 'independents', many of whom were close to President Touré, there were also representatives from a large number of political parties. In total, there were twenty-one ministers, eleven of whom were independents and ten of whom were representatives of no fewer than eight political parties (Baudais and Chauzal, 2006: 68). There were two ADEMA ministers, both of whom were present in an official capacity. There were also two ministers from the *Rassemblement pour le Mali* (Rally for Mali – RPM) party, which was the second largest party group in the legislature and whose leader, Ibrahim Boubacar Keïta, had come third, with 21.0 per cent of the vote, at the 2002 presidential election. The presence of both ADEMA and the RPM in the government was significant because the RPM was an offshoot from ADEMA, having been formed by Keïta when ADEMA refused to select him as their official candidate for the 2002 presidential election. Thus, like President Yalá in 2000, President Touré appointed what might be called a 'government of national union', though the president did not refer to it in this way, preferring to label it a 'government of consensus' instead (Ibid.: 76). That said, President Touré went one step further than President Yalá by forming an oversized coalition that included almost every political group in the legislature, including parties that only recently were extremely hostile to each other. There was no formal coalition pact or agreement, but President Touré did issue a '*lettre de cadrage*' (framework letter), which indicated, in very general terms, the policy priorities of the new government.

The situation in the National Assembly was similar. Art. 68 of the 1992 constitution states that the President (Speaker) of the National Assembly is elected for the duration of the legislature. According to the Assembly's standing orders (*règlement intérieur*), the legislature's business is managed by eight vice-presidents, two questors, and eight parliamentary secretaries that collectively form the Assembly's bureau.[40] The members of the bureau are elected at the beginning of each parliamentary year, and Art. 11 of the *règlement intérieur* states that the composition of the bureau should try to reproduce the relative strength of the parliamentary groups in the Assembly overall. In 2002 there was fierce competition for the election of the President of the National Assembly between Ibrahim Boubacar Keïta of the RPM and Moutanga Tall of the *Congrès national d'initiative démocratique* (National Congress for Democratic Initiative – CNID), both of which were constituent elements of the *Espoir 2002* coalition. With President Touré's backing, Keïta was elected as President of the Assembly, with Tall being elected to the post of first vice-president. For its part, ADEMA representatives were elected to minor posts on the bureau consistent with Art. 11 of the *règlement intérieur*. These events demonstrated that even though there was competition between the different parties in the legislature, there was no attempt by any party to adopt a winner-takes-all strategy. Moreover, while President Touré did make his preference for Speaker clear, he did not attempt to intervene more broadly to try to force the election of a slate of people who were close to him. Crucially, the election of the bureau took place in September 2002 prior to the formation of the second Hamani government. Undoubtedly, the election of Keïta facilitated the participation of the RPM in the government. Generally, even if parties had a neo-patrimonial incentive to take office (Ibid.: 78), President Touré's hands-off strategy in relation to the election of the Assembly's bureau reassured all political parties and helped the subsequent formation of a consensus government. The National Assembly unanimously adopted the government's declaration of general policy in December 2002 (Diarra, 2010: 219).

In April 2004, there was a change of prime minister. However, in contrast to the equivalent situation in Guinea-Bissau and contrary to the expectations of certain Malian observers, the change did not come about as the result of a political crisis or the collapse of the coalition. While there is little doubt that President Touré made it plain to Hamani that he would like to see a change of prime minister, there is also little sense that the prime minister was removed because of any overt conflict with the president.[41] Certainly, Hamani did not go public with any criticisms of the president, even if he had any. Moreover, the change of prime minister did not lead to a change of political strategy. Hamani's replacement was Ousmane Issoufi Maïga, who had been an independent minister in the previous administration. In addition, more than 60 per cent of the ministers from the previous government were reappointed.[42] While the number of ministers increased to twenty-eight, the proportion of independents to party ministers remained very similar, though ADEMA and the RPM now had three ministers each and CNID had two. In total, nine parties were now represented in the government (Ibid.: 68). Generally, the contrast with Guinea-Bissau is very stark. Unlike President Yalá, President Touré was willing to work with and maintain an oversized coalition government. He appointed a non-partisan prime minister not, like President Yalá, as a way of trying to construct a parliamentary majority by default after his original coalition had collapsed, but because it ensured that he could avoid being seen to privilege one party at the expense of any other, given the resources that the prime minister controlled. President Touré's strategy was extremely successful. Again, when the new prime minister presented his declaration of general policy to the legislature in June 2004, he won the support of all 138 deputies who took part in the vote.[43] Moreover, while Guinea-Bissau was marked by a revolving-door premiership from 2000 to 2003, in Mali Prime Minister Maïga remained in office with essentially the same set of government ministers until September 2007.

In the National Assembly, the relations between the executive and the legislature were relatively smooth. The government was never faced with a motion of no-confidence. Moreover, the president did not send back a bill to the legislature for a second reading. There were occasions when relations were somewhat more strained. For example, in December 2004 the Speaker of the Assembly, Ibrahim Boubacar Keïta, headed a parliamentary delegation that met with the prime minister to discuss the government's policy towards the Transrail railway company.[44] The members of Assembly were unhappy with the way in which the government was handling the matter. More generally, the Assembly interpellated the government on eight occasions in the period between the 2002 and 2007 elections (Diarra, 2010: 217). That is to say, the legislature requested that government ministers appear before the legislature to explain and defend specific policies. Even so, while Art. 92 of the Assembly's *règlement intérieur* states that an interpellation may be followed by a censure motion, no such motion was ever tabled. For one observer, the relatively high number of interpellations was a positive sign, indicating, especially in comparison with the 1992–2002 period, that the legislature was playing an active role (Ibid.: 219). Indeed, what is perhaps most noteworthy is that, in contrast to the situation in Guinea-Bissau, the government did not react negatively to the Assembly's activity by trying either to reduce its powers or to use its procedural prerogatives to dominate the legislative process.

While relations between the government and the legislature were relatively smooth, over time relations between the different parties in the legislature became increasingly tense. The annual election of the bureau regularly brought matters to a head. In 2003, the RPM tried to gain the post of questor, but to no avail. In 2004, ADEMA negotiated with the RPM such that both gained posts at the expense of other groups, though in the end there was no opposition to the deal.[45] However, in 2005 the situation changed. At that time the *Espoir 2002* coalition effectively collapsed. The CNID and other members of the coalition reached an agreement with ADEMA that left the RPM isolated within the Assembly.[46] The RPM party leader, Ibrahim Boubacar Keïta, maintained his position as Speaker, because he had been elected for the full term of the legislature, but the RPM was provided with only two minor positions on the bureau. In response, the RPM refused to take them up.[47] In effect, the election of the Assembly's bureau in October 2005 ended the political consensus in the legislature.[48] The RPM, by this time the largest party in the Assembly, was isolated. Indeed, this was no once-off event. In October 2006, when the final bureau of the 2002–7 legislature was elected, the composition remained exactly the same, indicating that the anti-RPM alliance that had been forged the previous year was still intact.[49]

To what extent did the breakdown of consensus in the legislature mark a sign of deteriorating executive/legislative relations? There is little doubt that President Touré always aimed to be re-elected. There is also little doubt that his personal popularity would have been sufficient to meet this aim. However, he wanted the support of a coalition of parties. As Baudais and Chauzal (2006) argue, President Touré was never 'a-partisan'. From 2002 to 2007, he was independent of any particular party, but he worked with parties very closely. Indeed, he was happy to meet with representatives of the main political parties on a formal basis at Koulouba, the presidential residence.[50] For the parties themselves, they had to calculate whether they stood to gain more by supporting Touré or by running their own candidate. All of the main parties were divided on the issue. Gradually, they began to make their choice. By 2005, ADEMA had come to the conclusion that it had no candidate who was likely to beat Touré and, therefore, calculated that it would benefit by openly supporting the president. However, the RPM, or at least its leader, Ibrahim Boubacar Keïta, made a different calculation. He was perhaps the only person other than Touré who had a general popularity. By the early part of 2005, it was assumed that Keïta would stand against the president[51] and he 'missed no opportunity' to make it known that he was unhappy with the way in which the president was governing.[52] Keïta too tried to forge alliances with various parties, including ADEMA at one point[53] and then the *Union pour la République et la Démocratie* (Union for the Republic and Democracy – URD), which was an offshoot of ADEMA and which had considerable support in some parts of the country.[54] In the end, though, other parties calculated that they had more to lose by not supporting Touré, the likely winner, than by joining with Keïta. Thus, the alliance in October 2005 between ADEMA and the non-RPM elements of the *Espoir 2002* coalition should not be viewed as the collapse of a coalition that was precipitated by inter-institutional rivalry between, on the one hand, the president and the government and, on the other, the Speaker of the Assembly. Rather, it should be seen as the *de facto* creation of a new majority that was designed to support the re-election of President Touré against his most likely and dangerous rival, Ibrahim Boubacar Keïta.[55] In short, the president was not working against parliament by rupturing a majority and going it alone. Instead, a new majority was being created that would allow the president and most of the political parties in the country to form a stable government in the longer term.

In Mali, the period from 2002 to 2007 is generally considered to be a period of consensus. While the RPM was forced into a minority position in the legislature in October 2005, the party's ministers remained in government. Moreover, even within the legislature the anti-RPM majority manifested itself most clearly in the votes for the Assembly's bureau than on legislative votes generally. For some, the period of consensus was problematic, particularly the presence of so many independents in the government.[56] For others, by contrast, President Touré's strategy was fundamentally beneficial: 'Its main strength is that it is based on an equilibrium of forces, since the parties are able to use the parliament as a way of controlling the government's action and, if necessary, as a counterweight the influence of the president'.[57] The fact that the policy of consensus was so closely associated with President Touré has led some observers to argue that Mali's democratic success was at least in part a function of Touré personally, or, rather, that Touré's charisma managed to stave off an institutional crisis at least temporarily (Villalón and Idrissa, 2005: 72). However, a premier-presidential reading of events during Touré's first term suggests otherwise. The president was aware that the only way for him to exercise any influence was through the government and the legislature. Therefore, it was rational for the president to pursue a consensual strategy. This situation can be compared with that of President Yalá in Guinea-Bissau. He was aware that he had the power to shape the government in the way that he wished. Faced with opposition, this encouraged him to rule against the legislature in the hope that he could force through reforms and eventually win the day. In the end, though, the strategy of isolation left Yalá even more powerless, and even more determined to act unilaterally. Finally, the military intervened to put an end to Yalá's term.

In 2007, President Touré was triumphantly re-elected, winning 71.2 per cent of the vote at the first ballot, thus dispensing with the need for a second round. For his part, Ibrahim Boubacar Keïta came second, winning 19.15 per cent of the vote. To date, President Touré's second term has been remarkably similar to his first. For example, in October 2007 the government of the new prime minister, Modibo Sidibé, contained representatives of civil society and eight political parties, though not the RPM.[58] This time, though, the government, in the form of the president's ADP coalition, has a clear majority in the legislature. Following his re-election, President Touré is now term limited. Even though he established a commission that in 2010 proposed a set of constitutional reforms, they did not include the abolition of term limits. Therefore, the president is due to step down in 2012.

Worryingly, though, the proposed reforms did include a change that would allow the president to be able to dismiss the prime minister.[59] If enacted, this would install a president-parliamentary form of semi-presidentialism in Mali. If the reforms are passed in their current form, the argument in this book suggests that the democratic future of Mali may not be so bright as it has been up to this point.

CONCLUSION

This chapter began with a puzzle. Why did two young democracies in West Africa experience two very different democratic outcomes? Why did democracy in Guinea-Bissau collapse when in Mali it survived? Moreover, why did these different outcomes occur when both countries had a long history of colonial rule but only a short history of democracy, when both had a very low level of economic development and a highly fragmented ethnic population, and when both experienced the situation where a highly popular newly elected president came to power without a legislative majority? The answer, in part, lies in the constitutional structure of these countries. In Guinea-Bissau, with a president-parliamentary form of semi-presidentialism, the president had little incentive to build an inclusive coalition. Instead, when faced with opposition, the president had an incentive to change the government in the hope that a new majority might somehow emerge or that the legislature would be bowed into submission in the face of the president's unilateral exercise of authority. Faced with the president's actions, the legislature responded by refusing to cooperate with the president and by trying to change the president's powers and by encouraging him to leave office. By contrast, in Mali, with a premier-presidential form of semi-presidentialism, the president had an incentive to build a working majority. The president was aware that if he decided to oppose the forces in the legislature, then he would be forced to operate with a government over which he had little control. Therefore, to maintain an influence over the system, he had an incentive to cooperate. The result was a strategy of consensus and a very stable period of government. Undoubtedly, the outcomes in both cases were not caused solely by the different institutional arrangements in each country. Moreover, by definition, the outcomes were at least in part endogenous to the choice of the different institutional structures in the first place. All the same, what is remarkable is that the story of the collapse and survival of these two democracies can be told in a way which is entirely consistent with the hypothesized expectations of the effects of the two different forms of semi-presidentialism that were identified in Chapter 2 and with the general statistical associations that were discovered in Chapter 3. In Chapter 6, a different methodological approach is taken to test the argument in this book even further.

NOTES

1. From 1991 to 1993 inclusive Guinea-Bissau is given a score of 5.5, but is officially recorded as Partly Free. For the purposes of this book, and in line with Freedom House's official classification schema, it assumed that the Partly Free category begins with a score of 5.
2. Figures from the World Bank's World Development Indicators.
3. Four of the five measured used here record democracy beginning at this time. Only FH F & PF records an earlier start.
4. Available in French at: http://confinder.richmond.edu/admin/docs/Guinea_Bissau_French.pdf (accessed 23 April 2010).
5. The 1996 version of the Constitution, which has been changed only slightly from the version amended in 1993, is available in Portuguese at: http://www.anpguinebissau.org/leis/constituicao/constituicaoguine.pdf (accessed 23 April 2010).
6. In fact, during this period 1994–8, the endogeneity problem was, arguably, less severe than it might at first appear. For example, prior to the 1993 constitutional reforms, there was a *Comissão multipartidaria de transição* (Multiparty Commission of Transition) in 1992. While there was often conflict and stalemate between the parties represented on the Commission, it did help to draw up the reforms that were subsequently passed in 1993 (Cardoso, 1995: 268). Moreover, the PAIGC was frequently accused of delaying the transition because it was afraid that it might lose power in free elections (Azevedo, 2009: 154). Indeed, Vieira nearly lost the 1994 presidential election to Yalá, winning only 52 per cent of the vote at the second ballot. Overall, while Vieira was clearly a powerful figure generally and did intervene in the writing of the constitution, including Art. 68 and the list of presidential powers (Azevedo, 2009: 144), the system was more fluid than a purely endogenous account of institutional choice would require.
7. For a more detailed summary, see Azevedo (2009: 144–52).
8. *Africa Research Bulletin: Political, Social and Cultural Series*, 1–31 May 1997, p. 12688. Vieira appointed the new Prime Minister, Carlos Correia, without consulting the parties in the legislature as required by Arts. 68-g and 98–1 of the Constitution. In October 1997, the Supreme Court ruled that Prime Minister Correia's appointment was unconstitutional. Facing pressure from the Assembly where all parliamentary work had been suspended in protest, President Vieira then dismissed Correia only to reappoint him a few days later after consultations with the Council of State and party leaders (*Guinea-Bissau: President dismisses Prime Minister Correia*, AFP news agency, Paris – 12 October 1997). Following Prime Minister Correia's reappointment President Vieira announced that he had corrected a 'constitutional error' (*Africa Research Bulletin: Political, Social and Cultural Series*, 1–31 October 1997, p. 12853).
9. 'Guinea-Bissau: Ntchama named new prime minister', 25 January 2000 (IRIN) (http://www.irinnews.org/Report.aspx?ReportId=11941).
10. Ibid.

11. *Africa Research Bulletin: Political, Social and Cultural Series*, 1–30 September 2000, p. 14109.
12. *Africa Research Bulletin: Political, Social and Cultural Series*, 1–31 January 2001, p. 14260.
13. 'Guinea-Bissau: Minority government sworn in', 26 January 2001 (IRIN) (www.irinnews.org/Report.aspx?ReportId=17122).
14. 'Guinea-Bissau: Talks aimed at saving ruling coalition continue', 24 January 2001 (IRIN) (www.irinnews.org/Report.aspx?ReportId=17053).
15. 'Guiné-Bissau terá novo primeiro-ministro', *Il Público*, 9 March 2001 (www.publico.pt/Mundo/guinebissau-tera-novo-primeirominiistro_14104).
16. 'Guinea-Bissau: Opposition calls on government to resign', 31 July 2001 (IRIN) (www.irinnews.org/Report.aspx?ReportId=24094).
17. Ibid.
18. *Africa Research Bulletin: Political, Social and Cultural Series*, 1–31 August 2001, p. 14512.
19. 'Guinea-Bissau: Constitutional crisis', 18 September 2001 (IRIN) (www.irinnews.org/Report.aspx?ReportId=26939).
20. 'Parliament prepares exit of Guinea-Bissau government', *Afrol News*, 22 April 2001 (www.afrol.com/News2001/gub005_imbala_opp2.htm).
21. 'Parlamento da Guiné-Bissau debate se vai votar moção de censura', *Il Público*, 30 April 2001 (www.publico.pt/Mundo/parlamento-da-guinebissau-debate-se-vai-votar-mocao-de-censura_21008).
22. *Report of the Secretary-General on developments in Guinea-Bissau and the activities of the United Nations Peace-building Support Office in that country*, point 7, available at: www.afrol.com/Countries/Guinea_Bissau/documents/un_bissau_220601.htm (accessed 28 April 2010).
23. Quoted from 'Guinea Bissau: President sacks Supreme Court judges', 11 September 2001 (IRIN) (www.irinnews.org/Report.aspx?ReportId=26688).
24. 'Guinea Bissau: Constitutional crisis', 18 September 2001 (IRIN) (www.irinnews.org/Report.aspx?ReportId=26939).
25. 'Guinea-Bissau towards political collapse', afrol news, 26 October 2001 (www.afrol.com/News2001/gub008_polit_crisis.htm).
26. 'Guinea Bissau: Opposition wants parliamentary debate on volatile situation', 2 October 2001 (IRIN) (www.irinnews.org/Report.aspx?ReportId=27406).
27. 'Guinea-Bissau towards political collapse', afrol news, 26 October 2001 (www.afrol.com/News2001/gub008_polit_crisis.htm).
28. 'Guinea Bissau in a state of 'institutional' uprising', PANA, 29 October 2001 (www.panapress.com/paysindexlat.asp?codepays=eng024&page=65).
29. *Africa Research Bulletin: Political, Social and Cultural Series*, 1–31 December 2001, p. 14659.
30. 'Guinea Bissau: Opposition want evidence of attempted coup', 6 December 2001 (IRIN) (www.irinnews.org/Report.aspx?ReportId=28954).

31. 'Guinea-Bissau premier accuses Yala of abusing power', PANA, 26 August 2002 (www.panapress.com/paysindexlat.asp?codepays=eng024&page=63).
32. 'Maiores partidos da oposição exigem demissão de Kumba Ialá', *Il Público*, 4 October 2002 (www.publico.pt/Mundo/maiores-partidos-da-oposicao-exigem-demissao-de-kumba- iala_187008).
33. 'Presidente da Guiné-Bissau vai dissolver Parlamento e convocar eleições antecipadas', *Il Público*, 14 November 2002 (www.publico.pt/Mundo/presidente-da-guinebissau-vai-dissolver-parlamento-e-convocar-eleicoes-antecipadas_196181).
34. 'Kumba Ialá convoca Conselho de Estado depois de anunciar eleições antecipadas', *Il Público*, 15 November 2002 (www.publico.pt/Mundo/kumba-iala-convoca-conselho-de-estado-depois-de-anunciar-eleicoes-antecipadas_196383).
35. The criteria for identifying Free and Partly Free countries have varied slightly over time.
36. Figures from the World Bank's World Development Indicators.
37. The text of the constitution is available in French at: www.koulouba.pr.ml/spip.php?article96
38. For a review of the constitution, see Pimont (1993).
39. In 2003, ADEMA split with the creation of the *Union pour la République et la Démocratie* (Union for the Republic and Democracy – URD). The URD group comprised seventeen former ADEMA deputies, reducing the ADEMA group to thirty-six deputies and making the RPM the plurality group in the legislature.
40. The *règlement intérieur* for this period is available at: www.assemblee-nationale.insti.ml/reglint/index1.htm
41. *L'Indépendant*, 6 May 2004, 'ATT donne les raisons du depart de AG Hamani' (www.malikounda.com/nouvelle_voir.php?idNouvelle=709).
42. *L'Indépendant*, 4 May 2004, 'Nouveau gouvernment: La grande désillusion' (www.malikounda.com/nouvelle_voir.php?idNouvelle=696).
43. *L'Essor*, 14 June 2004, 'Adoption de la déclaration de politique générale du gouvernement: Ousmane Issoufi Maïga fait le plein des voix' (www.malikounda.com/nouvelle_voir.php?idNouvelle=919).
44. *Le Républicain*, 14 December 2004, 'Vive tension au sommet de l'état. Chaude altercation entre IBK et Pinochet' (www.malikounda.com/nouvelle_voir.php?idNouvelle=2325).
45. *L'Essor*, 11 October 2004, 'Mise en place du bureau de l'Assemblée nationale. Le consensus a le dernier mot' (www.malikounda.com/nouvelle_voir.php?idNouvelle=1789).
46. *Les Echos*, 17 October 2010, 'Formation du bureau de l'Assemblee nationale. ADÉMA-CNID-ACC-CODI-MPR-PIDS: L'union fait la farce' (www.malikounda.com/nouvelle_voir.php?idNouvelle=4999).
47. *Le Républicain*, 19 October 2005, 'Consensus rompu à l'Assemblée nationale. Que peut faire IBK?' (www.malikounda.com/nouvelle_voir.php?idNouvelle=5026).
48. *Le Républicain*, 21 October 2005, 'Fin du consensus. Le temps des grandes manoeuvres politiciennes' (www.malikounda.com/nouvelle_voir.php?idNouvelle=5053).

49. *L'Essor*, 6 October 2006, 'Renouvellement du bureau de l'Assemblée nationale: statu quo complet' (www.malikounda.com/nouvelle_voir.php?idNouvelle=9300).
50. See, for example, the report in *Les Echos*, 10 March 2005, 'Rencontres ATT-partis politiques. Un petit tour de table et puis... C'est tout?' (www.malikounda.com/nouvelle_voir.php?idNouvelle=3049).
51. *Le Républicain*, 21 February 2005, 'Front politique. Le RPM se démarque', available at: www.malikounda.com/nouvelle_voir.php?idNouvelle=2890
52. *Les Echos*, 10 March 2005, 'Rencontres ATT-partis politiques. Un petit tour de table et puis... C'est tout?' (www.malikounda.com/nouvelle_voir.php?idNouvelle=3049).
53. *Le Républicain*, 13 September 2004, 'Politique. Le consensus à l'épreuve' (www.malikounda.com/nouvelle_voir.php?idNouvelle=1585).
54. *Le Républicain*, 29 September 2005, 'Fusion entre le RPM et l'URD. Déjà l'échec!' (www.malikounda.com/nouvelle_voir.php?idNouvelle=4830).
55. So, while the electoral coalition that supported Touré's re-election in 2007, the *Alliance pour la démocratie et le progrès* (Alliance for Democracy and Progress – ADP) was only formally announced in November 2006, it included all the groups that had broken the consensus in parliament a year earlier. See *Le Républicain*, 9 November 2006, 'Présidentielle. Une alliance pour ATT' (www.malikounda.com/nouvelle_voir.php?idNouvelle=9854).
56. *Le Républicain*, 7 June 2005, 'Consensus politique. La potion magique' (www.malikounda.com/nouvelle_voir.php?idNouvelle=3800).
57. *L'Essor*, 20 September 2005, 'Spécial 22 septembre 2005: l'avenir politique au Mali. Consensus: à usages multiples' (www.malikounda.com/nouvelle_voir.php?idNouvelle=4757).
58. *Nouvel Horizon*, 5 October 2007, 'Nouveau gouvernement. L'ADP et la société civile largement représentées' (www.malikounda.com/nouvelle_voir.php?idNouvelle=14151).
59. See the report at: http://web.me.com/relgie/The_Semi-presidential_One/Blog/Entries/2010/4/21_Mali_-_Local_elections_2.html.

6

The Performance of Democracy under Semi-Presidentialism – Country Narratives

Chapter 5 examined two semi-presidential countries that were similar in many economic, social, and cultural respects, but that varied in terms of their semi-presidential design. By controlling for as many factors as possible, the aim was to focus on the effect of institutional variation within semi-presidentialism. These controlled case studies provided strong evidence to suggest that the collapse of democracy in Guinea-Bissau was consistent with a president-parliamentary reading of events, whereas the survival of democracy in Mali was consistent with a premier-presidential narrative. This chapter takes a similar but different approach. Again, this chapter uses controlled case studies to examine the effect of institutional variation within semi-presidentialism, but it does so on the basis of two 'natural-like experiments'. In social science, a 'natural experiment' is an observational study in which a treatment is applied 'as if' randomly to some subjects but not to others (Dunning, 2008). If the outcome in the treatment group varies from the outcome in the control group, then the grounds for drawing an inference about the causal effect of the treatment are strengthened. This chapter does not claim to be describing a true natural experiment. However, it does observe the effect of applying a certain treatment – an institutional change – to a particular subject – a democracy. If the outcome is observed to be consistent with the expected effect of the treatment, then there are grounds to suggest that the causal process has been correctly specified.

This chapter examines two cases: one where a democracy with a premier-presidential form of semi-presidentialism switched to a president-parliamentary form, and one where a democracy with a president-parliamentary form switched to a premier-presidential form. Chapter 4 demonstrated that, within the set of democracies, countries with a president-parliamentary form of semi-presidentialism performed worse than those with a premier-presidential form. By focusing on two 'natural-like experiments', the expectation is that in the country where there was a switch from premier-presidentialism to president-parliamentarism, democratic performance should have worsened, even if democracy did not collapse altogether. By contrast, the further expectation is that in the country where there was a switch from president-parliamentarism to premier-presidentialism, democratic performance should have improved. Thus, like Chapter 5, this chapter examines two controlled case studies. However, in this chapter the controls are applied by studying individual countries in which there has been institutional variation over time. In this way, the application of a certain treatment to a particular subject is being observed. This is the sense in which the cases in this chapter constitute 'natural-like experiments'.

Only two countries have ever switched directly from a premier-presidential form of semi-presidentialism to a president-parliamentary form.[1] As identified in Table 2.3, they are Madagascar in October 1995 and Senegal in January 2001. Beginning in either 1992 or 1993, Madagascar was classed as a democracy by all five of the indicators used in this book. Following the switch from premier-presidentialism to president-parliamentarism in 1995, Madagascar's Polity and Freedom House scores declined. Indeed, FH ED records a collapse of democracy in 2008 and Polity records the same in 2009 when there was a coup against the incumbent president. Given this chapter focuses on the performance of democracies, Madagascar is excluded from consideration. This leaves Senegal. All five indicators have continuously classed Senegal as a democracy from 2000 onwards. There is evidence from both Freedom House and Polity that the quality of Senegal's democracy has disimproved since 2001. Therefore, even though the period of democracy under premier-presidentialism prior to the switch is very short, this chapter focuses on the case of Senegal from 2000 to 2010 inclusive.

Only a slightly larger number of countries have switched directly from a president-parliamentary form of semi-presidentialism to a premier-presidential form. They are Armenia in November 2005, Croatia in November 2000, Portugal in September 1982, São Tomé e Príncipe in January 2003, and Ukraine in May 2006. When it made the switch to premier-presidentialism in 2005, Armenia was classed as a democracy by only three of the five indicators used in this book. Given this chapter focuses on the performance of democracies, Armenia is excluded from any consideration. Similarly, Polity $\geq$+6 records the start of democracy in Croatia only in 2000. Again, therefore, there is some ambiguity as to whether there was democracy in Croatia prior to the switch to premier-presidentialism. Therefore, Croatia is excluded. For its part, São Tomé e Príncipe is too small to be included in the Polity data set. Therefore, it is excluded too. This leaves Portugal and Ukraine. They are both recorded as democracies by all five indicators in the period before and after the switch to premier-presidentialism. Therefore, they are both potential candidates for consideration. Indeed, they both register improvements in their average Polity and Freedom House scores under premier-presidentialism compared with their average scores under president-parliamentarism. Given space constraints, though, only one country can be studied. This chapter examines the case of Portugal from 1976 to 1986. All five indicators record the beginning of democracy there in 1976. Thus, during this period, Portugal was still a nascent democracy. While the improvement in Portugal's Polity and Freedom House scores was relatively small in the decade after democratization, the Portuguese case provides a good opportunity to examine the switch from president-parliamentarism to premier-presidentialism.

In this context, this chapter examines the switch from premier-presidentialism to president-parliamentarism in Senegal and the switch from president-parliamentarism to premier-presidentialism in Portugal. Consistent with the logic outlined in Chapter 2, there is the expectation that, while remaining democratic, the political process in Senegal should have become more unstable over the course of the period 2000–10. This is because under president-parliamentarism, actors have fewer incentives to stick to political deals. For example, presidents are aware that they have the ability to change the terms of a deal, perhaps by dismissing the prime minister and the government. Given this awareness, there is always the temptation to strike a new deal in the hope of gaining an additional benefit. However, over time the resultant instability is likely to be detrimental to the performance of democracy. By contrast, there is the expectation that the political process in Portugal should have become more stable over the course of the period 1976–86. Under premier-presidentialism, actors have fewer incentives to break an agreement. For example, once appointed, presidents cannot change the government. Therefore, they are likely to invest more resources in the formation of the government in the first instance, providing all actors with greater incentives thereafter to stick to the deal that has been negotiated. In other words, the political process is likely to be more stable under premier-presidentialism, not simply because the president has fewer powers to act unilaterally but because the president has fewer incentives to try to renegotiate agreements that have been reached with other political actors. Starting with Senegal, to what extent has the performance of democracy been consistent with the logic of a switch from one form of semi-presidentialism to another?

PRESIDENT-PARLIAMENTARISM AND DEMOCRATIC PERFORMANCE: THE CASE OF SENEGAL

As noted in Chapter 5, Senegal gained independence from France in June 1960 as part of the Federation of Mali. However, Senegal withdrew from the Federation in August 1960. In September 1960, Léopold Sédar Senghor was elected as President of Senegal.[2] He represented the *Union progressiste sénégalais* (Senegalese Progressive Union – UPS), which was the sole party represented in parliament. Over the next few years, even though opposition parties were still legal, a combination of the electoral system, the fusion of the UPS with smaller parties, and the banning of parties that were considered to be subversive meant that the UPS's position was reinforced. Indeed, when the direct election of the president was introduced in 1963, President Senghor was re-elected unopposed. The same result occurred in

1968 and 1973. Thereafter, the political situation changed. Previously, there was no constitutional limitation on the number of political parties and yet the UPS, which in 1976 was renamed the *Parti socialiste sénégalais* (Senegalese Socialist Party – PS), was the only party to win representation. In 1976, even though the number of parties was constitutionally limited to a maximum of three (four in 1978), the system was liberalized to allow for a degree of competition between them. Consequently, while President Senghor was easily re-elected at the 1978 presidential election, he faced real competition from Abdoulaye Wade, the leader of the newly formed *Parti démocratique sénégalais* (Senegalese Democratic Party – PDS), who won 17.4 per cent of the vote.

In December 1980, President Senghor stepped down and was replaced by Abdou Diouf. One of President Diouf's first acts was to end the restriction on the number of political parties and in April 1981 a constitutional amendment was passed to this end. There were five candidates at the 1983 presidential election, though President Diouf was easily returned winning 83.5 per cent of the vote. Similarly, at the legislative election, which was held at the same time, the PS won 111 of the 120 seats in the *Assemblée nationale* (National Assembly). Throughout the course of the 1980s and 1990s, the transition process moved forward very slowly. During this time, there was 'the regular organization of at least partially free elections, without a significant threat to the ruling party's hold on power' (Villalón, 1994: 163). For example, in 1993 Abdoulaye Wade won 32.0 per cent of the vote at the presidential election, but President Diouf was re-elected at the first ballot, winning 58.4 per cent. Similarly, following the 1998 legislative election, eleven parties were represented in the National Assembly, but the PS gained an overwhelming majority winning 93 of the 140 seats. In the 1990s, President Diouf invited various opposition parties to enter a government of national union and several of them, including Abdoulaye Wade's PDS, agreed to do so on a number of occasions, notably in 1991 and 1993 (Tirera, 2006: 213–22). All the same, by the time of the 2000 presidential election, Senegal had experienced either single-party rule or dominant-party rule by the UPS/PS for forty consecutive years.

In the run-up to the 2000 presidential election, the hegemony of the PS was challenged (Diop et al. 2000). In July 1998, prior to the legislative election of that year, Djibo Kâ split from the PS, forming the *Union pour le renouveau démocratique* (Union for Democratic Renewal – URD). In July 1999, Moustapha Niasse followed suit, forming the *Alliance des forces du progrès* (Alliance of the Forces of Progress – AFP). Both declared their intention to stand at the presidential election. Once again, though, the most dangerous challenge to President Diouf came from Abdoulaye Wade, who was standing at his fifth presidential election with the slogan 'sopi', or 'change'. On this occasion, for various economic, social, and political reasons (Sidibé, 2006: 67–102), Wade's coalition for change was better placed than at any previous time. At the first ballot, President Diouf topped the poll winning 41.3 per cent of the vote, while Wade came second with 31.0 per cent, well ahead of Niasse who won 16.8 per cent and Kâ who won 7.1 per cent.

Prior to the second ballot, an agreement was reached between Wade and Niasse, whereby the latter agreed to support the former in return for the post of prime minister.[3] At the second round, Wade won 58.5 per cent of the vote. President Diouf conceded defeat gracefully and on 1 April 2000 Abdoulaye Wade was inaugurated as President of Senegal.

President Wade took office in the context of a constitution that had already been revised many times (Fall, 2009). In 1960, Senegal had a parliamentary constitution. The president was elected by an electoral college, comprising deputies and representatives of local and regional councils (Art. 21), and the legislature could dismiss the prime minister and government by a vote of no-confidence (Art. 52). In 1963, a new constitution was adopted. The president was directly elected (Art. 21), the position of prime minister was abolished, and the government was no longer responsible to the Assembly. Thus, it was purely presidential. The 1963 constitution was still extant in 2000, but during this time it had undergone a number of fundamental revisions that had changed the nature of the regime on more than one occasion.[4] In 1970, following ongoing social unrest (Bathily, 1992: 143–4), an amendment was passed that reintroduced the post of prime minister (Art. 36) and that made the prime minister and government explicitly responsible both to the president (Art. 43) and to the legislature (Art. 75), thus installing a president-parliamentary form of semi-presidentialism. However, in 1983 the constitution was amended again, this time abolishing the prime minister and any mention of government responsibility to the legislature, so reinstating a presidential regime. In 1991, there was a return to the status quo ante. Once more against a background of social unrest, the post of prime minister reappeared (Art. 36) and the government was again made responsible to the legislature (Art. 75), so re-establishing a semi-presidential regime, though this time there was no mention of the prime minister and government being responsible to the president. Thus, in April 2000, Abdoulaye Wade assumed power in the framework of a premier-presidential constitution, but one in which the president was the dominant actor.[5] According to the constitution, the president determined the policy of the nation, which the government applied 'under the direction of the prime minister' (Art. 36). The prime minister had the administration at his/her disposal (Art. 38), as well as the right to propose the names of government ministers to the president (Art. 43) and to propose that a referendum be held on a given issue (Art. 46), but the prime minister had no other constitutional prerogatives.

During the 2000 election campaign, both Wade and Niasse, who was duly appointed prime minister on 5 April, had promised constitutional reform (Fall, 2009: 90). Immediately following the election, plans for a new constitution were drawn up. For Wade and the government, the problem was that the PS still held a majority in the Assembly as a result of the 1998 legislative election. At the time, the constitution only allowed the Assembly to be dissolved if it voted a motion of censure against the government. However, faced with the prospect of an early election at which they might lose their seat, PS deputies sat tight. The only way for

President Wade to engineer a dissolution was to pass a completely new constitution that would change the terms under which the Assembly could be dissolved (Fall, 2006: 20–3). The constitution could be submitted directly to a referendum on the basis of Art. 46 and so the government did not have to worry that the Assembly would refuse to pass the reform.[6] Therefore, while constitutional reform was an electoral promise, it was also politically expedient. That said, the new constitution was supported by all the major parties, including the PS (Galvan, 2001: 55), and was approved in a referendum on 7 January 2001 by 94.0 per cent of those who voted and with a turnout of 65.7 per cent.

The 2001 constitution is explicitly president-parliamentary. The government, which comprises the prime minister as head of government and government ministers, is responsible to the president and to the Assembly (Art. 53). In some senses, the prime minister has more power under the new constitution than under the previous one. For example, the constitution still states that the president 'determines the policy of the nation' (Art. 42), but it now states that the 'government leads and coordinates the policy of the nation under the authority of the prime minister' (Art. 53). The prime minister's role as head of government is also specified somewhat more clearly, for example, in terms of the power to issue regulations and to make certain public appointments (Art. 57). Even so, the powers of the president remained virtually intact, closely resembling those of the French president under the 1958 constitution. For example, the president is the 'guardian of the constitution' and the 'guarantor of the regular functioning of public institutions, national independence and the integrity of the territory' (Art. 42). The president has explicit prerogatives in the area of defence and foreign affairs (Arts. 45 and 88) and may assume emergency powers when the nation is threatened (Art. 52). The president may also dissolve the National Assembly, although not within the first two years of the legislature (Art. 87). Almost immediately following the passage of the new constitution, President Wade used this power. Elections were held in April 2001 and the president's supporters, led by his PDS party, gained 89 of the 120 seats in the parliament.

There is some evidence that the performance of democracy in Senegal has declined since the change to president-parliamentarism in 2001. For Polity IV, the 2000 election marked the country's transition to democracy with its score increasing from 1 in 1999 to +8 in 2000. In 2007, Senegal's Polity score was reduced to +7, indicating a decline in democratic quality.[7] The overall Polity score is an aggregate of sub-scores. Interestingly, the decline in Polity's overall score for Senegal was the result of a decline in its so-called XCONST sub-score, which 'refers to the extent of institutionalized constraints on the decision-making powers of chief executives, whether individuals or collectivities' (Marshall and Jaggers, 2009: 23) and which is concerned 'with the checks and balances between the various parts of the decision-making process' (Ibid.). Thus, the decline in Senegal's Polity score would appear to be directly related to the functioning of the executive and the legislature. For their part, Freedom House classed Senegal as

Partly Free from 1975 to 2001 inclusive. They then recorded the country as Free from 2002 to 2007 inclusive. However, in 2008 they downgraded Senegal to Partly Free once again. This classification was also recorded in the 2010 report for events in 2009. Therefore, while the early years of the Wade presidency were associated with better democratic performance, the later years have witnessed a decline. This point holds true, necessarily, when the overall status is expressed numerically (see Table 6.1). Particularly noteworthy is the recent decline of the Freedom House sub-score for Political Rights (PR sub in Table 6.1). This category measures elements such as the electoral process, political pluralism and participation, and the functioning of government. Like Polity's XCONST sub-score, these are the areas where president-parliamentarism is most likely to have an observable effect.

Overall, there is no doubt that Senegal has remained a democracy and that any decline in the country's democratic performance has been relatively small. All the same, there is some evidence of a disimprovement. Moreover, it might be added that country experts have been increasingly outspoken in their condemnation of President's Wade presidency, classing it now as 'mere electoral authoritarianism' (Mbow, 2008: 156) and accusing Wade himself of acting like an 'absolute monarch' (Gaye, 2010: 82). Given the 'natural-like' nature of this case study, many of the standard variables associated with democratic performance have remained stationary since President's Wade election in 2000. For example, there has been no change in the level of ethnic fragmentation, or the country's former colonial status. Moreover, it might be noted that GDP per capita increased from \$620 in 2000 to \$677 in 2009.[8] Therefore, any decline in Senegal's democratic performance is not associated with a decline in the country's economic performance. Instead, what did change during this time was the country's institutional structure. What is the evidence that the switch from premier-presidentialism to

TABLE 6.1 *Freedom House scores for Senegal, 2000–9*

	2000	2001	2002	2003	2004	2005	2006	2007	2008	2009
Status	PF	PF	F	F	F	F	F	F	PF	PF
Score	3.5	3.5	2.5	2.5	2.5	2.5	2.5	2.5	3	3
PR, CL	3, 4	3, 4	2, 3	2, 3	2, 3	2, 3	2, 3	2, 3	3, 3	3, 3
PR sub	–	–	–	31	34	34	33	33	30	29
CL sub	–	–	–	37	41	42	43	43	43	43

Legend:
Status: The overall status – PF = Partly Free, F = Free;
Score: Combined aggregate score for Political Rights and Civil Liberties;
PR, CL: Aggregate scores for Political Rights (PR) and Civil Liberties (CL);
PR sub: Sub-score for Political Rights (max = 40, higher = better performance);
CL sub: Sub-score for Civil Liberties (max = 60, higher = better performance).

Source: http://www.freedomhouse.org/template.cfm?page=15 (accessed 1 June 2010).

president-parliamentarism caused any decline in democratic performance following President's Wade election in 2000?

The period of premier-presidentialism following Wade's victory was extremely short, lasting less than a year. Nevertheless, some aspects of this period were consistent with a premier-presidential reading of events. For example, following his election, Wade formed a wide-ranging coalition that included Niasse's AFP party and a number of smaller parties. Indeed, the government included representatives of more parties than ever before,[9] suggesting that considerable political resources had been sunk into the coalition deal. That said, the coalition did not include either the PS or the URD, whose leader, Djibo Kâ, had rallied to Abdou Diouf between the first and second ballot of the presidential election. However, it did include dissidents from the URD and it might be noted that the party's ruling committee had voted overwhelmingly to oppose Kâ's decision to support Diouf (Belmessous, 2000: 143). In addition, while the PS was the main opposition party and while it enjoyed an overwhelming majority in the legislature, the relationship between the government and the Assembly was relatively benign.[10] No government bills were voted down (Thomas and Sissokho, 2005: 106). No motion of censure was lodged. As noted previously, there is no doubt that PS deputies wanted to avoid a confrontation that might trigger a new election. There is also no doubt that the government 'avoided presenting controversial legislation' (Ibid.) for fear that it would be defeated or heavily amended. All the same, it is noteworthy that faced with a potentially hostile parliamentary majority, President Wade did not provoke a confrontation, preferring to bide his time and prepare the new constitution. What is more, while the constitution failed to weaken the powers of the president to any significant degree and while Wade was very closely involved in preparing the document (Fall, 2009: 96), the fact that the powers of the prime minister were somewhat reinforced may be taken as a sign that Wade was honouring the power-sharing arrangement that he had brokered with Prime Minister Niasse (Creevey et al., 2005: 487). For his part, Niasse was also included in the drafting process and the AFP party had no hesitation in backing the constitution at the referendum.[11] Generally, while the president and the prime minister were clearly preoccupied with trying to maximize support for their respective parties at the forthcoming general election and while their alliance may have been purely tactical (Coulibaly, 2003: 110), there were no major disagreements between them in public at least.[12] Indeed, Prime Minister Niasse was criticized within his own party for not being more assertive vis-à-vis President Wade.[13] In these ways, despite the very short period between Wade's election and the passage of the new constitution, there is some evidence that the system operated in a manner that is consistent with the logic of premier-presidentialism.

With the passage of the president-parliamentary constitution in January 2001, the style of governing changed almost immediately. On 3 March, Prime Minister Niasse was dismissed. Two days before, the prime minister had been critical of

President Wade in a meeting of the AFP political executives (Ibid.: 111) and subsequently Niasse reported that he had been expecting to be sacked,[14] but at the time the prime minister's dismissal came out of the blue (Ibid.: 113). Clearly, the stakes were very high in the run-up to the Assembly election. All the same, even though this context may have determined the particular timing of Prime Minister Niasse's departure, subsequent events suggest that the outcome itself was merely the first manifestation of a repeated pattern of behaviour. In the period until 2010, there were five other prime ministers. The departure of Prime Minister Cheikh Hadjibou Soumaré in April 2009 meant that up to that point the average lifespan for a prime minister since the introduction of president-parliamentarism was a mere twenty months. This prime ministerial merry-go-round has not been propelled by conflict between the executive and the legislature. As noted earlier, the 2001 legislative election returned an overwhelming majority for the PDS-led sopi coalition. Indeed, the 2007 Assembly election resulted in an even greater proportion of seats for Wade's supporters because the main opposition grouping, which included Niasse's AFP party, boycotted the election. Instead, the instability has been caused by Wade's own interventions. For example, in April 2004, Prime Minister Idriss Seck was sacked by President Wade.[15] Seck had been the president's chief adviser immediately after the 2000 election and was seen as the presidential *dauphin*. Indeed, for one observer, this was exactly the reason why he was dismissed (Diop, 2006: 118). A similar motivation was the reason at least in part why Prime Minister Macky Sall was removed in June 2007, though he was also blamed for the low turnout at the Assembly election in that month.[16] Overall, the high turnover of prime ministers suggests that the position is not viewed by the president as part of a deal that has been negotiated and that needs to be honoured but rather as a clientelistic resource that can be given out or taken away at any time the president considers there is a benefit to be gained from so doing.

This point applies even more clearly to the government as a whole. In a recent interview, President Wade remarked that, for him, 'a government is like a football team and it is necessary to make changes to it'.[17] True to this aphorism, the period since January 2001 has been marked by almost continuous ministerial and cabinet reshuffles. For example, on 30 April 2009, Souleymane Ndéné Ndiaye was named as prime minister and the next day President Wade issued the decree that formally announced the composition of the new government. In the eight-month period to the end of the year, no fewer than nine further decrees were issued, reshuffling the government.[18] The first change came on 4 May 2009, less than a week after the formation of the new government, when the Minister of Mines, Industry and Small and Medium Enterprises departed. There were two further changes in May alone. True, this instability did not begin with the passage to president-parliamentarism. The Minister of Education named in Niasse government was not in office long enough to attend her first Council of

Ministers meeting (Niang, 2006: 103). However, such instability has been ongoing since 2001. One Minister of Culture lasted less than a month. By 2005, the Ministry of Health and the Ministry of Culture had both experienced six different ministers in five years (Ibid.).

The explanation for this prime ministerial and governmental instability lies in the failure to build a stable coalition. The Niasse government may have included the largest number of parties in any government up to that point, but since 2001 the partisan nature of the coalition has constantly varied and the inclusiveness of the coalition has tended to diminish. For example, the AFP left the government when Niasse was dismissed as prime minister in March 2001. In March 2005, the small left-wing *Ligue Démocratique/Mouvement pour le Parti des Travailleurs* (Democratic League/Movement for the Workers' Party – LD/MPT) was 'defenstrated' from office (Seck, 2006: 69). In April 2004, Djibo Kâ's URD party joined the governing coalition.[19] In February 2007, ministers from *And-Jëf/Parti Africain pour la démocratie et le socialisme* (And-Jëf/African Party for Democracy and Socialism – AJ/PADS) left the government, only to rejoin in March 2008 before leaving again in May 2009. Rather than building a stable coalition, President Wade has preferred to offer ministerial posts to political 'nomads' from other parties, including the PS. This so-called '*transhumance*' has been particularly prevalent under his presidency (Niang, 2004: ch. 4). Undoubtedly, the relatively personalistic rather than ideological nature of political parties in Senegal, the neo-patrimonial desire to assume office, and party political positioning in the context of electoral campaigns have all encouraged such instability. However, President Wade has used his power to hire and fire prime ministers and ministers to construct short-term alliances rather than long-term deals. This is entirely consistent with a president-parliamentary logic where there is little incentive to reach a long-term political arrangement, but where, instead, there is an incentive to derive short-term benefits from the regular distribution of political resources.

The contingent nature of the political process under president-parliamentarism can also be seen in the seemingly constant revisions to the 2001 constitution itself. As outlined above, the passage of the new constitution marked a rupture with the previous regime. This was not only because of the change from one form of semi-presidentialism to another and because it allowed President Wade to engineer a loyal parliamentary majority but also because it changed other elements of the constitution of which the former opposition had been critical. For example, the Senate, which had been created by a constitutional amendment in 1998, was abolished. Similarly, the president's term of office was reduced from seven years to five years. Therefore, even though prior to 2001 Senegal had a history of frequent constitutional amendments, there is some reason to believe that 'Wade's constitution' would remain stable for a period of time. This was not the case. There were four constitutional amendments prior to the re-election of President Wade in March 2000. Most notably, the amendment in June 2003 created a new institution, the *Conseil de la République pour les Affaires économiques et sociales* (Council of the Republic for Economic and Social Affairs – CRAES). This institution was criticized for being a *de facto* replacement for the Senate that had been abolished only two years ago. Prior to his election in 2000, Wade had criticized the Senate for being an institution that served no purpose other than to act as a neo-patrimonial 'resting home' for former deputies and/or political friends of the president. This accusation was now turned against Wade himself (Niang, 2006: 278–9). Following his re-election in 2007, the pace of constitutional reform accelerated. There were no fewer than nine constitutional amendments between May 2007 and June 2009. Again, the nature of some of these reforms suggests the essential instability of the regime under Wade. For instance, in May 2007 the Senate was re-established. Similarly, in October 2008 the president's term of office was increased to seven years once again. Then, in August 2008 the CRAES was abolished by one constitutional law only for another law on the same day to create an ostensibly similar institution, the *Conseil Économique et Sociale* (Economic and Social Council – CES). The background to the creation of the CES is noteworthy. Thiam (2007: 150–1) reports that President Wade had persuaded a senior but often disaffected PDS figure, Aminata Tall, to withdraw from the competition for the presidency of the Senate, offering her, in return, the presidency of the CRAES. However, the incumbent president of the CRAES refused to resign. Therefore, one institution was abolished and a similar institution was created, though by the time the decision was made, Tall was no longer the president's preferred candidate. Thus, the 'banalization' (Fall, 2009: 156) of constitutional reform can be seen as another element of President Wade's short-term, clientelistic approach to decision-making. The final constitutional amendment in this period can also be understood in this way. In June 2009, an amendment was passed that created the position of Vice-President. Interestingly, though, more than a year after the amendment was passed, no appointment had yet been made, creating the suspicion that President Wade would make an appointment only when it was politically expedient to do so and even raising the spectre of the introduction of a quasi-monarchical system, whereby the president's son, Karim Wade, would be appointed Vice-President and *de facto* successor (Diop, 2009).

The final example that illustrates the dynamics of president-parliamentarism under President Wade is the serial postponement of elections since 2001. The delaying of elections has occurred in many countries. However, what is noticeable about the practice in Senegal is that it has happened repeatedly and in a short space of time. In 2001, local elections scheduled for that year were delayed until May 2002. Indeed, the law that delayed the elections also allowed the government in the meantime to dissolve local councils, many of which were dominated by the PS (Seck, 2006: 71). In January 2006, a constitutional amendment was passed to extend the life of the National Assembly for another year so that presidential and legislative elections could be held simultaneously in February 2007. In the bill to amend the constitution, the official reason for delaying the election was that torrential rains had put such a strain on the economy that it was necessary to save money by holding the two elections simultaneously.[20] However, there is little doubt that the president hoped to benefit from simultaneous elections, though, in the end, a court ruling meant that the elections could not be held together and another amendment had to be passed extending the Assembly's term until June 2007. Finally, in 2007 the local elections scheduled for that year were once again delayed. Originally postponed until 2008, they were then delayed once again. Eventually, they took place in March 2009 and were a setback for Wade's PDS party and what remained of the sopi coalition.

Under president-parliamentarism, there is little incentive to reach an inclusive political deal and there is always the prospect that change may bring about a short-term benefit. The case of Senegal illustrates this point very well. While the period of democracy under premier-presidentialism was very short, there was no change of prime minister and relative ministerial stability. The government prepared a new constitution and the text then allowed the Assembly to be dissolved, but the executive did not seek conflict with the Assembly and did not try to force through its reforms as quickly as it might have done. By contrast, during the period of democracy under president-parliamentarism, there have been regular changes of prime minister and even more regular government reshuffles. There have been frequent constitutional amendments and elections have been regularly delayed. Interestingly, this pattern of behaviour in Senegal is remarkably reminiscent of the behaviour of President Yalá in Guinea-Bissau (see Chapter 5). He, too, was quick to change prime ministers, dismiss coalition partners, and delay elections, though he did not have the support in the legislature to try to change the constitution to his advantage. While in Guinea-Bissau, Yalá's actions contributed to the collapse of democracy, in Senegal democracy has survived. However, there is also evidence that the high level of political instability at the elite level has undermined the democratic process. Overall, there is reason to believe that the switch from premier-presidentialism to president-parliamentarism in Senegal may have hindered the performance of certain aspects of democracy there since 2001.

PREMIER-PRESIDENTIALISM AND DEMOCRATIC PERFORMANCE: THE CASE OF PORTUGAL

In 1911, following the overthrow of the monarchy in the revolution of the previous year, Portugal adopted a new parliamentary constitution. From this time until a coup in 1926, Portugal was a democracy.[21] However, with the coup and the subsequent establishment of the '*Estado Novo*' (New State), the country experienced a long period of authoritarianism, which lasted until the so-called 'Carnation Revolution' beginning on 25 April 1974. The revolution was led by the *Movimento das Forças Armadas* (Armed Forces Movement – MFA), which mainly comprised left-leaning elements of the military. In April 1975, elections were held for a Constituent Assembly, which, in conjunction with the MFA, was responsible for drafting a new constitution. In February 1976, the MFA reached an agreement with the political parties in the Constituent Assembly about the main points of the constitution, which was eventually promulgated on 2 April 1976. Later that month, a legislative election was held, returning the *Partido Socialista* (Socialist Party – PS) as the largest party but with only a relative majority in parliament. In June 1976, António Ramalho Eanes was elected at the first round of the presidential election, winning 61.6 per cent of the vote. He was a leading member of the MFA who ran as an independent candidate at the election. In July 1976, the first so-called 'constitutional government' was formed with President Eanes appointing the leader of the PS, Mário Soares, as prime minister. This point marks the beginning of Portugal's second and now consolidated period of democracy.

The 1976 constitution established a president-parliamentary form of semi-presidentialism.[22] The original wording of the constitution stated that the government and the prime minister were politically responsible to both the president and the National Assembly (Arts. 193 and 194). Thus, the system of dual responsibility was clear. However, in September 1982, a major revision of the constitution occurred.[23] This revision established a premier-presidential form of semi-presidentialism. The defining element in this regard was the result of a change in the wording of Arts. 193 and 194. The former now stated that the government was responsible to both the president and the National Assembly, but with no mention of political responsibility. The latter specified that the prime minister was responsible to the president but was politically responsible to the National Assembly. The rewording of these Articles was deliberately designed to indicate that while the prime minister formally tendered his or her resignation to the president and, in this sense, was responsible to the head of state, only the National Assembly had the power to force the prime minister and the government to resign. True, Art. 198 was also amended and a clause was added stating that the president could dismiss the government when it becomes necessary to do so in order to ensure the normal functioning of the democratic institutions. All the same, the wording of this Article was explicitly designed to indicate that such a power could be invoked only in exceptional circumstances. Thus, whereas previously the constitution allowed the president to dismiss the prime minister and government at any time, this was no longer the case after the 1982 constitutional reform. This is the basis for the change from president-parliamentarism to premier-presidentialism at that time (Neto and Lobo, 2009: 250).

The Portuguese constitution has been revised on six occasions since 1982. However, the form of semi-presidentialism has remained unchanged. While the performance of democracy could be considered for the whole period 1976–2010, this study examines only the period 1976–86 inclusive. During this period, GDP per capita increased substantially from $8,140 in 1976 to $10,322 in 1986.[24] Therefore, it is plausible that any improvement in democratic performance was caused by an improvement in economic development. That said, restricting the period under consideration does control for certain other potentially important explanatory factors. For example, this period marks the presidency of António Ramalho Eanes, who was succeeded in March 1986 by Mário Soares following the latter's victory at the second round of the presidential election in February of that year. Thus, examining the 1976–86 period controls for the personality of the president as an explanatory variable. Moreover, this period also marks the end of the implicit military clause (Pereira, 1984: 42) that was part of the basis for the agreement between the MFA and the political parties in 1976 (Jalali, 2010). This clause implied that the first president of the new Republic should be a military figure, whereas this was no longer a *de facto* political requirement in 1986. Therefore, the presidential election of that year marks the definitive 'civilianization' of Portuguese political life. In addition, Portugal joined the European Union (EU) on 1 January 1986. While prospective membership may have had an impact on Portuguese politics between the application to join in March 1978 and accession nearly eight years later, at least one writer argues that EU membership only started to have a big impact on domestic policymaking from the late 1980s onwards (Amorim Neto, 2003: 567). In this way, examining the period 1976–86 controls for the impact on the development of Portugal's political system of the main external actor in the region. Finally, the July 1987 legislative election returned the first single-party majority government under the new Republic. Consequently, for the whole period under consideration here, the 'parliamentary system was in flux' (Magone, 2000: 529), allowing the impact of the different forms of semi-presidentialism to be isolated in this regard. In all of these respects, limiting the focus of attention to the period 1976–86 in Portugal maximizes the extent to which the change from one subtype of semi-presidentialism to another can be treated as a natural-like experiment.

There is good evidence to suggest that the performance of democracy in Portugal improved somewhat in the period 1976–86. Indeed, without implying any causal relationship at this point, there is evidence to suggest that the improvement was directly related to the switch from president-parliamentarism to premier-presidentialism in 1982. For example, on the basis of the Polity measure of democracy, Portugal records a score of +9 from 1976 to 1981 inclusive and a score of +10 from 1982 onwards. This once-off improvement was the result of a change in the XCONST sub-category score. In other words, according to Polity, the improvement in the performance of democracy was related to the change in the relationship between the president and the legislature when the constitution was amended in 1982. The situation with regard to Freedom House is similar. Freedom House classifies Portugal as Free for the whole period since 1976. However, from

1976 to 1980 inclusive, Freedom House records an aggregate score of 2, comprising individual scores of 2 for both political rights and civil rights. However, for the period January 1981–August 1982 onwards, the aggregate score improved to 1.5 as a result of a decrease in the individual score for political rights from 2 to 1. Given the constitutional reform was promulgated in September 1982, the improvement in the Freedom House score incorporates the period when the constitutional amendment was agreed. Moreover, the improvement resulted from a change in the score for political rights at this time, which is the element that would be expected to improve if the change was associated with the switch from president-parliamentarism to premier-presidentialism. Overall, while on the basis of both Polity and Freedom House measures, the improvement in the performance of democracy was only small in the period 1976–86, there was nevertheless an improvement and the timing is consistent with the switch from one form of semi-presidentialism to another. What is the evidence to suggest that political life in Portugal was consistent with the hypothesized effects of the two subtypes of semi-presidentialism during this time?

The period of president-parliamentarism from 1976 to 1982 demonstrated a number of characteristics that are typically associated with this subtype of semi-presidentialism. The first relates to the types of government that were formed during this period. (For a list of governments from 1976 to 1987, see Table 6.2.) The most noticeable element in this regard is the presence of three short-lived presidential governments from August 1978 to December 1979. In July 1978, the coalition between the PS and the *Centro Democrático e Social* (Democratic and Social Centre – CDS) collapsed. At this point, Prime Minister Soares made it clear to President Eanes that he was willing to form a minority Socialist government perhaps including representatives of the CDS in an individual capacity (Avillez, 1996: 78). However, without attempting to see whether or not any such government could survive in the legislature, President Eanes dismissed Soares and decided to form his own so-called 'government of presidential initiative'. For one observer, this decision 'can be considered the apex of presidential power' (Magone, 2000: 535). When the government headed by Alfredo Nobre da Costa was appointed, Eanes argued that the country needed governmental stability, that such stability could only be achieved by way of a new political agreement, and that one of the aims of the new government was to create the conditions for the emergence of such an agreement (quoted in Lopes and Barroso, 1980: 49). The problem with this strategy was that it was adopted without any prior agreement with the political parties in the legislature. Rather than working with the parties to ensure an agreement and stability, the president was seen to be working against the parties, attempting to impose his own preferences upon them. This interpretation of events was clearly present when the legislature met to approve the Nobre da Costa government. The constitution states that a new government must present its programme to the legislature. The government is considered to be approved unless an absolute majority of deputies votes to reject the programme.[25] During the

TABLE 6.2 *Governments in Portugal, 1976–87*

Prime Minister	PM's party	Dates	Government composition
Soares I	PS	July 1976–Dec. 1977	PS minority
Soares II	PS	Jan. 1978–July 1978	PS–CDS
Nobre da Costa	N/P	Aug. 1978–Sep. 1978	Presidential
Mota Pinto	N/P	Nov. 1978–June 1979	Presidential
Pintasilgo	N/P	July 1979–Dec. 1979	Presidential
Sá Carneiro I	PSD	Jan. 1980–Oct. 1980	PSD–CDS–PPM
Sá Carneiro II[1]	PSD	Oct. 1980–Jan. 1981	PSD–CDS–PPM
Balsemão I	PSD	Jan. 1981–Aug. 1981	PSD–CDS–PPM
Balsemão II	PSD	Sept. 1981–Dec. 1982	PSD–CDS–PPM
Soares III	PS	June 1983–July 1985	PD–PSD
Cavaco Silva I	PSD	Nov. 1985–Aug. 1987	PSD minority

Note:
[1]Sá Carneiro died in Dec. 1980. The government formally ended in Jan. 1981.
Legend:
CDS – Democratic and Social Centre;
N/P – No Party;
PPM – People's Monarchist Party;
PS – Socialist Party;
PSD – Social Democratic Party.
Source: Magone (2000: 540).

debate, Mário Soares declared that '[if] it is not easy to govern against the express will of the President of the Republic, it is practically impossible to do so against the will of the parties represented in the legislature' (quoted in Lopes and Barroso, 1980: 50). Proving Soares correct, in the subsequent vote 141 of 252 deputies voted to reject the programme (Salgado de Matos, 1992: 780). Thus, the government fell after only two weeks in office.

The reaction of President Eanes to the rejection of the Nobre da Costa government is also instructive. Again, the president preferred to appoint a government of presidential initiative, this time headed by Carlos Mota Pinto, rather than try to construct a party-based legislative majority. On this occasion, the president's rhetoric was somewhat more consensual, emphasizing that he hoped that the new government would 'evolve in time into a form of cross-party agreement' (quoted in Miranda, 1984: 214). That said, the choice of Mota Pinto was controversial. He had been a non-party minister in the first Soares government. For this reason, his appointment was designed to appeal to the Socialists, and the PS abstained when the government's programme was presented to the legislature (Salgado de Matos, 1992: 780), thus effectively ensuring the government's appointment. However, Mota Pinto was a dissident within the *Partido Social Democrata* (Social Democratic Party – PSD) and was 'incompatible' (Lopes and Barroso, 1980: 57) with the then party leader, Francisco de Sá Carneiro.[26]

Indeed, for Lopes and Barroso, who were themselves close to the PSD,[27] the choice of Mota Pinto was deliberately designed to 'attack' (Ibid.: 58) the PSD by exacerbating tensions within the party and weakening the leadership of Sá Carneiro whom Eanes opposed. Thus, even though the president's rhetoric was perhaps more consensual this time, the choice of Mota Pinto was interpreted as a deliberate challenge to the authority of one of the two main parties in the system. Without any formal agreement with the Socialists and having alienated the leader of the PSD, the Mota Pinto government was in a precarious position. After only six months in office, the government faced two votes of no-confidence, one tabled by the communists and one by the PS. Faced with certain defeat, Mota Pinto resigned. In this context, President Eanes announced that the National Assembly would be dissolved and then appointed another government of presidential initiative, headed by Maria de Lourdes Pintasilgo, but this time as an interim administration.

The governments of presidential initiative neatly demonstrate the dynamics of president-parliamentarism. There were no negotiations with the parties in the legislature. The composition of the governments was not based on any formal or informal agreement between the president and any of the parties in the legislature. Indeed, arguably, at least one government was formed with the deliberate aim of destabilizing one of the main parties in the system. The parties in the legislature may have calculated that refusing to accept the programme of the Mota Pinto government would have damaged their standing and legitimized the president's strategy. Six months later, though, they were willing to vote the government out of office, calculating that the president would be the one who would be blamed for the instability.[28] The president may have been genuinely motivated by the long-term aim of greater political stability. Nonetheless, the result was a series of very unstable governments. This instability is characteristic of president-parliamentarism.

While presidential governments in the context of a fragmented legislature are symptomatic of president-parliamentarism, another characteristic of this subtype of semi-presidentialism can be found in the fluid nature of party political alliances generally from 1976 to 1982. While the 1976 legislative election failed to return a single-party or pre-election coalition majority, post-election majorities were equally difficult to manufacture or maintain. The first government was a single-party minority PS government. This government relied on shifting majorities to pass its legislation. For example, Miranda (1984: 211, fn 28) cites figures indicating that of the seventy-three laws passed during the Soares I administration, twenty-eight were supported by the PS, PSD, CDS, and the *Partido Comunista Português* (Portuguese Communist Party – PCP); fifteen by the PS, PSD, and CDS; six by the PS, PSD, and PCP; five by the PS and PCP; three by the PS, CDS, and PCP; three by the PS and PSD; and thirteen by the PS alone with all other parties abstaining. This vote-by-vote strategy may have worked well for a while, but the absence of a formal or even informal political agreement between the PS and any other party meant that the government was very susceptible to the legislature. Indeed, the Soares I administration was brought down when the PSD, CDS, and PCP combined to vote against a government-sponsored motion of confidence. At that point, Soares did begin negotiations with other parties, talking first to the PCP and then to CDS (Magone, 2000: 538). However, no deal was possible with the PCP. Therefore, Soares turned to the CDS more by default than design (Avillez, 1996: 70–1). In the end, the PS did reach a deal with the CDS and three ministers from that party were appointed to the government. However, the government lasted only six months, the CDS ministers then withdrawing and precipitating the three presidential governments. While there were persistent policy disagreements between the PS and the CDS during the short lifetime of the government, the pragmatic nature of the alliance was an indication that it was unlikely to last long. Indeed, despite his initial confidence, Soares himself came to realize very early on that the agreement was fragile (Ibid.: 72).

The final characteristic that is consistent with a president-parliamentary reading of events is the interventionist role of the president. Given the absence of a comprehensive political deal, all actors, including the president, had an incentive to destabilize any agreement that had been reached in an attempt to derive an incremental benefit from any new arrangement that could be brokered. This description neatly captures the behaviour of President Eanes from 1976 to 1982. For example, while Soares recalls that the president applauded the idea of an agreement between the PS and the CDS in January 1978 (Ibid.), less than three months later during his speech to commemorate the Carnation Revolution of 25 April and when he could see that the CDS ministers were likely to leave the government, President Eanes began to prepare the way for the dismissal of Soares and the appointment of the presidential governments (Braga da Cruz, 1994: 245). In other words, even though the government consisted of the two parties that the president most wished to see in office together, when there were clear difficulties between them, the president was a destabilizing force.

The disruptive nature of presidential interventions can be seen most clearly during the lifetime of the coalition majority governments from January 1980 to December 1982. When the president dissolved the legislature following the fall of the Mota Pinto government, the PSD, CDS, and the *Partido Popular Monárquico* (People's Monarchist Party – PPM) formed a pre-electoral coalition that won a bare majority of seats at the election in December 1979. When the constitutionally mandated legislative election was then held in October 1980, the so-called *Aliança Democrática* (Democratic Alliance – AD) slightly increased its majority. Therefore, in January 1980, President Eanes was obliged to appoint the leader of the centre-right PSD party and *de facto* leader of the AD, Francisco de Sá Carneiro, as prime minister. The president, though nominally independent, was opposed to the PSD, which he saw as being too right-wing, and his relations with Sá Carneiro personally were poor. There followed a period of 'institutional guerrilla warfare' (*guerrilha institucional*) between the president and the government/majority

(Campinos, 1986: 214). While Lopes and Barroso (1980: 80–1) provide a long list of disputes between the president and the Sá Carneiro I government, perhaps the main site of the conflict generally was in the Council of the Revolution. This was an institution that had been created as part of the deal between the MFA and the political parties. Comprising members of the armed forces and chaired by the President of the Republic, the Council was mainly an advisory body. However, it had the power to rule on the constitutionality of government decrees. In 1980, the Council struck down three government decrees that aimed to open up public companies to the private sector by modifying the 1977 law that prevented them from operating in certain economic areas (Campinos, 1986: 215). This decision was a direct challenge to the government's legitimacy. Following Sá Carneiro's sudden death on 4 December 1980 and President Eanes's re-election on 7 December, relations between the president and the new PSD/AD prime minister, Francisco Pinto Balsemão, were more cordial (Barroso, 1986: 243). However, for one observer, the intensity of the 'institutional guerrilla warfare' increased (Campinos, 1986: 215). For example, Eanes was accused of engaging in a 'parallel diplomacy' (Barroso, 1986: 44), particularly in relation to Portugal's policy towards its former colonies in Africa, and also on matters of international political economy and security policy.

While presidential interventions continued throughout the AD governments, the most intense period of conflict surrounded the preparation of the 1982 constitutional reform itself. By January 1981, the prospect of constitutional reform was very much on the horizon. At that time, faced with the threat of a reduction in his powers, President Eanes issued a particularly provocative threat. He said that he would promulgate such a reform, but that he would then resign, propose his own candidate for the presidency, and present himself for the post of prime minister (Ibid.: 251). This was a challenge to the political parties and an attempt to scare them into amending the reform proposals. When the reform was eventually passed, the president's powers were weakened, though the wording of certain clauses was amended to address some of the president's concerns, notably Arts. 193 and 194 relating directly to the subtype of semi-presidentialism (Opello, 1990: 89). In the end, President Eanes promulgated the reform, but he made it clear that he would not have done so if he had a choice in the matter (Ibid.). Generally, the evidence from Portugal suggests that the president intervenes more during periods of cohabitation than during periods of unified government (Jalali, 2010). While, as a non-partisan figure, the Eanes presidency cannot be classified as a period of cohabitation, it is not surprising that presidential interventions were ongoing during the AD governments. The centre-right parties had forged a majority coalition, even if relations between and, particularly, within the governing parties were often strained. The president was not part of the coalition deal. Indeed, more so than under the governments from 1976 to 1979, Eanes was excluded from the deal. He was faced with a government whose policies he opposed and a constitutional reform that was at least partly designed by the main parties with the personality of Eanes in mind (Balsemão quoted in Araújo, 2003: 86). This situation motivated the president to try to destabilize the status quo. Again, therefore, presidential interventions during the AD administrations can be interpreted in a way that is consistent with a president-parliamentary reading of events.

The 1982 constitutional reform resulted in an overall reduction in the powers of the presidency (Shugart and Carey, 1992: 155). Moreover, the Council of the Revolution was abolished. For the purposes of this book, though, the key change in 1982 was not so much the general reduction in the powers of the president, but the shift from president-parliamentarism to premier-presidentialism and the greater degree of stability that this latter subtype of semi-presidentialism is expected to generate. There is good evidence that generally there has been an increase in political stability in Portugal since the 1982 reform. For example, Moreira (2005: 30) demonstrates that governments have on average remained in power much longer. However, it is likely that the onset of majority governments and economic development, perhaps partly the result of EU membership, have been key sources of such stability. For that reason, the focus here is on the period 1983–6 inclusive. This is the period from the promulgation of the constitutional reform in September 1982 to the election of Mário Soares as president in February 1986. This is a very short period of time in which to observe the effects of the shift from one subtype of semi-presidentialism to another, especially when the impact of institutional change may be lagged. However, this period was chosen with a view to controlling for as many other independent effects as possible. Moreover, there are some signs that the political process was indeed consistent with a premier-presidential reading of events during this short period.

The first sign was the presence of relative political stability during the PS–PSD coalition from June 1983 to July 1985. The period immediately following the passage of the 1982 constitutional reform was one of political instability. There were severe tensions within the PSD and, following a relatively poor performance at the local elections in December 1983, Prime Minister Balsemão resigned. He proposed Vítor Crespo from the PSD as his replacement. However, President Eanes refused the recommendation, preferring to dissolve the Assembly instead (Morais et al., 1984: 132). This action was entirely consistent with political practice prior to the reform a few months earlier. However, when the election failed to return a majority, the result was a PS–PSD coalition that lasted for more than two years. The nature of the arrangement between the two parties was different from previous governments. For example, unlike the CDS previously, the PSD rejected the idea of a loose arrangement, preferring a formal agreement (Stock, 1986: 55). Thus, this was the first left–right coalition since democratization. Moreover, Mário Soares, whose position within the PS was certainly more secure at that point than it had been on certain occasions previously, was able to secure internal party support for the coalition by way of a ballot of party members (Ibid.). Therefore, there was a firm commitment to the coalition from both parties. In addition, President Eanes had long supported the idea of a 'central block' (*bloco central*) government. Thus, while the coalition was negotiated without presidential involvement, there was not the sense, as there had been with the previous AD administration, that the new government was actively opposed to the president. Overall, in contrast to any previous administration, the main political actors had sunk a not insignificant amount of political costs into the government and had an incentive to ensure that it lasted.

When the government did collapse, the circumstances were also quite specific. Carlos Mota Pinto, who had taken over the leadership of the PSD in 1984 and who had negotiated the coalition deal with Soares (Avillez, 1996: 175–8), died in May 1985. Mota Pinto's replacement as party leader, Aníbal Cavaco Silva, wanted to pursue a different political strategy from his predecessor, preferring a bipolarization of the party system rather than a grand coalition. Therefore, following his election as party leader in June 1985, Cavaco Silva withdrew the PSD ministers from the government and President Eanes dissolved the Assembly. In other words, the 'central block' coalition fell not because of tensions between representatives of the various institutions but because of an exogenous event, the death of one of the coalition leaders, and the election of a new leader with a different strategy. The PSD gained seats at the 1985 election, allowing it to form a single-party minority government, and then won an overall majority at the 1987 election, ushering in the period of single-party majority governments.

The other main sign of the changing political system relates to the role of President Eanes. Following the 1982 constitutional reform, the president restricted himself 'to exercising, essentially, protocol powers and limited powers of arbitration' (Blanco de Morais, 1997: 154). Similarly, for one observer at least, when President Eanes dissolved the Assembly following the collapse of PD–PSD coalition, this was less a sign that the president was trying to destabilize the political process and more an indication that the idea of presidential governments 'was a thing of the past' (Salgado de Matos, 1992: 783). More substantively, Amorim Neto and Lobo (2009: 248) show that President Eanes used his veto much less frequently after 1982 than he had done previously, vetoing only 1 of 303 laws from 1983 to 1985 compared with 10 of 341 laws from 1976 to 1980, including three vetoes during the AD administration led by Sá Carneiro,[29] and 5 of 119 laws from 1980 to 1983, and this is notwithstanding the fact that the 1982 constitutional revision actually increased the president's veto power (Ibid.: 247). The president's political strategy changed as well. In 1985, President Eanes formed the *Partido Renovador Democrático* (Democratic Renovator Party – PRD). The party contested the 1985 local elections and held the balance of power following the 1985 legislative election with forty-five deputies. The formation of the PRD was clearly motivated by the fact that Eanes was term limited and was seeking to create a political vehicle for himself when his mandate ended in 1986. However, the creation of the PRD also ended any notion that the president was non-partisan. In November 1985, when the president's party abstained on the motion to reject the government's programme, the PRD effectively kept the minority PSD administration in power. In so doing, and in stark contrast to the three presidential governments, which were formed against the political parties, the president was willing to keep the PSD in power. This 'demilitarization' (Braga da Cruz, 1994: 251–2) of political life came at the very end of the Eanes presidency and was, no doubt, caused by the conjunction of multiple factors. Nonetheless, it is consistent with a premier-presidential interpretation of the Portuguese system after the 1982 constitutional reform.

The switch from president-parliamentarism to premier-presidentialism in 1982 generated a change in the dynamics of Portuguese politics. This change predated the onset of single-party majority government in 1987. Under president-parliamentarism, President Eanes was willing to resort to presidential governments, coalition building was often ad hoc, and the president was a destabilizing force. Under premier-presidentialism, President Eanes did not resort to presidential government when the opportunity to do so arose, there was a broader governing coalition, and at the end of his term the president formed his own political party, which supported the incumbent minority government. While the president seemed to act against some of or all of the main political parties prior to 1982, afterwards he seemed willing to tolerate the choices made by them and towards the end he actively participated in the coalition-building process. These changes may have been facilitated by a more benign economic situation. The Soares government collapsed in 1977 when the country was under pressure from the International Monetary Fund, whereas by 1986 the country was more developed economically. All the same, there is evidence that the change in the country's institutional arrangements in 1982 helped to establish the new dynamics of Portuguese politics. Prior to this time, the president had little incentive to work with the government and calculated that there were benefits to be gained from opposing some or all of the main political forces in the legislature. After the reform, the president's only way of influencing the political process was to work through the government. The president responded by playing a less active role, allowing the government to govern and intervening only to dissolve the legislature when the coalition had broken down. The performance of democracy improved in the period coinciding with the switch from president-parliamentarism to premier-presidentialism. The dynamics of the new system suggest that the change from one subtype of semi-presidentialism to the other was instrumental in generating this improvement.

CONCLUSION

In Chapter 5, two controlled case studies demonstrated that, in one case, the collapse of democracy was consistent with a president-parliamentary interpretation of events and that, in another, the survival of democracy was consistent with a premier-presidential interpretation. In this chapter, two natural-like experiments have provided evidence that, in Senegal, the shift from premier-presidentialism to president-parliamentarism was associated with a decline in the performance of democracy and that, in Portugal, the switch from president-parliamentarism to premier-presidentialism coincided with an improvement in democratic performance. In both of these cases, the change in the performance of democracy was only small. Moreover, in each case the time period under one of the subtypes of semi-presidentialism was very short, making it difficult to provide a full comparison of the change from one subtype of semi-presidentialism to another. All the same, in both Senegal and Portugal there were clear signs that the dynamics of the political process and, in particular, the nature of the deals that were reached between the various actors were consistent with the hypothesized effects of the two subtypes. These elements of the political process resulted, no doubt, from the combination of various factors and were not caused solely by the institutional change that occurred at a certain point. However, there is evidence from both countries that the political system operated very differently after the change than it had done before. Thus, there is reason to believe that the move from one form of semi-presidentialism to another was at least part of the reason why the operation of the political process varied over time. So far, the argument in this book has relied on large-n statistical evidence and in-depth case studies. In Chapter 7, the general experience of various other countries is examined. To what extent is there general evidence to suggest that countries operate different under one subtype of semi-presidentialism than under the other?

NOTES

1. In a number of cases, countries have switched from one form of semi-presidentialism to another, but only following an interim constitution usually provoked by a coup. For example, Mauritania was premier-presidential from 1991 to 2005. However, in August 2005 there was a coup, the constitution was suspended, and there was a new constitutional charter. In July 2006 a semi-presidential constitution was readopted and this time it was president-parliamentary. Therefore, even though there was a switch from one form of semi-presidentialism to the other, the switch was not direct.
2. For an overview of Senegalese political history from 1960 to the 1980s, see Hesseling (1985).
3. Agence France Press, 'M. Niasse accepterait "a certaines conditions" d'être Premier ministre', 8 March 2000.
4. There were eighteen constitutional amendments from 1963 to 2000 inclusive.
5. The text of the 1963 constitution following the 1998 amendment, which was the final change before Wade took power in 2000, is available at: http://mjp.univ-perp.fr/constit/sn1963.htm (accessed 1 June 2010).

6. That said, Fall (2009: 96–101) does question the constitutionality, or at least the regularity, of the process that was chosen.
7. The decline was made retrospectively in the 2010 update of the Polity data. In the 2009 version, Senegal's Polity score for 2007 and 2008 was still +8.
8. See ERS International Macroeconomic Data Set, Real 2005 GDP Per Capita ($).
9. *Jeune Afrique Économie*, 'Sénégal. Casting de 'cohabitension', 17–30 April 2000, p. 6.
10. See, for example, the report in *Jeune Afrique/L'Intelligent*, 'Quand Niasse affronte ses anciens amis', no. 2064, 1–7 August 2000.
11. *Jeune Afrique Économie*, 'Dix mois après l'arrivée d'Abdoulaye Wade à la tête de l'État, la veritable alternance ne semble devoir voir le jour qu'au lendemain des legislatives de mars 2001', 20 November–3 December 2000, p. 43.
12. There are reports of disagreements in private. See, for example, the history of Wade's proposed reshuffle in July 2000 in Coulibaly (2003: 106–8).
13. Ibid., p. 44.
14. *Agence France Presse*, 'Le president Wade limoge M. Niasse et nomme une femme Premier ministre', 3 March 2001.
15. *RFI*, 'Wade change de premier ministre', 23 April 2004, available at: www.rfi.fr/actufr/articles/052/article_27606.asp
16. *Nettali*, 'Faible taux de participation aux legislatives: Le camp de Karim Wade accuse Macky Sall', 8 June 2007, available at: www.seneweb.com/news/article/10650.php
17. *L'Observateur*, '10 ans de l'alternance: Les confessions du President Wade', 20 March 2010, available at: www.seneweb.com/news/article/30158.php
18. Information taken from www.gouv.sn/spip.php?rubrique3 (accessed 2 June 2010).
19. *Africa Research Bulletin: Political, Social and Cultural Series*, 1–30 April 2004, p. 15709.
20. *Loi constitutionnelle N° 2006–11 du 20 janvier 2006 prorogeant le mandat des députés élus à l'issue des élections du 29 avril 2001*, available at: www.gouv.sn/spip.php?article680
21. Portugal registered a Polity2 score of +7 from 1911 to 1925 inclusive. Similarly, Svolik records a period of democracy between these dates.
22. The original text of the 1976 constitution is available in Portuguese at: www.tribunalconstitucional.pt/tc/content/files/crp/crp1976.pdf (accessed 23 August 2010).
23. The text of the 1976 constitution as revised in 1982 is available in Portuguese at: http://app.parlamento.pt/LivrosOnLine/Vozes_Constituinte/cons1982.html (accessed 23 August 2010).
24. See ERS International Macroeconomic Data Set, Real 2005 GDP Per Capita ($).
25. This is Art. 192 of the current constitution and Art. 195 of the original constitution.
26. At this time, the PSD was known as the *Partido Popular Democrático* (Democratic People's Party).

27. At the time, Barroso and Lopes were writing as academics, but both soon featured in PSD governments from the mid-1980s and both led the PSD thereafter – Barroso from 1999 to 2004 and Lopes from 2004 to 2005.
28. As a non-partisan figure, there was no opportunity to sanction the president at the legislative election, but the presidential election was only just over a year away and the parties may have calculated that the voters would have the opportunity to blame him then. In the end, Eanes was comfortably re-elected.
29. Figures kindly supplied by the Directorate of Documentation, Information and Communication Services, Legislative and Parliamentary Information Division, Assembly of the Republic, Portugal.

7

Premier-Presidentialism, President-Parliamentarism, and Democratic Performance: Indicative Case Studies

In Chapter 2, a detailed causal mechanism was outlined generating the expectation that democratic performance in countries with president-parliamentary constitutions was likely to be worse than in those with premier-presidential constitutions. Chapters 3 and 4 provided statistical evidence to support this expectation based on a large-n analysis of all semi-presidential democracies since 1919. Chapters 5 and 6 then provided descriptive evidence to back up this expectation based on the in-depth analysis of the performance of four semi-presidential democracies. The advantage of a large-n statistical analysis is that it can provide robust evidence for a general association between particular variables. The disadvantage is that it misses the context of specific cases. By contrast, the advantage of an in-depth qualitative analysis is that it can capture the specificities of particular cases. The disadvantage, though, is that it encourages generalizations to be made from the study of only a small number of countries. By adopting a mixed-method research strategy, this book has tried to maximize the benefits to be gained from the advantages of both types of analysis in a way that counteracts the limitations associated with their disadvantages. This chapter aims to extend this research strategy even further by providing a 'mid-level' empirical analysis of the link between varieties of semi-presidentialism and democratic performance. To this end, this chapter presents a set of indicative case studies that illustrate the consequences of the two forms of semi-presidentialism, thus increasing the overall number and range of countries under discussion.

The chapter begins by examining the dynamics of president-parliamentarism and then moves on to an examination of premier-presidentialism. For both, evidence from cases that appear to conform to the hypothesized dynamics of each type of semi-presidentialism is presented first. Then, a number of confounding cases are presented. These are cases where the performance of democracy seems to run counter to the hypothesized effect of the two forms of semi-presidentialism, namely cases where democracy has thrived under president-parliamentarism and where it has collapsed under premier-presidentialism. To what extent do such cases pose a fundamental challenge to the thesis presented in this book? If there are a large number of confounding cases and if the nature of political competition in these cases runs counter to the expectations that were detailed in Chapter 2, then they would indeed pose a serious problem. However, if there are only a small number of cases and if the nature of political competition there is broadly consistent with the hypothesized dynamics of the two forms of semi-presidentialism, then even though the outcome of these cases runs counter to the one predicted they would not be unduly damaging, especially given the range of supporting evidence provided throughout the book as a whole. To begin, the performance of democracy under president-parliamentarism is considered.

PRESIDENT-PARLIAMENTARISM AND DEMOCRATIC PERFORMANCE: CONFIRMING CASES

So far, this book has identified the problems of president-parliamentarism in Guinea-Bissau, Mauritania, and Senegal. These cases provided evidence to support the causal mechanism that was ascribed to president-parliamentarism in Chapter 2. These cases, though, are not the only ones where this form of semi-presidentialism has been associated with a decline in democratic performance. Table 7.1 provides a list of president-parliamentary countries where at least three of the five measures of democracy identified in Chapter 3 (Polity $\geq$+1, Polity $\geq$+6, FH F & PF, FH ED, and ACLP/DD) have recorded either a collapse of democracy and/or a decline in democratic performance.[1] To illustrate the dynamics of political competition under president-parliamentarism and its negative effect on democratic performance, an indicative study of Russia is presented.

Russia

In December 1993, Russia adopted a semi-presidential constitution.[2] Art. 81–1 states that the president shall be directly elected for a four-year term.[3] Art. 117–3 states that if the Russian parliament, the Duma, passes a vote of no-confidence in the government on two occasions within three months, then the president must either announce the resignation of the government or dissolve the Duma. Art. 117–4 indicates that the same outcome occurs if the government asks for a vote of confidence and loses it. The net result is that the government is collectively responsible to the Duma. Certainly, the Duma knows that if it wishes to dismiss the government, then it risks its own dissolution. This may create a powerful disincentive to pass a vote of no-confidence. However, there is no constitutional barrier to the collective dismissal of the government. Moreover, if the majority in the Duma believes that the resulting election will strengthen its position vis-à-vis the president or at least not weaken it, then there may be a political incentive to

TABLE 7.1 *President-parliamentary countries with a decline in democratic performance for at least three indicators of democracy*

Country	Indicators of democracy
Armenia	Polity ≥+1 and Polity ≥+6 collapse in 1995–6 and a decline in FH F & PF performance in 1996
Central African Republic	Polity ≥+1, FH F & PF, FH ED, and ACLP/DD collapse in 2001–3
Comoros	Polity ≥+1 and ACLP/DD in 1995 and a decline in FH F & PF performance in 1997
Georgia	FH ED collapse in 2008 and decline in Polity ≥+1, Polity ≥+6 and a decline in FH F & PF performance in 2007
Guinea-Bissau	Polity ≥+1, FH ED, and ACLP/DD collapse in 2003
Kyrgyzstan	FH F & PF and FH ED collapse in 2000 and a decline in FH F & PF performance in 1998
Mauritania	Polity ≥+1, FH F & PF, FH ED, and ACLP/DD collapse in 2008
Peru	Polity ≥+1, Polity ≥+6, FH F & PF, FH ED, and ACLP/DD collapse in 1990–2
Russia	Polity ≥+6, FH F & PF, and FH ED collapse in 2004–7 and a decline in Polity ≥+1 performance in 2007
Sri Lanka	Polity ≥+6 collapse in 1982 and 2003 and a decline in Polity ≥+1 and FH F & PF performance in 1981–2 and 2003–6
Ukraine	Polity ≥+6 collapse in 1993 and a decline in Polity ≥+1 and FH F & PF performance in 1993. A decline in Polity ≥+1, Polity ≥+6, and FH F & PF performance in 2000

call the president's bluff.[4] In addition to Arts. 81 and 117, Art. 83-c provides a clear statement of president-parliamentarism: the president of the Russian Federation shall 'decide the resignation of the Government of the Russian Federation'. Thus, from 1993, Russia has had a president-parliamentary form of semi-presidentialism.

From 1993 to 1997 inclusive, Freedom House gave Russia a score of 3.5 and a rating of Partly Free. From 1998, the rating declined one-half point per year for three years to reach a score of 5 in 2000. In 2004, Freedom House recorded a score of 5.5 and Russia was classed as Not Free. During the same 1993–2003 period, Freedom House classed Russia as an Electoral Democracy. However, in 2004 this status was removed. Thus, both Freedom House indicators used in this book record a collapse of democracy in 2004. In 2000, Polity increased its score for Russia from +3 to +6. From 2000 to 2006 inclusive, Russia's Polity score remained stable. However, in 2007, Russia's Polity score declined to +4, at which time on the basis of the Polity ≥+6 indicator, democracy collapsed. The ACLP/DD indicator has never classed Russia as a democracy. Overall, three indicators record a period of democracy in Russia followed by a collapse at around the same point in time. To what extent are the dynamics of the Russian case consistent with a president-parliamentary interpretation of events?

In 1991, prior to the introduction of semi-presidentialism, Boris Yeltsin was elected as president of the Russian Federation. In 1996, he was re-elected and in 2000 and 2004 Vladimir Putin was returned. There were legislative elections in December 1993, as well as in 1995, 1999, and 2003. In the period 1994–2001, the executive failed to enjoy majority support in the legislature. It is difficult to calculate the exact levels of party support for the president in the Duma during this period because of the fluid nature of party politics. However, Chaisty (2008: 438) estimates that pro-executive parties comprised between 12 and 35 per cent of the total number of deputies during this time. Whatever the precise level of support, prior to the spring of 2001 when a four-party majority coalition was formed that supported President Putin (Ibid.: 439), the executive enjoyed only minority support in the Duma. That said, at no point did an opposition party enjoy majority support. Remington (2008: 969) states that 'opposition forces generally had a majority' in the period 1994–9. Even so, the opposition usually lacked cohesion. Overall, prior to the emergence of a majority in 2001, the president and the legislature needed to work with each other in order to govern effectively. The causal mechanism outlined in Chapter 2 suggests that there is little incentive under president-parliamentarism for such cooperation to occur. In Russia, conflict between the president and the legislature was clearly observable during this period.

The appointment and dismissal of the prime minister and government ministers generally are prime indicators of conflict between the executive and the legislature. There were five separate prime ministers in the period 1994–2000, as well as a number of reshuffles that can, in effect, be counted as new governments. In their study, Morgan-Jones and Schleiter (2004) identify eight cases where the president's preferences regarding governmental change can be reliably identified. They find that four of these cases correspond to those where the president's preferences predominated, whereas the four others went against the president's preferences. The former may be interpreted as presidential governments, the latter as legislative governments. For example, in April 1998, Yeltsin proposed Sergei Kiriyenko as prime minister. The constitution requires the Duma to consent to the president's choice of prime minister (Art. 103–1a). This means that the president's candidate needs the support of 226 of the 450 deputies in the Duma. If the Duma refuses to consent to the president's prime ministerial candidate on three successive occasions, then 'the President of the Russian Federation shall appoint a Chairman of the Government of the Russian Federation, dissolve the State Duma and call a new election' (Art. 111–4). On 10 April 1998, Kirienko received the support of 143 deputies, while on 17 April he received the support of only 115 deputies (Mazo, 2005: 39–40). If the Duma refused to consent to the president's appointment for a third time, then it could be dissolved. When the vote was taken on 24 April, Kirienko received 251 votes and was approved. Thus, the president was able to force a prime minister on a reluctant legislature. However, in August 1998, President Yeltsin dismissed Prime Minister Kirienko in the context of a major financial crisis. As Kirienko's replacement, Yeltsin proposed the appointment of former Prime Minister, Viktor Chernomyrdin. At the first investiture vote on 31 August, Chernomyrdin received 94 votes, while at the second he received 138 votes (Ibid.: 43–5). At this time, a dissolution would have weakened the president because of his increasing unpopularity. Therefore, the Duma held the upper hand. The result was the nomination of Evgenii Primakov. At the investiture vote on 11 September 1998, Primakov received 315 votes. In this way, the legislature was able to force a prime minister on a reluctant president.

The legislature's often-hostile attitude towards the president can be seen in other ways too. For example, there were three votes of no-confidence against Prime Minister Viktor Chernomyrdin and his government from October 1994 to July 1995. None of the votes was successful, but each was a sign that the Duma was willing to flex its muscles against the president. Undoubtedly, though, the clearest example of the legislature's hostile attitude came with the votes to impeach the president in May 1999. Art. 93 of the constitution states that the Duma may charge the president with impeachment and that the charges are passed if they receive the support of two-thirds of the total number of deputies in the Duma, or 300 votes. The impeachment process began in June 1998 (Remington, 2001: 515). In the end, there were five charges. When the vote was taken on 15 May 1999, none of the charges received the required number of votes, though 283 deputies did support the one relating to Yeltsin's purported responsibility for the conflict in Chechnya.[5] There is little doubt that one of the reasons why none of the impeachment votes succeeded was that President Yeltsin dismissed Prime Minister Primakov from office on 12 May 1999 (Ibid.). This meant that the Duma would face another investiture process. This time, a dissolution of the legislature risked strengthening the president at least partly because the legislature was seen to be to blame for exacerbating the country's crisis. In the end, the Duma approved Primakov's replacement, Sergei Stepashin, at the first investiture vote, at least partly because Stepashin was signalled as a temporary appointment. In August 1998, Vladimir Putin's nomination as prime minister was approved by 233 deputies again at the first investiture vote.

While there is good evidence of the legislature's hostility towards the president in the period 1994–2001, there is equivalent evidence of the president's hostility towards the legislature. For instance, Chandler (2001: 509–16) records no fewer than 219 presidential vetoes of Duma legislation in the period July 1994–February 1999. Remington (2008: 970) singles out the example of the so-called 'trophy art' law, which the president vetoed twice in March and May 1997. On both occasions, the veto was overridden by the legislature. President Yeltsin still refused to sign the bill until a decision by the Constitutional Court required him to do so. Another good example of the president acting against the legislature was the frequent recourse to decree laws. Protsyk (2004) identifies thousands of presidential decrees in the period 1994–2000, many of which related to minor appointments, but some of which concerned economic and social policy legislation. Protsyk also notes that there was a decline in the number of published decrees after 1997, but at this point the number of unpublished decrees increased (Ibid.: 653). As with vetoes, the use of decrees suggests that the president is acting against parliament rather than cooperating with it.

Generally, in the 1994–2000 period, there was considerable conflict between the president and the legislature. This conflict did not prevent the passage of important legislation (Chaisty and Schleiter, 2002). Moreover, while each side flexed its constitutional muscles, this behaviour was often designed to force a compromise rather than to block the political process altogether. For example, presidential vetoes did not necessarily kill legislation. Most bills were finally passed following further negotiations between the president and the legislature (Troxel, 2003: 99). That said, each side needed to engage in brinksmanship precisely because there was no formal coalition or partnership agreement. The Duma may have acted as a check on presidential power in the 1994–2000 period, but this was not the benign result of a system of separation of powers and checks and balances. It was the outcome of an institutional battle for control over the political system. When President Putin managed to form a majority government in 2001, and particularly following the legislative election in December 2003 that returned a solid and cohesive majority for Putin's United Russia party, the battle was won. President Putin was able to pass legislation that centralized power, including control of the media. United Russia used its position to control the distribution of political resources in the Duma and changed the rules of parliamentary procedure to ensure a monopoly of power there. Chaisty (2008: 447) reports that only three bills remained vetoed in the 2003–7 Duma compared with more than 100 in the period 1996–2000. The electoral system was changed to reduce the number of political parties likely to enter the Duma and to make it more difficult for independents to be elected. Together, these developments ensured that Putin and United Russia maintained their hold on power, but only at the expense of democracy.

The president-parliamentary system in Russia meant that the president and the legislature did not have a joint stake in the system. The president was willing to try to rule against the legislature and vice versa. This situation created considerable instability, which was reflected in the turnover of prime ministers, the switch from presidential to legislative governments, presidential vetoes and veto overrides, votes of no-confidence, and impeachment charges. Such instability took place in the context of considerable economic uncertainty in the mid-1990s and, increasingly, in the context of a difficult security situation, including terrorist attacks in Moscow itself. The absence of a democratic tradition, the problems with managing such a vast and heterogeneous country, the presence of windfall oil revenues after 2001 that allowed the state to buy the loyalty of potential opponents, all of these factors and no doubt others contributed to the decline in democratic performance. However, Russia's president-parliamentary system created a situation in which political leaders believed that they had little to lose and much to gain from taking the country in a more authoritarian direction. In this way, the election of Putin did not begin the move towards authoritarianism. The choice of Putin as Yeltsin's successor was itself a sign that such a move was likely to occur anyway. The speed of the change was undoubtedly affected by the emergence of a majority in 2001. Again, though, the fact that such a majority emerged at that time was a sign that parties had calculated that they had more to gain both politically and materially from such an agreement than from the continuation of a chronically unstable system. The legislature was complicit in the move towards authoritarianism. These dynamics closely match the causal mechanism that was outlined in Chapter 2 and suggest that Russia's president-parliamentary system was at least partly responsible for the collapse of democracy there.

PRESIDENT-PARLIAMENTARISM AND DEMOCRATIC PERFORMANCE: CONFOUNDING CASES?

While this book has provided large-n statistical evidence and in-depth case study evidence to support the argument that democratic performance is likely to be worse under president-parliamentarism than under premier-presidentialism, if a large number of individual cases are inconsistent with this evidence then the overall argument in this book would be weakened. Moreover, if the dynamics of political competition in the cases were inconsistent with the hypothesized effects of president-parliamentarism and premier-presidentialism, then the argument would be weakened further still. To address this issue, this section examines some potentially confounding cases.

Table 7.2 provides a list of president-parliamentary countries where democratic performance has either improved or remained stable over time on the basis of at least three of the five indicators of democracy identified in Chapter 3.[6] The number of confounding cases in Table 7.2 is smaller than the number of confirming cases

TABLE 7.2 *President-parliamentary countries with an improvement or no decline in democratic performance for at least three indicators of democracy*

Country	Indicators of democracy
Austria	Polity ≥+1, Polity ≥+6, FH F & PF, FH ED, ACLP/DD
Guinea-Bissau	Polity ≥+1 and Polity ≥+6 since 2006, FH ED since 2005, ACLP/DD since 2004
Iceland	FH F & PF, FH ED, and ACLP/DD
Namibia	Polity ≥+1, Polity ≥+6, FH F & PF, FH ED
Peru	Polity ≥+1, Polity ≥+6, FH F & PF, FH ED, and ACLP/DD since 2001
Senegal	Polity ≥+1, Polity ≥+6, FH ED, ACLP/DD
Sri Lanka	Polity ≥+1, Polity ≥+6, and FH F & PF since 2006, FH ED, ACLP/DD
Taiwan	Polity ≥+1, Polity ≥+6, FH ED, ACLP/DD

in Table 7.1, suggesting that the central thesis of this volume is fundamentally sound. Moreover, it should be noted that Guinea-Bissau and Sri Lanka are included in Table 7.2 only because they have been stable on the basis of various indicators since 2005 and 2006 respectively. At this point, therefore, they scarcely constitute major challenges to the main argument of this book. In addition, even though various measures indicate that democracy in Peru has been either stable or improving since 2001, Peru experienced a collapse of democracy prior to this time under a remarkably similar constitution to its current one. So, judgement on the impact of president-parliamentarism in Peru should perhaps be reserved at this point. Finally, the case of Senegal has been dealt with in a previous chapter. To recap, it should be noted that this book uses the Polity data set that was issued in 2009 and that records the score for countries until 2008 inclusive. In 2010, Polity updated its data set to include democratic performance in 2009. When it did so, it retrospectively lowered Senegal's Polity 2 score from 2007 onwards. Thus, Senegal is only included in Table 7.2 because the 2008 data set is being used. As Chapter 6 demonstrated, various indicators of democracy now agree that democratic performance in Senegal has actually declined under president-parliamentarism. If these countries are excluded, then there are only four potentially confounding cases: Austria, Iceland, Namibia, and Taiwan. This is a reassuringly small number. Even so, to what extent has political competition in these countries been consistent with a president-parliamentary reading of events? If it has not, then is there a particular reason why? To begin, the situation in Taiwan is analysed.

Taiwan

The constitution of Taiwan dates back to 1947.[7] In 1948, a set of so-called Temporary Provisions were enacted, establishing an authoritarian system. In 1991, the Temporary Provisions were repealed and a set of so-called Additional Articles were added to the original text of the 1947 constitution. There were amendments to the Additional Articles in 1992, 1994, 1997, 2000, and 2005.[8] In 1994, the Additional Articles were revised to allow for the direct election of the president (Add. Art. 2).[9] The first direct election was held in 1996. In 1997, the Additional Articles were amended once again.[10] From this point on, the legislature (Legislative Yuan) has been empowered to table a vote of no-confidence against the government (Executive Yuan). The constitution states: 'Should more than one-half of the total number of Legislative Yuan members approve the motion, the president of the Executive Yuan shall tender his resignation within ten days, and at the same time may request that the president dissolve the Legislative Yuan' (Add. Art. 3–3). The constitution further states: 'The president may, within ten days following passage by the Legislative Yuan of a no-confidence vote against the president of the Executive Yuan, declare the dissolution of the Legislative Yuan after consulting with its president' (Add. Art. 2). Thus, rather like the Russian case, the prime minister (president of the Executive Yuan) and government are collectively responsible to the legislature, but the legislature risks its own dissolution if it wishes to dismiss the cabinet. Finally, there is a relatively clear statement of president-parliamentarism. The constitution states: 'Presidential orders to appoint or remove from office the president of the Executive Yuan . . . and to dissolve the Legislative Yuan, do not require the countersignature of the president of the Executive Yuan' (Add. Art. 2). Thus, the constitution implies that the president can order the removal of the prime minister and, indeed, this has happened on a number of occasions without any legal challenge. In this way, Taiwan has had a president-parliamentary form of semi-presidentialism since 1997.

The theory proposed in this book implies that democratic performance in Taiwan should have declined after 1997. However, this has not been the case. While some measures class Taiwan as a democracy prior to this time, all five indicators used in this book have consistently classed Taiwan as a democracy since this date. Both the FH ED and ACLP/DD indicators record democracy as beginning in 1996. Polity records a score of +8 in 1996, +9 from 1997 to 2003 inclusive, and a score of +10 thereafter. The situation with regard to Freedom House is more complicated. Freedom House gives Taiwan a score of 2 from 1996 to 1999 inclusive and then records an improvement in democracy in 2000 and 2001 with a score of 1.5. The Freedom House rating falls back to a score of 2 in 2002 and 2003, only for it to improve to 1.5 in 2004 and to 1 in 2005. There is then another decline to 1.5 in 2006, but the score remains stable thereafter. Thus, there is variation in the Freedom House ratings over time but no significant decline. Moreover, Freedom House has consistently classified Taiwan as Free since 1996. Generally, therefore, Taiwan's democratic performance has improved or remained stable under president-parliamentarism, confounding the main expectation of this book. That said, the dynamics of Taiwanese politics have exhibited some of the standard characteristics associated with a president-parliamentary form of semi-presidentialism and most notably from 2000 to 2008.

In March 2000, Chen Shui-bian from the Democratic Progressive Party (DPP) was elected as president of Taiwan. He inherited a legislature in which the opposition Kuomintang (KMT) party had a majority, holding 114 of the 225 seats, and in which the so-called 'Pan-Blue' opposition block as a whole controlled 139 seats. Since the 1997 constitutional amendments, the appointment of the prime minister does not require an investiture vote. In this context, President's Chen's strategy was entirely predictable. He appointed a so-called 'government of all the people' led by a KMT prime minister, Tang Fei, and including a number of KMT ministers, all of whom agreed to serve in a personal capacity (Wu, 2005: 112). However, the appointment angered the KMT (Copper, 2008: 181), which preferred a formal coalition.[11] The KMT was highly critical of the prime minister in the legislature, but it did not want to provoke a general election by voting a motion of no-confidence. Thus, President Chen was able to avoid cohabitation by relying on the fact that he could appoint a prime minister without the need for an investiture vote and by calculating that the government would be safe in office because the opposition would prefer to avoid a new election. In addition, he hoped that Prime Minister Tang would be able to manufacture a majority in the legislature with the support of friendly KMT deputies and that this strategy would allow the president's programme to be passed. In this way, President Chen governed against the legislature.[12]

In December 2001, the legislative election weakened the 'Pan-Blue' camp and the KMT in particular, but the opposition retained a total of 115 of the 225 seats in the legislature. In March 2004, President Chen was re-elected, but the December 2004 legislative elections again returned a 'Pan-Blue' majority with 114 seats. Thus, throughout his term of office, President Chen faced an opposition majority in the legislature, even if, at least following the December 2001 election, no single opposition party enjoyed majority support there. In this context, President Chen's governments continued to include KMT representation in a personal capacity, even after Prime Minister Tang resigned in October 2000 (Wu, 2005: 117). Moreover, even though President Chen appointed a succession of DPP prime ministers from this point on, his governments always included a considerable proportion of non-partisan figures. For example, in the period 2000–7, one expert calculates that in addition to KMT ministers serving in a personal capacity and ministers who were nominally independent but who were known to be close to the KMT, genuinely non-partisan independents comprised between 17.7 and 33.3 per cent of the total number of government ministers.[13] Certainly, President Chen did call for a coalition on certain occasions. For instance, following the 2004 legislative elections, President Chen proposed a coalition with the People First Party (PFP), which was part of the 'Pan-Blue' camp.[14] However, the PFP, itself an offshoot of the KMT, declined the proposal, calculating that its supporters would punish the party for joining a formal coalition with the DPP and would switch their vote to the KMT at the next election. In fact, there were often suspicions that the president's calls for a coalition were merely a strategy to try to divide the opposition rather than a genuine call for a broad-based government.[15] Overall, the desire to avoid cohabitation and the decision to support a minority government as a way of avoiding a coalition with opposition parties is entirely consistent with the expectations of president-parliamentarism.

More generally, there was a high degree of conflict between the executive and the legislature in the period 2000–8. For example, Wu (2007: 213) records that during the 1998–2001 Legislative Yuan, 72.7 per cent of all government bills were passed prior to the election of President Chen compared with 38.5 per cent following his election. Similarly, Huang (2006: 384) states that in 2004 only 15.4 per cent of the government's priority programmes were approved by the legislature. Chan (2006: 65–6) recounts the example of the deal to buy US weapons that was delayed by executive–legislative conflict. The government approved the weapons package, but the 'Pan-Blue' majority in the legislature blocked it. Chan (2006) notes that the weapons deal 'failed to make its way onto the legislative agenda on no more than 30 occasions'. It is certainly the case that in 2005 there was cooperation between the DPP and the KMT on the issue of constitutional reform, but only because by cooperating each party was able to secure long-term dominance over its respective block. So, in 2005, elections were held for the National Assembly, which was an institution that was convened mainly for the purpose of constitutional reform. Following the election, the combined support of the DPP and the KMT in the National Assembly meant that they could pass a package of reforms that would make it more difficult for smaller parties to win representation in the Legislative Yuan (Ibid.: 67). However, once the reforms were passed and the National Assembly was dissolved, the conflict between the DPP and the KMT and the 'Pan-Blue' opposition in the Legislative Yuan resumed. For example, Kucera (2006: 41) states that the 'number of bills passed through the Legislative Yuan is constantly dropping . . . Almost no important bills were passed during this spring session 2006, leaving many very important bills on hold'.

The conflict between the executive and the legislature can be seen very clearly in the repeated attempts by the opposition to recall and/or impeach President Chen. Art. 2 of the Additional Articles states: 'Recall of the president or the vice president shall be initiated upon the proposal of one-fourth of all members of the Legislative Yuan, and also passed by two-thirds of all the members. The final recall must be passed by more than one-half of the valid ballots in a vote in which more than one-half of the electorate in the free area of the Republic of China takes part.' Prior to a reform in 2005, the same article stated that: 'Should a motion to impeach the president or the vice president initiated and submitted to the National Assembly by the Legislative Yuan be passed by a two-thirds majority of all delegates to the National Assembly, the party impeached shall forthwith be dismissed from office.' In November 2000, the opposition began an impeachment process when President Chen announced that the country's proposed fourth nuclear reactor, which had already been approved by the legislature, was going to be cancelled.[16] In the end, the process was dropped because of adverse public reaction to it. Similarly, in June 2006 the KMT presented a motion to recall the president, following allegations of corruption against the president and his family.[17] In October 2006, another recall motion was debated, again on foot of persistent corruption allegations.[18] Then in November 2006, yet another recall motion was debated for the same reason.[19] All three motions failed to achieve the required two-thirds majority in the Legislative Yuan. All the same, each was a clear indication of the absence of cooperation between the executive and the legislature.

In many respects, the situation in Taiwan from 2000 to 2008 resembled the situation in Russia from 1994 to 2001. The executive did not have the support of a majority in the legislature; there was conflict between the two institutions; and this conflict manifested itself in extremes of behaviour, including attempts to remove the president from power. The difference is that in Russia democracy collapsed, whereas in Taiwan it did not. In the January 2008 legislative election, the KMT won a large majority in the Legislative Yuan and in the March 2008 presidential election, the KMT candidate, Ma Ying-jeou, won an easy victory over his DPP rival. Therefore, unified majority government was restored. Unlike the majority situation in Russia under President Putin, President Ma's term in office has not been marked by any significant decline in democratic performance. For this reason, Taiwan confounds the general logic of the effect of president-parliamentarism. That said, the fact that there were remarkable similarities between the dynamics of the two countries during the periods under consideration here does suggest that the causal mechanism associated with president-parliamentarism is sound. It also suggests that the survival of democracy in Taiwan is the result of powerful forces that have counteracted the potentially damaging effects of president-parliamentarism. These forces may have been political. In Taiwan, the KMT clearly expected to be returned to office with a majority. It had hoped that this would be the case in 2004, but as President Chen became more and more unpopular during his second term, the likelihood of a KMT victory in the 2008 round of elections was almost inevitable. For that reason, there was little incentive to turn to authoritarianism to secure power. The forces may also have been economic. Taiwan has an advanced industrial economy and is not reliant on windfall resource revenues, such as oil and gas. The economic costs of a move towards authoritarianism would have been great. The forces may also have been external. Taiwan is dependent on the United States for its security and the United States would have been unlikely to support an authoritarian move. Moreover, even though so much of Taiwanese politics revolves around whether or not there should be closer or more distant relations with China, even those, like the KMT, who are seen to be more sympathetic to the mainland do not believe that China's authoritarianism is a model for Taiwan to follow. Overall, while Taiwan is a confounding case in terms of the trajectory of its democratic performance, the nature of political competition has been entirely consistent with the hypothesized effects of president-parliamentarism, meaning that it does not seriously undermine the logic of the argument in this volume.

Austria, Iceland, and Namibia

Austria, Iceland, and Namibia have president-parliamentary constitutions. In Austria, Arts. 60 and 74 of the constitution provide a clear statement of the direct election of the president and the government's collective responsibility to the legislature respectively.[20] In addition, Art. 67(1) states: 'Save as otherwise provided by the Constitution, all official acts of the Federal President shall be based on recommendation by the Federal Government or the Federal Minister authorized by it . . . ', while Art. 70(1) states: 'No recommendation is requisite to the dismissal of the Federal Chancellor or the whole Federal Government'. Thus, the president has the unilateral power to dismiss the government. In Iceland, the constitutional situation is a little more complicated.[21] Art. 5 establishes the direct election of the president, while Art. 14 states that 'Ministers are accountable for all executive acts', and Art. 17 makes it clear that there is a prime minister. There is no explicit clause which states that the government is responsible to the legislature, though Art. 1 classifies Iceland as a 'Republic with a parliamentary government'. Therefore, it can be assumed that government is responsible to the legislature. In addition, Art. 15 states that the 'President appoints Ministers and discharges them', implying that Iceland is president-parliamentary. In Namibia, the constitutional situation is more straightforward.[22] The direct election of the president is stated in Art. 28(1), while Art. 35(1) makes it clear that there is a prime minister. Art. 41 then states: 'All Ministers shall be accountable individually for the administration of their own Ministries and collectively for the administration of the work of the Cabinet, both to the President and to Parliament', thus establishing a president-parliamentary form of semi-presidentialism.

Iceland has been semi-presidential since 1944 and Austria returned to semi-presidentialism in 1945. Iceland is not included in the Polity data set, but Polity has consistently recorded a score of +10 for Austria since 1946. For its part, Freedom House has given a maximum score of 1 to both countries since the first recorded year in 1972. Austria and Iceland have also been recorded as democracies in the FH ED data set since the first recorded year in 1989 and by the ACLP/DD data set since 1945. In Namibia, a semi-presidential system was adopted in 1990. The ACLP/DD data set has not recorded Namibia as a democracy at any point since this time. However, Polity has recorded a score of +6 for Namibia since 1990. Freedom House has classified the country as Free since this time and recorded a slight improvement in its FH F & PF score from 2.5 from 1990 to 2004 to 2 in 2005 and thereafter.[23] The FH ED data set also records Namibia as a democracy since 1990. Therefore, in terms of their democratic performance these three countries are confounding cases. To what extent does the nature of political competition in these cases pose a problem for the argument presented in this book?

The Austrian and Icelandic cases demonstrate characteristics that are far removed from the standard expectations of president-parliamentarism. For example, Austria has a tradition of grand coalitions between the two main opposing forces in the legislature, the Social Democrats and the Austrian People's Party. In the period from 1945 to 2010, there was a grand coalition between these parties for no fewer than forty-one years. In 1998 and 2010, one of the parties in the grand coalition declined to stand a candidate at the presidential election, thus ensuring that the other party's candidate would be successful. In 1953 and 1959, presidents used their influence to maintain grand coalitions when an alternative majority might have been available (Müller, 1992: 106). The president has never dismissed a prime minister. The president has never refused to sign a law (Müller, 1999: 38). The president has never used his unilateral power of parliamentary dissolution. In other words, Austria has never experienced the type of behaviour generally associated with president-parliamentary systems. The same point applies to Iceland. Here, there has been a tradition of broad-based coalition governments (Indridason, 2005: 444). There have been four minority governments, but three of these were caretaker governments (Ibid.: 451). Indeed, presidents have encouraged the formation of majority governments when parties may have preferred other options (Kristinsson, 1999: 93). The presidential veto has been used only twice, in 2004 and in 2010.[24] The president has been involved in the premature dissolution of the legislature, but has never done so unilaterally against the wishes of the parliamentary majority. Again, the Icelandic experience is very different from other examples of president-parliamentarism that have been encountered so far in this book.

In Namibia, the dynamics of the political process have been very different from those in Austria and Iceland. Again, though, the Namibian case exhibits few, if any, of the expected characteristics of president-parliamentarism. The key element of the Namibian case is the dominance of the SWAPO party. In 1989, SWAPO enjoyed the support of 57.3 per cent of the total number of deputies in the legislature. In 1994, this figure increased to 73.9 per cent and it has remained remarkably stable around that figure ever since.[25] In 1989, the president was unanimously elected by the constituent assembly. In the four direct presidential elections since 1994, the SWAPO candidate has been elected at the first ballot, winning very close to 76 per cent on each occasion. Therefore, Namibia has a dominant party system that has led to a long period of unified majority government. This situation has generated considerable political stability. There have been only three prime ministers since 1990. There has been a small proportion of non-partisan ministers in government, but unsurprisingly SWAPO representatives have dominated the cabinet (Woldendorp et al., 2002: 392–3). Thus, president-parliamentarism in Namibia has not generated the instability that is often characteristic of this form of semi-presidentialism.

These sketches confirm that Austria, Iceland, and Namibia are confounding cases. However, they also hint at the reason why. These countries are all highly unusual cases. In practice, Austria and Iceland operate as *de facto* parliamentary systems. This does not mean that they have weak presidents. On the contrary, the Austrian and especially the Icelandic presidents have considerable constitutional powers. For example, the Austrian president has the power to dissolve the legislature and to veto legislation by refusing to sign a law. The president has a role to play in government formation. The president is also the commander-in-chief of the armed forces and has the power to accept or reject the government's foreign policy decisions. Instead, it means that even though both the Austrian and Icelandic presidents have considerable constitutional powers, by convention the president exercises none of these powers. So, Müller (1999: 22) states about the Austrian case: 'The cabinet's routine offer of its resignation to each newly elected or re-elected president as a rule has been turned down. In practice it is no more than an act of politeness and is by no means meant to be more'. The reasons for the gap between the president's powers in the constitution and powers in practice are well known. They relate to historical factors in Austria and Iceland and the context in which semi-presidentialism was (re-)introduced in the two countries (Kristinsson, 1999: 88–90; Müller, 1999: 23–6). Whatever the reasons, the overriding and 'self-perpetuating' (Müller, 1992: 107) norm that the president should be a passive 'authority-in-reserve' (Ibid.) figure means that the usual dynamics of president-parliamentarism have no room whatsoever to play out.

The situation in Namibia is very different but the result is the same. The utter dominance of SWAPO has meant that the country has not had to face any potentially destabilizing conflict between the executive and the legislature. Indeed, the particularity of the Namibian case is exacerbated by the fact that the large-sized single-party SWAPO government comprises ministers who also have seats in the relatively small-sized legislature. The effect is that 'as far as the ruling party is concerned, the National Assembly is little more than the Executive in disguise' (Keulder, quoted in Bauer, 2001: 38). While there have been examples of the president acting unilaterally without consulting parliament (Ibid.), the dominance of SWAPO has meant that the executive and the legislature have acted in unison, thus avoiding any potentially destabilizing conflict.

So, to what extent do the Austrian, Icelandic, and Namibian cases pose a problem for the central thesis of this book? On the one hand, these three countries are indeed confounding cases. Like Taiwan, they have not recorded any decline in democratic performance. Unlike Taiwan, though, they have not demonstrated any of the characteristics typically associated with president-parliamentarism. So, they provide absolutely no evidence to support the claims made in this volume. On the other hand, the peculiarity of the political situation in Austria, Iceland, and Namibia is also reassuring. In his pioneering study, Duverger (1980: 179) notes that the biggest gap between presidential power in the constitution and presidential power in practice can be found in Iceland. In their study of presidential, parliamentary, and semi-presidential countries, Samuels and Shugart (2010) acknowledge that Austria is semi-presidential, but exclude it from their study because of the aberrant nature of the system there. For its part, Namibia is one of a cluster of Southern African countries where there are dominant-party democracies, including Botswana and South Africa. These countries buck the trend in the sense that *de facto* one-party countries usually descend into authoritarianism, yet in these countries democracy has survived. Whatever the reason why these Southern African countries have managed to remain democratic, there is little doubt that Namibia is one of a small number of unusual cases. Overall, therefore, the very particular nature of the Austrian, Icelandic, and Namibian cases means that they do not fatally damage the argument of this book.

PREMIER-PRESIDENTIALISM AND DEMOCRATIC PERFORMANCE: CONFIRMING CASES

This book has already examined both the case of Mali, a premier-presidential country where democracy has survived, and the case of Portugal, a country that switched from president-parliamentarism to premier-presidentialism and where the level of democratic performance subsequently improved. Table 7.3 provides a full list of premier-presidential countries where democratic performance has improved or where democracy has at least survived. Countries are included if they have experienced an improvement in the level of democratic performance using the Polity ≥+1, Polity ≥+6, and FH F & PF indicators and/or if democracy has survived using the FH ED and ACLP/DD indicators. The countries recorded in Table 7.3 are those that meet these requirements for at least three of these five indicators of democracy. These countries are the ones where the outcomes most clearly support the predictions made about the effect of premier-presidentialism relative to president-parliamentarism, though it should be noted that Serbia has only been included in the various data sets since 2006. To what extent have the predicted dynamics of premier-presidentialism been present in this set of countries? Table 7.3 contains a large number of former-communist countries in Eastern and Southern Europe. Therefore, a country from this region is chosen. From this set of countries, Poland is selected not least because, as will be shown, from 1990 to 1995 it represents a potentially 'difficult' case for the theory presented in this book.

Poland

Poland became semi-presidential in 1990 with the passage of amendments to the 1952 constitution.[26] The first post-communist constitution was adopted in October 1992.[27] This was an explicitly interim document that was known as the 'Little Constitution'. In this document, Art. 29(1) stated that the president shall be elected by the nation, Art. 53(1) established a Council of Ministers with a prime minister as the chair, and Art. 64 stated that the 'Prime Minister shall submit the resignation of the Government to the President' if a 'vote of confidence has not been granted to the Council of Ministers by the House of Representatives', or if a 'vote of no confidence has been passed by the House of Representatives'. This Article provided two other circumstances in which the government must resign and the power of the president to dismiss the government was not mentioned as one of them. Therefore, the 'Little Constitution' formalized a premier-presidential system. In April 1997, a consolidated constitution was passed.[28] Art. 127(1) states that the president shall be elected by the nation, Art. 147(1) indicates that the prime minister is the president (chair) of the Council of Ministers, and Art. 157(1) states that the Council of Ministers shall be collectively responsible to the

TABLE 7.3 *Premier-presidential countries with an improvement or no decline in democratic performance for at least three indicators of democracy*

Country	Indicators of democracy
Bulgaria	Improvement in Polity ≥+1 and Polity ≥+6 since 2001, FH ED, ALCP/DD
Cape Verde	Improvement in FH F & PF since 2003, FH ED, ALCP/DD
Croatia	Improvement in Polity ≥+1 and Polity ≥+6 since 2005 and FH F & PF in 2001 and 2009, FH ED, ALCP/DD
East Timor	Improvement in Polity ≥+1 and Polity ≥+6 since 2006, FH ED, ALCP/DD
Finland	Improvement in Polity ≥+1 since 1944 and FH F & PF in 1987 and since 1988, FH ED, ALCP/DD
France	Improvement in both Polity ≥+1 and Polity ≥+6 since 1986, FH F & PF since 2002, FH ED, ALCP/DD
Ireland	Improvement in Polity ≥+1 and Polity ≥+6 since 1952, FH ED, ALCP/DD
Lithuania	Improvement in FH F & PF since 2006, FH ED, ALCP/DD
Macedonia	Improvement in Polity ≥+1 and Polity ≥+6 since 2002, and FH F & PF since 2002, FH ED, ALCP/DD
Mongolia	Improvement in Polity ≥+1 and Polity ≥+6 since 1996, and FH F & PF since 2002, FH ED, ALCP/DD
Poland	Improvement in Polity ≥+1 and Polity ≥+6 in 1995 and since 2002, and FH F & PF in 1995 and since 2005, FH ED, ALCP/DD
Portugal	Improvement in FH F & PF since 1991, FH ED, ALCP/DD
Romania	Improvement in Polity ≥+1 in 1996, Polity ≥+1 and Polity ≥+6 since 2004, and FH F & PF since 2004, FH ED, ALCP/DD
Serbia	Improvement in FH F & PF in 2009, FH ED, ALCP/DD
Slovakia	Improvement in Polity ≥+1 and Polity ≥+6 since 2006, and FH F & PF since 2004, FH ED, ALCP/DD
Slovenia	Improvement in FH F & PF since 2002, FH ED, ALCP/DD
Ukraine	Improvement in Polity ≥+1 and Polity ≥+6 since 2006, FH ED, ALCP/DD

legislature. Nowhere in the list of the president's powers is there any mention of the ability to dismiss the prime minister or the government and no such power is listed in Art. 162 which identifies the circumstances in which the government must resign. Again, therefore, Poland has a premier-presidential system.

Since 1990, democracy in Poland has survived and its democratic performance has improved. The FH ED and ACLP/DD indicators both record a continuous period of democracy since 1990. Polity records a score of +5 in 1990. This score then increases to +8 in 1991, +9 in 1995, and +10 in 2002. Freedom House gives Poland a score of 2 in 1990. This score then improves to 1.5 in 1995 and to 1 in 2004. Unequivocally, therefore, the performance of democracy in Poland has ameliorated since 1990. However, such a trajectory was not necessarily inevitable. Writing in the mid-1990s, Linz and Stepan (1996) were not overly optimistic about the prospects for democratic consolidation in Poland. Moreover, they included the country's semi-presidential constitution as one of the factors that was working against the consolidation of democracy at that time. They stated

(Ibid.: 255): 'the new democracy's origins in an ethical civil society, a pacted transition, and, very rapidly, a semipresidential system with a directly elected charismatic leader created a legacy of ambivalence toward political society which must be transcended before Poland can consolidate democracy'. Thus, for Linz and Stepan there was nothing inevitable about the eventual consolidation of Polish democracy, and semi-presidentialism was one of the problematic factors facing the country in the process of democratic transition.

This book argues that the country's premier-presidential form of semi-presidentialism was more conducive to the survival of democracy and an improvement in democratic performance than would have been the case under president-parliamentarism. To what extent have the dynamics of Polish politics since 1990 been consistent with such a premier-presidential reading of events? To address this question, the main focus is on events during the presidency of Lech Wałęsa from 1991 to 1995. Wałęsa was elected president in December 1990, inheriting a so-called 'contract legislature' that had been elected under partly free conditions in June 1989. At the time of Wałęsa's election, there was now an anti-communist majority in the Sejm, but there was no coherent majority supporting the president. The first free legislative election was held in October 1991. This election returned an extremely fragmented legislature in which the largest party group enjoyed the support of only 13.5 per cent of the seats in the Sejm (Sanford, 1993). In September 1993, the premature dissolution of the legislature returned a much less fragmented institution, but one in which the party closest to Wałęsa, the Nonpartisan Bloc for Support of Reforms (BBWR), enjoyed only 3.5 per cent of the seats (Millard, 1994). The Wałęsa presidency came to an end in November 1995 when he was defeated at the second ballot of the presidential election. Therefore, similar to President Yeltsin in Russia and President Chen Shui-bian in Taiwan, President Wałęsa was unable to rely on the support of a parliamentary majority at any point during his term in office. If the central theme of this book is correct, then the dynamics of politics during the Wałęsa presidency should be different from those outlined previously in Russia and Taiwan.

At first blush, Poland exhibits few of the standard characteristics of premier-presidentialism during this period. Wałęsa was a charismatic figure (Jasiewicz, 1997: 165) who 'frequently tried to go beyond his constitutional powers' (McMenamin, 2008: 125), particularly regarding appointments to and dismissals from public sector offices. There was considerable governmental instability, including five prime ministers, during Wałęsa's term. There was conflict between the president and the legislature. For example, when Prime Minister Hanna Suchocka's government was brought down by a vote of no-confidence, '[t]o general consternation' (Millard, 2008: 373) President Wałęsa preferred to dissolve the Sejm rather than nominate a replacement prime minister who could try to construct a majority for the government. Wałęsa issued twenty-four legislative vetoes during his presidency in addition to the eight occasions when he requested the country's Constitutional Tribunal to rule on a particular piece of legislation (Wyrzykowski and Cielen, 2006: 260). For its part, in October 1994 the legislature issued an unprecedented 'Address to the President', asking him to 'avoid actions that might violate the law' (quoted in Jasiewicz, 1997: 152) in what was 'only a step short of a threat of impeachment' (Ibid.). Governmental instability, presidential vetoes, and the threat of impeachment are all characteristics of president-parliamentarism rather than premier-presidentialism.

Undoubtedly, there was a highly charged political atmosphere in Poland in the period 1990–5. However, the dynamics of the Polish system were different from those described in previous president-parliamentary cases. The process of prime ministerial appointment is a case in point. While Wałęsa often had very clear preferences regarding the choice of prime minister, the Sejm dominated the appointment process (McMenamin, 2008: 129). For instance, following the October 1991 legislative election, Wałęsa nominated Bronisław Geremek from the Democratic Union (UD) as prime minister. However, it was clear that he would not win the support of an absolute majority in the legislature as required for the appointment of a government. Therefore, the Sejm nominated Jan Olszewski who was subsequently approved. This may look like a case of the legislature appointing a government against the president. However, it was much more the result of party calculations in the context of a highly fragmented legislature: the UD 'did not want to form the initial government because of its internal neo-liberal and social-democratic divisions; it knew that the parliamentary arithmetic would make it continually vulnerable, and it preferred its competitors to harvest the unpopularity of democratic capitalism's growing pains' (Sanford, 1993: 116–17). Similarly, following the 1993 legislative election, President Wałęsa asked the two leading parties in the Sejm to provide him with a list of three prime ministerial nominees from which he would choose one. The parties refused, as was their right, and insisted that the president name Waldemar Pawlak. Wałęsa did so. Again, this tug-of-war might be interpreted as the legislature forcing a government on the president. As Jasiewicz (1997: 150) observes, though, Wałęsa was aware that he 'would not be able to force any candidacy against the will of these parties'. In other words, under Poland's premier-presidential system the option of forming a presidential government was simply absent.[29] Therefore, even if the president tried to manipulate the nomination process to maximize the chances of the appointment of a prime minister who was most favourable to him, if the parties in the legislature could agree a candidate between themselves then there was nothing the president could do to prevent such a candidate from being appointed. Thus, unlike the situation in Russia, there was no alternation of presidential and legislative governments in Poland. Moreover, unlike the situation in Taiwan, there was a continuous period of cohabitation during the Wałęsa presidency.

The dismissal of prime ministers during Wałęsa's term of office also confirms that the dynamics of political competition in Poland were consistent with a premier-presidential interpretation of events. In this regard, McMenamin (2008: 130) states that the 'Sejm has been even more important in the removal of prime ministers than it has in their appointment'. For example, Hannah Suchocka's government was brought down by a vote of no confidence in May 1993. President Wałęsa took the unusual step of supporting the no-confidence vote by writing to the Speaker of Sejm requesting the immediate dismissal of the government (Van Der Meer Krok-Paszkowska, 1999: 180). However, Suchocka's survival depended not on the president but on party competition in the legislature (Nalewajko and Wesołowski, 2007: 73). The motion of no-confidence was passed by one vote and was supported by a disparate coalition of forces, including one party that had no intention of bringing the government down but which miscalculated and voted in favour of the motion (Jasiewicz, 1997: 148). The downfall of the Pawlak government in March 1995 is another case in point. As outlined above, Wałęsa was opposed to his appointment in October 1993. During his term as prime minister, Wałęsa 'conspired against Pawlak' (McMenamin, 2008: 130). All the same, when the prime minister was finally forced to resign, it was because he had lost the support of the largest party in the Sejm, the Democratic Left Alliance (SLD), rather than because the president forced him out of office (Ibid.). Indeed, Pawlak's case is particularly telling. As part of his attempt to destabilize the Pawlak government, Wałęsa claimed that the prime minister was not up to the task and made it known that 'if he had had the right to recall the prime minister he would have done so' much earlier (Van Der Meer Krok-Paszkowska, 1999: 184). So, there is no doubt that if Poland had a president-parliamentary system, then President Wałęsa would have used his power to dismiss Pawlak. Indeed, in 1992, during another crisis period, President Wałęsa stated: 'we probably all agree that the only situation for Poland is an above-party government, a government we will form out of specialists' (quoted in Linz and Stepan, 1996: 281). The parties in the legislature did not agree. What is clear, though, is that President Wałęsa expressed the same motivations as President Yeltsin and President Chen. However, unable to dismiss the prime minister and form a presidential government, Wałęsa had to cohabit, albeit unwillingly, with opposition prime ministers. Summing up Wałęsa's presidency, Bernhard (2005: 227) concludes that his strategy was 'completely self-defeating. The president was incapable of ruling without parliamentary support'. This is the essence of premier-presidentialism.

Instability in Poland did not end with Wałęsa's defeat at the 1995 presidential election. Indeed, his successor, Aleksander Kwaśniewski, issued as many vetoes during his second term of office from 2000 to 2005 as Wałęsa had from 1990 to 1995 and requested even more reviews of government legislation from the Constitutional Tribunal (Wyrzykowski and Cielen, 2006: 260). Like Wałęsa, though, when the opposition won the 1997 legislative election, President Kwaśniewski had no option but to accept a cohabitation government. Generally, Kwaśniewski was a more consensual figure than Wałęsa. Indeed, his 'idea of the presidency was in many respects the opposite' of his predecessor (McMenamin, 2008: 125). Thus, even if he had the power, he may not have been motivated to appoint a presidential government. However, the key point is that he did not have the power. He had to cohabit. In so doing, like Wałęsa, Kwaśniewski had to decide either to work with the government that had been selected by the legislature or to oppose it. Broadly speaking, Kwaśniewski preferred the former course of action and Wałęsa the latter. At no time, though, could the president decide either to replace the government with a presidential administration or refuse to cohabit. This generated a different dynamic in Poland than equivalent situations in president-parliamentary countries.

Overall, the Polish case demonstrates that premier-presidentialism does not necessarily generate harmony and cooperation. In particular, it shows that during periods of cohabitation the relationship between the president, on the one side, and the prime minister and the legislature, on the other, may be extremely conflictual. However, under premier-presidentialism, unless the president calculates that the benefits of seizing power unlawfully outweigh the costs of cohabiting with the opposition, then the president has to accept the legislature's choice of government. The Polish case also neatly demonstrates the importance of thinking counter-factually about the effects of the two forms of semi-presidentialism. Wałęsa was not a dictator. On the contrary, he made his reputation by standing up against authoritarianism at considerable risk to his personal security. However, if he had been president and Poland had had a president-parliamentary system in the early 1990s, there is little doubt that he would have dismissed the prime minister and that he would have appointed a non-partisan presidential government. This may have led to a similar outcome as in Russia where the authoritarian tendency became so overwhelming that the process of democratization was derailed altogether. Of course, it may also have been the case that the democratic momentum was already so strong that, as in Taiwan, a president-parliamentary Poland may still have consolidated. Neither form of semi-presidentialism has deterministic effects. With the counterfactual in mind, the Polish case again demonstrates that the logic of political competition under premier-presidentialism is different from the dynamics of president-parliamentarism.

PREMIER-PRESIDENTIALISM AND DEMOCRATIC PERFORMANCE: CONFOUNDING CASES?

Table 7.4 records the set of premier-presidential countries that have experienced a decline in democratic performance and/or a collapse of democracy for at least three of the five indicators used throughout this book. Of all the countries that are included in the various data sets, only three meet these criteria – Congo-Brazzaville in 1997, Haiti in 2000, and Niger in 1996.[30] Compared with the number of cases that are consistent with the predicted effect of premier-presidentialism, this is a reassuringly small number indeed. Even so, to what extent has the nature of political competition in these countries been consistent with a premier-presidential

TABLE 7.4 *Premier-presidential countries with a decline in democratic performance for at least three indicators of democracy*

Country	Indicators of democracy
Congo-Brazzaville	Polity ≥+1, FH F & PF, FH ED, ALCP/DD, all collapse in 1997
Haiti	Polity ≥+1 and Polity ≥+6 decline in 1999 and collapse in 2000, FH F & PF decline in 1998 and collapse in 2000, FH ED collapse in 2000
Niger	Polity ≥+1 and Polity ≥+6, FH F & PF, FH ED, ALCP/DD, all collapse in 1996

interpretation of events, even if their eventual outcome confounds the hypothesized effect of this form of semi-presidentialism? The three countries are considered together.

Congo-Brazzaville, Haiti, and Niger

Congo-Brazzaville, Haiti, and Niger are all unequivocal cases of premier-presidentialism. The 1992 Constitution of Congo-Brazzaville stated that the president was elected by universal suffrage (Art. 68), and that if the National Assembly passed a motion of no-confidence or if it rejected a new government's programme, then the prime minister had to tender the government's resignation to the president (Art. 123). Moreover, the constitution made it clear that these were the only circumstances in which the government must resign (Art. 89).[31] The 1987 Constitution of Haiti also states that the president is directly elected (Art. 134) and that the government is responsible to parliament (Art. 156), detailing the procedures for lodging and passing a motion of no-confidence (Art. 129). There is no mention of any responsibility to the president and the president is empowered to end the prime minister's term of office only when the government presents its resignation (Art. 137–1).[32] The 1992 Constitution of Niger was very similar to its Congo-Brazzaville and Haiti counterparts. The direct election of the president was clearly stated (Art. 38). The constitution also stated that the government was responsible to the National Assembly (Art. 62) and specified the precise circumstances in which the legislature could bring down the government (Arts. 88 and 89). There was no mention of the government's responsibility to the president and, as in Haiti, the president could end the prime minister's term of office only when the government presented its resignation collectively (Art. 47).[33]

The decline in the democratic performance of all three countries is equally unequivocal. Of the five indicators used in this book, only the Polity ≥+6 indicator fails to record the beginning of a period of democracy in Congo-Brazzaville in 1992.[34] Moreover, the four indicators that do register a period of democracy at that time all record a collapse in 1997. The situation in Niger is even more straightforward. Here, all five indicators specify the beginning of a period of democracy in

1992 and all five record a collapse in 1996. In Haiti, the ACLP/DD indicator does not identify a period of democracy at all. However, Polity ≥+1 and Polity ≥+6 record the start of a period of democracy in 1994, with Polity ≥+6 then registering a collapse in 1999 and Polity ≥+1 registering a decline in 1999 and a collapse in 2000. The FH F & PF and FH ED indicators also record the onset of democracy in 1994 and a collapse in 2000, but FH F & PF also records a prior decline in democratic performance in 1998. Thus, in all three cases the trajectory of democratic performance runs counter to the central expectation of this book. What were the dynamics of political competition in these three cases?

The situation in Haiti is genuinely confounding. In June/September 1995, legislative elections returned a majority for the Lavalas Political Organisation (*Organisation Politique Lavalas* – OPL). In December 1995, René Préval of the OPL was elected president. While the combination of these elections would appear to have returned a unified OPL majority, it was a very disparate organization. Gradually, the OPL block fractured, splitting into various opposing groups and depriving President Préval of a working majority (Moestrup, 2011: 255). By 1997, the legislature was gridlocked. Lacking support, Prime Minister Rosny Smarth resigned in June 1997. President Préval nominated four prime ministers, but none were approved by the legislature (Fatton, 2000: 23). Haiti was without a functioning government for eighteen months. To break the deadlock, President Préval suspended the legislature in January 1999, appointed a prime minister unilaterally, and ruled by decree. There were elections in 2000, but they were not considered to be free and fair and democracy in Haiti collapsed. In this way, not only did the outcome of Haiti's democratic experiment run counter to the central argument of this book, but also President Préval's decision to suspend the legislature and rule by decree also resembles more closely the behaviour of a president in a president-parliamentary system than in a premier-presidential context. True, the president had tried to work through the legislature and the legislature was so divided that it was unable to present a coherent cohabitation government, which President Préval would then have had to decide whether or not to accept. All the same, neither the outcome of Haiti's short-lived premier-presidential democracy nor the nature of political competition from 1995 to 2000 provides evidence to back up the central thesis of this volume. For one writer, this is evidence that semi-presidentialism in general was partly to blame for Haiti's troubles (Moestrup, 2011). For another writer, though, in the Haitian context, '[i]nstitutions simply do not soar above the material and political structures of society. They reflect the balance of forces governing class relations and interests, and their workings are severely constrained by the material environment within which they operate' (Fatton, 2000: 28). Overall, it is hard to escape the conclusion that the collapse of democracy in Haiti was overdetermined. Certainly, the presence of premier-presidentialism did not help to improve democratic performance.

In contrast, in Congo-Brazzaville there is at least some evidence to suggest that the dynamics of premier-presidentialism were present. In June/July 1992, National

Assembly elections returned a legislature in which no single party enjoyed a majority and where the largest group was the Pan-African Union for Social Democracy (*Union Panafricaine pour la Démocratie Sociale* – UPADS) with 39 of the 125 seats. In the August presidential election, Pascal Lissouba of UPADS was elected president at the second ballot, beating Bernard Kolelas of the Congolese Movement for Democracy and Integral Development (*Mouvement Congolais pour la Démocratie et le Développement Intégral* – MCDDI). Lissouba was victorious at least partly because he reached an agreement with the third-placed candidate at the first ballot, Denis Sassou-Nguesso of the Congolese Party of Labour (*Parti congolais du travail* – PCT), whereby Sassou-Nguesso would support Lissouba at the second round in return for seats in the government (Kouvibidilia, 2000: 158–9). However, when the government was finally named, the PCT received only three ministerial posts (Ibid.: 187). As a result, Sassou-Nguesso joined the opposition, which now had the support of a majority in the legislature. With Lissouba unwilling to form a cohabitation government, in October 1992 the opposition passed a motion of no-confidence in the government (Ibid.: 200). In November, Lissouba responded by dissolving the legislature. The new elections in May/June 1993 returned a slim majority for UPADS.

At face value, these events seem to run counter to the predictions of premier-presidentialism. Under this form of semi-presidentialism, the president would be expected to accept a period of cohabitation. However, having appointed a prime minister under somewhat dubious constitutional circumstances (Ibid.: 184), President Lissouba dissolved the Assembly on an even more dubious constitutional pretext (M'Paka, 2007: 204–5). That said, it is notable that prior to the legislative elections in May/June 1993, an agreement was reached whereby 60 per cent of government seats would go to the opposition and 40 per cent would go to the president's representatives (Kouvibidilia, 2000: 244–50). This agreement was consistent with the logic that the president can only govern with the support of the legislature under premier-presidentialism. When the opposition contested the results of 1993 election, the situation descended into civil war. Following a peace accord in 1994, a new government of '*ouverture*' (openness) was formed in January 1995. The government included representatives from Kolelas' MCDDI and a number of smaller parties (M'Paka, 2005: 233), again indicating that the president was aware that the government required a stable majority in the legislature in order to govern.

Overall, President Lissouba was aware that unless he seized power unconstitutionally, which he may have calculated that militarily he was unable to do, he would have to accept the reality of the balance of forces in the legislature. He tried his best to change that balance by dissolving the legislature and by including representatives of minor opposition parties often serving in a personal capacity in all of his governments. However, he could not govern against the legislature in quite the way that, for example, President Yalá was able to do in Guinea-Bissau. Obviously, there are many reasons for the collapse of democracy in Guinea-Bissau

(Clark, 2008). Moreover, given its collapse, Congo-Brazzaville is undoubtedly a confounding case for this book. All the same, there are signs that events in Congo-Brazzaville had a somewhat different dynamic to those in president-parliamentary countries that collapsed.

The same point applies even more clearly to the case of Niger. Here, legislative elections were held in February 1993. They returned a fragmented legislature in which the National Movement for the Society of Development (*Mouvement National pour la Société du Développement* – MNSD) was the largest single group with twenty-nine of the eighty-three seats in total, but where an alliance of parties led by the Democratic and Social Convention (*Convention démocratique et sociale* – CDS) was returned with the largest block of seats, the CDS returning twenty-two of the alliance's fifty deputies. The presidential election was held very soon afterwards. Mahamane Ousmane of the CDS was elected at the second ballot ahead of Mamadou Tandja of the MNSD. Ousmane owed his election to the support he gained from Mahamadou Issoufou of the Nigerien Party for Democracy and Socialism (*Parti Nigérien pour la Démocratie et le Socialisme* – PNDS), which was part of the majority block in the legislature. Following his election, President Ousmane appointed Issoufou as prime minister following an agreement that had previously been reached (Issa Abdourhamane, 1996: 7). However, in September 1994, Prime Minister Issoufou resigned and the PNDS formed an alliance with the MNSD, leaving President Ousmane's CDS party in a minority position in parliament. The president appointed a prime minister from the CDS as Issoufou's replacement, but the new majority in the legislature passed a motion of no-confidence in the government in October 1994. President Ousmane immediately dissolved the Assembly and elections were held in January 1995. Contrary to the president's hopes and/or expectations, the elections confirmed an opposition majority. In February 1995, President Ousmane responded by appointing an MNSD prime minister, but one who was unacceptable to the party leader, Mamadou Tandja. Consequently, the opposition passed a motion of no-confidence in the government, forcing the president to appoint the MNSD's preferred choice, Hama Amadou, at the head of a cohabitation government (Maignan, 2000: 94). Relations between the president and the government were poor. There was an ongoing stand-off between the two parts of the executive. As Villalón and Idrissa (2005: 38) put it: 'both president and prime minister went "on strike," refusing to carry out duties prescribed by the constitution for the normal functioning of the government, a near-total breakdown in constitutional procedures resulted'. The president was waiting to dissolve the Assembly for a second time, being unable to do so until a year had passed since the previous legislative election. Meanwhile, on 26 January 1996, former prime minister Mahamadou Issoufou lodged a request with the Supreme Court for the president to be removed from office because of an alleged incapacity to govern (Ibrahim and Niandou Souley, 1998: 164). In this context, the military stepped in and took power, thus ending Niger's first experiment with democracy.

Again, in one respect Niger is undoubtedly a confounding case. The constitutional system was clearly premier-presidential, but democracy collapsed. That said, more so even than the Congo-Brazzaville case, events in Niger followed the expected premier-presidential path. The president was only able to govern through the legislature. The president tried to generate a majority in his favour by prematurely dissolving the Assembly. However, when the legislature was shown to be irrevocably opposed to the chief executive, the president had no option but to accept a period of cohabitation. Thus, even though the outcome in Niger runs counter to the central expectation of this book, the key point is that the political process there was fundamentally consistent with the expected dynamics of premier-presidentialism.

CONCLUSION

The central thesis of this book is that democratic performance should be positively associated with premier-presidentialism and negatively associated with president-parliamentarism. This chapter has provided more evidence to support this contention. There was a long list of cases where president-parliamentarism was associated with a decline in the performance of democracy and/or the collapse of democracy altogether. There was also a long list of cases where premier-presidentialism was associated with an improvement in democratic performance and/or the survival of democracy. Moreover, indicative case studies showed that the dynamics of political competition in Russia and Poland were generally consistent with the hypothesized effects of the two forms of semi-presidentialism. In president-parliamentary Russia, there was ongoing executive–legislative conflict that eventually led to the calculation that there was more to be gained from a move to authoritarianism than from maintaining a democratic system. In contrast, even though there was also executive–legislative conflict in premier-presidential Poland, the nature of such conflict confirmed that the president was only able to govern through the legislature. When President Wałęsa refused to do so, then he found that he still had to cohabit with a prime minister and government that the legislature had chosen. This chapter also identified a number of seemingly confounding cases. These are cases where democratic performance improved under president-parliamentarism and declined under premier-presidentialism. Reassuringly, the list of confounding cases is relatively small. Moreover, in these cases, the dynamics of political competition were usually consistent with the hypothesized effects of president-parliamentarism and premier-presidentialism. Indicative case studies showed that in president-parliamentary Taiwan, there has not been any decline in democratic performance but the political process has demonstrated features that are quintessentially president-parliamentary. By the same token, in

Congo-Brazzaville and Niger, both of which were premier-presidential, democracy collapsed but characteristics of premier-presidential competition were clearly observable. In Austria, Iceland, and Namibia, the dynamics of president-parliamentarism are totally absent, but these cases are also notoriously unusual. In Austria and Iceland, the norms of parliamentary competition are so strong that they supervene on any president-parliamentary characteristics. In Namibia, the presence of a dominant party has generated a type of competition that is specific to a particular region of the world. Thus, these cases do not suggest that there is a fatal flaw to the central thesis of this book. Indeed, only the case of Haiti was shown to be genuinely confounding. Given that democracy in Haiti has to operate in almost insupportable conditions and given the overwhelming evidence mustered throughout this book as a whole, it is reasonable to suggest that, overall, there is genuine and irrefutable evidence to show that in countries with a semi-presidential constitution the level of democratic performance is at least partly determined by the particular form of semi-presidentialism under which those countries have chosen to operate.

NOTES

1. Table 7.1 is based on the 2009 version of the Polity data set that records scores up to and including 2008. In the 2010 update of the Polity data set, the score for Madagascar declines from +7 to 0 in 2009. This would mean that Madagascar would be included in Table 7.1 if the Polity period was extended a further year. This point would also apply to Senegal if the 2010 update of the Polity data set were used.
2. The text of the 1993 constitution is available at: www.constitution.ru/en/10003000–01.htm (accessed 7 October 2010).
3. In 2008 the constitution was amended and the term extended to six years. The text of the amended version is available at: http://constitution.garant.ru/english/ (accessed 7 October 2010).
4. Mazo (2005) also notes that there are times when the president is constitutionally prohibited from dissolving the legislature. Therefore, during these periods the president would, presumably, have no option but to announce the resignation of the government.
5. The figures for each of the five votes are provided in Brown (2000: fn. 250).
6. Given the FH ED and ALCP/DD measures are dichotomous, countries are included if they are still classed as democratic in the last recorded year of these two data sets.
7. The text of the 1947 constitution is available at: www.taiwandocuments.org/constitution01.htm (accessed 8 October 2010).
8. For an overview of the constitutional revisions up to 2000, see www.taiwandocuments.org/constitution07.htm (accessed 8 October 2010).
9. The text of the 1994 amendments is available at: www.taiwandocuments.org/constitution03.htm (accessed 8 October 2010).

10. The text of the 1997 amendments is available at: www.taiwandocuments.org/constitution02.htm (accessed 8 October 2010).
11. Goh Sui Noi, 'Chen rejects KMT call for a coalition', *The Straits Times* (Singapore), 16 July 2000.
12. In fact, the new government lasted fewer than five months. In October, Prime Minister Tang resigned for health reasons, but also following a public disagreement with President Chen over the decision to scrap a proposed nuclear power station that the prime minister supported.
13. Figures kindly supplied by Jung-Hsiang Tsai of the Department of Political Science at the National Chung Cheng University, Taiwan.
14. Jacky Hsu, 'Taiwan's bitter rivals might form coalition', *South China Morning Post*, 8 January 2005.
15. See, for example, Goh Sui Noi, 'Taiwan's Chen ready to form coalition', *The Straits Times* (Singapore), 8 May 2001.
16. Lawrence Chung, 'Lawmakers begin moves to impeach Chen', *The Straits Times* (Singapore), 8 November 2000.
17. Lawrence Chung, 'Respite for Chen as opposition move to oust him falls short', *South China Morning Post*, 28 June 2006.
18. Lawrence Chung, 'Unrest to drag on as Chen recall vote fails; Opposition now looking to a no-confidence vote in bid to topple the cabinet', *South China Morning Post*, 14 October 2006.
19. Lawrence Chung, 'Third opposition bid to oust Chen fails; Motion calling for a referendum on the Taiwanese leader is thwarted by DPP lawmakers' boycott', *South China Morning Post*, 25 November 2006.
20. The text of the Austrian constitution is available at: www.ris.bka.gv.at/Dokumente/Erv/ERV_1930_1/ERV_1930_1.pdf (accessed 14 October 2010).
21. The text of the Icelandic constitution is available at: www.government.is/constitution/ (accessed 14 October 2010).
22. The text of the Namibian constitution is available at: www.parliament.gov.na/acts_documents/135_act_7_of_2010.pdf/ (accessed 14 October 2010).
23. A score of 2 was also recorded for 1992.
24. See Robert Elgie, 'Iceland – Supposedly powerless president vetoes bill and provokes referendum', 8 January 2010, available at: www.semipresidentialism.com (accessed 15 October 2010).
25. All figures from http://en.wikipedia.org/wiki/Elections_in_Namibia (accessed 15 October 2010).
26. Following the 1990 amendments, Art. 32-a1 stated that 'The President is chosen by the nation', and Art. 37–1 stated that 'The Sejm [legislature] appoints and dismisses the government of the Polish Commonwealth – Council of Ministers or particular members thereof on the nomination of the President of the Council of Ministers presented after agreement with the President [of the Commonwealth]. The Sejm may dismiss the Council of Ministers or particular members thereof on its own initiative.' Thanks to Iain McMenamin for this translation.

27. The text of the 1992 Polish constitution is available at: www.servat.unibe.ch/icl/pl02000_.html (accessed 18 October 2010).
28. The text of the 1997 Polish constitution is available at: www.servat.unibe.ch/icl/pl00000_.html (accessed 18 October 2010).
29. The only presidential government was formed immediately after Wałęsa's election under the contract legislature. This government, which comprised mainly non-partisan ministers, lasted until the first free elections in October 1991.
30. It should be noted that Finland in the 1930s is a candidate for inclusion. The Polity data set records a decline in Finland's score from +10 in 1929, to +7 in 1930, to +4 in 1931. Finland's score then improves to +10 in 1944 and has remained at that level ever since. Given that of the five indicators used in this book, only Polity records democracy scores in the 1930s, it is highly likely if Freedom House or ACLP/DD had a longer time-series, then they too would record a decline in democratic performance or a collapse of democracy in Finland in the 1930s. However, to be consistent with the methodology used in Tables 7.1–7.3, Finland is not included as a confounding case in Table 7.4. In addition, it should also be noted that if the Polity 2010 update had been used, then a second collapse in Niger would also be recorded. The FH F & PF indicator records a decline in democratic performance in Niger in both 2007 and 2009. The FH ED indicator records a collapse in 2009. This book uses the Polity 2009 data set, which records country scores up to and including 2008. In this data set, Niger had not yet recorded a decline. Indeed, its Polity performance improved in 2004. However, if the 2010 update had been used, then on the basis of both the Polity ≥+1 and Polity ≥+6 indicators, Niger would have recorded a collapse in 2009. Again, though, for consistency it is not included in Table 7.4.
31. The text of the 1992 Congo-Brazzaville constitution is available in French at: http://mjp.univ-perp.fr/constit/cg1992.htm (accessed 21 October 2010).
32. The text of the 1987 Haiti constitution is available in French at: http://mjp.univ-perp.fr/constit/ht1987.htm (accessed 21 October 2010).
33. The text of the 1992 Niger constitution is available in French in Raynal (1993: 180–99).
34. Congo-Brazzaville recorded a Polity 2 score of +5 from 1992 to 1996 inclusive.

8

Conclusion

The stated aim of this book was to understand why democratic performance is better in some countries than in others. Specifically, the aim was to understand why democratic performance has varied within the set of countries with semi-presidential constitutions. In answering this question, the assumption was made that many factors are likely to have affected the performance of democracy, notably the level of economic development. However, controlling for other such factors, it was proposed that the design of executive–legislative relations has had a fundamental impact. Crucially, and building on Shugart and Carey's distinction (1992), it was suggested that democratic performance has been affected by the particular form of semi-presidentialism that a country has chosen to adopt: whether it has adopted a premier-presidential form of semi-presidentialism, where the prime minister and cabinet are responsible solely to the legislature, or a president-parliamentary form, where the prime minister and cabinet are responsible both to the legislature and to the president. This choice has been so important, it was proposed, because under premier-presidentialism the president can govern only through the legislature. By contrast, under president-parliamentarism the president and the legislature have an incentive to govern against each other. Therefore, it was hypothesized that the president and the legislature were more likely to cooperate under premier-presidentialism than under president-parliamentarism. The relative absence of such cooperation under president-parliamentarism may lead to instability and it may even lead actors to calculate that some degree of authoritarianism is preferable, thus democratic performance declines.

To test this intuition, this book has provided a definitive account of democratic performance in semi-presidential countries, including evidence from the countries that first adopted this type of constitution in 1919 to those that operate with it in the present day. The book has operationalized democratic performance by comparing cases where democracy has survived to those where it has collapsed, as well as by distinguishing between better- and worse-performing democracies. The case selection has always been made on the basis of more than one indicator of democracy, including indicators that are composed of different constitutive criteria as well as those that are based on the same criteria but with different boundary points. The book has used a variety of different types of evidence, ranging from large-n comparative studies to in-depth case studies of particular countries. The book has presented descriptive statistics as well as more sophisticated estimation techniques. When examining democratic performance within the set of democracies, a variety of estimation techniques were used. In the in-depth case studies, the book has provided both a narrative of the collapse of democracy in a president-parliamentary country and a narrative of the survival of democracy in a premier-presidential country that operated under very similar historical, social, and cultural conditions. The book has examined two natural-like experiments, identifying the effect on democratic performance of a switch from one form of semi-presidentialism to the other. The book has also presented mid-level indicative case studies, including the discussion of what would appear to be confounding cases. Generally, to ensure the most rigorous and robust test of the central hypothesis of this book, a mixed-method approach has been adopted and, within each method, different types of research design have been applied.

Across all of these measures and methods, strong support was found for the main argument of this book. Countries with president-parliamentary constitutions have performed worse than those with premier-presidential constitutions. This outcome was shown particularly clearly in the statistical models. Using descriptive statistics as well as more sophisticated and varied estimation techniques, there was a clear association between the type of semi-presidentialism and the performance of democracy. Moreover, strong support was found for the causal mechanism that was outlined in Chapter 2. Both the in-depth case studies and the indicative case studies showed that presidents and legislatures in president-parliamentary systems have tried to govern against each other, whereas under premier-presidentialism there has been a greater degree of cooperation. For example, in president-parliamentary countries there was evidence of presidents forming non-partisan governments when they failed to enjoy majority support in the legislature. There was also evidence of the legislature trying to impeach the president. Finally, when seemingly confounding cases were examined, most demonstrated characteristics that were consistent with the hypothesized causal mechanism, even if the outcome was different from the one expected. In the small number of confounding cases where these characteristics were absent, the countries were shown to be highly unusual and were generally acknowledged as such. Overall, the balance of evidence was overwhelmingly in favour of the basic intuition on which this project is founded.

That said, it should be stressed that the argument in this book is probabilistic and not deterministic. This book generates a strong policy recommendation: if a country wishes to adopt a semi-presidential constitution, then it should adopt a premier-presidential form of semi-presidentialism. All the same, there is no guarantee that a premier-presidential democracy will perform well. All that can be said is that, all else equal, premier-presidential democracies are likely to perform better than president-parliamentary democracies. What is more, this book makes no claim about any association between the form of semi-presidentialism and economic development, corruption, social equality, or any other such performance indicator. This book hypothesized a relationship between the form of semi-presidentialism and democratic performance. No other claim was made. Finally, this book does not allow any conclusion to be drawn about democratic performance under semi-presidentialism relative to the equivalent performance under presidentialism or parliamentarism. Thus, while this book generates a strong policy recommendation in favour of premier-presidentialism relative to president-parliamentarism, it does not generate any such recommendation relative to presidentialism or parliamentarism. That is a study for another day.

This book ends by revisiting the standard problems of semi-presidentialism that were identified in Chapter 1 and placing them in the context of the findings about premier-presidentialism and president-parliamentarism that have been identified over the course of the book as a whole. This exercise generates a number of questions. For example, why was so little support found for the problem of cohabitation and a divided executive? To what extent is minority government a problem for semi-presidential countries? What is the relationship between presidential power and the form of semi-presidentialism? Addressing these and other questions will help to generate a research agenda for the next generation of semi-presidential studies.

THE STANDARD 'PROBLEMS' OF SEMI-PRESIDENTIALISM REVISITED

In Chapter 1, four standard criticisms of semi-presidentialism were identified: the problem of a dual executive, cohabitation, divided minority government, and hyper-presidentialism. What does the evidence in this book tell us about these problems?

In the literature on semi-presidentialism, the two most commonly cited criticisms of semi-presidentialism are the problem of cohabitation and the problem of a dual executive. The empirical work in this book has provided little or no empirical evidence to back up either of these claims. True, democracy collapsed during a period of cohabitation in Niger. Generally, though, the survival model in Chapter 3 provided absolutely no evidence of any significant association between cohabitation, where the president and the prime minister are from different parties and where the president's party is not represented in the cabinet, and the duration of semi-presidential democracies. Moreover, in Chapter 4 when cohabitation was found to have a significant effect, it was always in the opposite direction to the one hypothesized. In other words, when cohabitation was a significant predictor of democratic performance, it was found to have a positive effect. The same conclusion can be drawn about the problem of a divided (or dual) executive. There was no evidence of any significant negative association between a divided executive, where the president and the prime minister are from different parties but where the president's party is represented in the cabinet, and the duration of semi-presidential democracies. What is more, while in one model (Table 4.11, Model 7) there was, as expected, a negative correlation between a divided executive and democratic performance, in seven models there was a positive association. On balance, therefore, like cohabitation, a divided executive was usually associated with better democratic performance. This evidence confounds the received wisdom about the two problems that are most commonly associated with semi-presidentialism.

Why is this the case? The answer lies in the distribution of the observations for cohabitation and a divided executive. For example, using the Polity ≥+1 data set there are 740 observations in total (i.e. years of semi-presidential democracy) and 100 observations for cohabitation. However, eighty-seven of the cohabitation observations occur in countries with a Polity score of +9 or +10. Using this indicator of democracy, the highest score recorded by a country in the year prior to its collapse was +8, which occurred both in Austria in 1932 before it collapsed in 1933 and in Niger in 1995 before it collapsed in 1996. What this means is that cohabitation has overwhelmingly occurred in countries that are, in effect, consolidated democracies where it is extremely unlikely that a collapse will ever occur. A similar story applies to observations of a divided executive. Again using the Polity ≥+1 data set, there are 113 observations for a divided executive and seventy-four of these observations occurred in countries with a score of +9 or +10. These figures confirm that semi-presidential democracies have experienced both cohabitation and a divided executive. Indeed, they show that they have experienced them 13.5 and 15.3 per cent of the time respectively. However, these figures also show that these situations tend to be experienced in consolidated democracies. Thus, critics of semi-presidentialism who believe that cohabitation and a divided executive are dangerous for the survival of democracy have made this argument on the basis of a faulty assumption. They have assumed that these situations will be distributed evenly across the range of semi-presidential democracies and that when they occur in young democracies the political system may not be able to survive their impact. In fact, though, the figures demonstrate that the distribution of these potentially problematic situations is heavily skewed towards the set of democratically consolidated countries. Therefore, neither cohabitation nor a divided executive is likely to be generally problematic for the survival of young democracies.

Why, though, is the distribution of cohabitation and a divided executive skewed towards consolidated democracies? The answer lies with the dynamics of president-parliamentarism vs. premier-presidentialism that were outlined in Chapter 2. Under premier-presidentialism, the president can govern only through the legislature. If the legislature is implacably opposed to the president, then the president will have to accept a period of cohabitation. However, under president-parliamentarism the president has an incentive to govern against the legislature. This is particularly so when there is the possibility of cohabitation. Faced with this threat, presidents are likely to appoint non-partisan prime ministers who will try to construct ad hoc majorities in the legislature. This logic is entirely consistent with the intuition in the recent book by Samuels and Shugart (2010: 45), who state that they 'expect cohabitation to almost never occur under president-parliamentarism'. They argue that this is both because, by definition, the president can dismiss the prime minister and try to avoid cohabitation in such countries and also because parties in president-parliamentary countries are likely to be more presidentialized with the effect that the threat of cohabitation is likely to be less frequent overall. The evidence confirms these arguments. Using the Polity ≥+1 data set, only 13 of the 100 cohabitation observations occurred in countries with a president-parliamentary form of semi-presidentialism. Moreover, eight of these thirteen observations occurred in Austria, which, as was seen in Chapter 7, is a highly anomalous case.[1] Using the same data set, 45 of 113 divided executive observations occurred in president-parliamentary countries. Thus, there would appear to be a more even distribution. However, 34 of these 113 observations again occurred in Austria. If Austria is excluded, then only 11 of 79 observations of a divided executive occurred under president-parliamentarism. Thus, like cohabitation, a divided executive is much more likely to occur under premier-presidentialism than under president-parliamentarism.

Overall, the critics of semi-presidentialism are undoubtedly correct to point out that countries with this type of constitution are likely to experience both cohabitation and a divided executive. Indeed, the figures for the Polity ≥+1 indicator show that one or other of these situations was experienced 28.5 per cent of the time in all semi-presidential democracies from 1919 to 2008 inclusive. However, they miss the fact that these types of situations are least likely to occur in the countries that are most likely to collapse. This does not mean that semi-presidentialism is a good choice for young democracies. It simply means that when semi-presidential democracies collapse they are more likely to do so for reasons other than the standard problems of cohabitation and a divided executive. To put it another way, the very reason why president-parliamentarism is dangerous for democracy, namely the incentive for presidents to try to govern against the legislature, is also the reason why both cohabitation and a divided executive are likely to be much less prevalent in such countries and, therefore, why president-parliamentarism is a much stronger predictor of poor democratic performance.

The literature on semi-presidentialism also identified the problem of divided minority government. In Chapters 3 and 4, this problem was tested by the inclusion of a minority government variable in the various estimations and models. Like the result for cohabitation, the finding was unequivocal. Controlling for all other factors, there was absolutely no support for the expected negative association between minority government and democratic collapse or performance generally. Instead, in Chapter 4 in the small number of models where there was a statistically significant result, it showed that there was a positive relationship between minority government and democratic performance.

Why was there no empirical support for the problem of minority government? The answer lies, necessarily, in the distribution of observations. Again using the Polity $\geq$+1 indicator, there were 740 observations in total and 173 observations of minority government (or 23.4 per cent of the time that there has been democracy under semi-presidentialism). Of these 173 observations, 115 occurred in countries with a Polity score of +8 or more. Therefore, the distribution of minority government observations was skewed towards the better-performing democracies. As before, though, this conclusion merely begs the question of why the distribution was skewed in this way. The answer can be found in the general literature on minority government. It is now commonly understood that the formation of a minority government may be a rational choice for parties in the legislature (Strom, 1990). Furthermore, Cheibub et al. (2004: 574) have demonstrated that minority government has occurred almost evenly across presidential and parliamentary systems. Extrapolating from this work, it is reasonable to expect that minority government would be observed in both premier-presidential and president-parliamentary systems. The evidence supports this contention. There were ninety-nine observations of minority government under premier-presidentialism (or 22.7 per cent of all premier-presidential observations) and seventy-four under president-parliamentarism (or 24.4 per cent of all president-parliamentary observations). Thus, there was little empirical support for the problem of minority government because even though minority government was observed under president-parliamentarism, there were sufficient observations of minority government under premier-presidentialism to ensure that the negative association with democratic performance that was predicted by the standard literature on semi-presidentialism did not materialize.

While the general literature on minority government provides a compelling reason why, overall, the negative association between minority government and democratic performance was not supported, this finding remains potentially puzzling. The logic underpinning this book implies that president-parliamentarism is entirely consistent with the formation of minority governments. With an incentive to govern against the legislature under this form of semi-presidentialism, the president may try to appoint a minority presidential government or a minority non-partisan government as a way of trying to avoid cohabitation and/or a divided executive and maximize influence over the cabinet. If the president can seize the initiative in this way, it may be difficult for the legislature to vote down the government for fear of being blamed for any subsequent political crisis. What is more, the effect of minority government is likely to be damaging under president-parliamentarism. Even if the legislature tolerates the minority presidential government, it may systematically block the president's policy proposals in the chamber. If the gridlock is protracted, then democratic performance may suffer and there may even come a time when actors calculate that authoritarianism is a more attractive option and democracy may collapse altogether. Thus, even if the presence of minority government under premier-presidentialism means that, overall, there is unlikely to be a negative association between minority government and democratic performance, there should be evidence that when minority government occurs under president-parliamentarism, democratic performance is challenged.

What is the evidence for this contention? Sticking with the Polity ≥+1 indicator, there were specific examples of president-parliamentary countries experiencing minority government in the year when they collapsed. This occurred in Armenia in 1996, Burkina Faso in 1980, and Mauritania in 2008. In addition, Weimar Germany experienced minority government in years prior to its collapse, though not in the year when democracy failed. Furthermore, evidence from the in-depth case studies and indicative studies showed that the causal mechanism that was outlined in Chapter 2 accurately predicted the observed pattern of executive/legislative relations in various president-parliamentary countries. For example, in Guinea-Bissau when it became clear that President Yalá had only minority support in the legislature, he resorted to the standard tactic of appointing a government of 'presidential initiative' before finally dissolving the legislature but then failing to call new elections. In Mauritania, the prime minister resigned when it became clear that he no longer had the support of a majority in the legislature. However, the president merely reappointed him in defiance of the legislature, provoking a coup almost immediately. In Russia, there were tit-for-tat presidential and legislative governments during the presidency of Boris Yeltsin who enjoyed only minority support in the Duma. To sum up, whereas cohabitation and a divided executive were very rare under president-parliamentarism, minority government was not. This was entirely predictable. Similarly, even though there was, understandably, no general association between minority government and poorer democratic performance, there was good evidence to suggest that when minority government occurred under president-parliamentarism, it coincided with periods of intense executive/legislative conflict. This is consistent with the central thesis of this volume.

Overall, the critics of semi-presidentialism are correct to point out that minority government can occur under semi-presidentialism. However, Skach (2005) is wrong to argue that minority government is semi-presidentialism's most dangerous subtype. Generally, controlling for other factors, the presence of minority government is not dangerous for semi-presidentialism. In fact, the evidence clearly shows that minority government is most prevalent in semi-presidential democracies that have performed well. All the same, there is evidence to suggest that when minority government occurs under president-parliamentarism, then democratic performance has declined. It would be tempting to conclude from this observation that the interaction of minority government and president-parliamentarism is most detrimental to democratic performance. However, the statistical evidence does not support this intuition. For example, including an interaction variable in the survival model in Chapter 3 did not significantly increase the explanatory power of the model. Instead, it is better to conclude that president-parliamentarism is the real problem of semi-presidentialism. When the executive and the legislature come into conflict under this form of semi-presidentialism, one of the president's strategies is to try to maximize control over the cabinet by appointing a minority presidential government. Similar to other strategies such as ruling by decree, the appointment of a minority government is likely merely to exacerbate the conflict between the two institutions. This may lead to a decline in democratic performance. Thus, Skach (2005) and Colton and Skach (2005) are correct that minority government in the Weimar Republic in the 1920s and Russia in the 1990s did coincide with a decline in democratic performance. However, the reason for the decline was not the presence of minority government per se. Minority government occurred because it was a rational strategy under president-parliamentarism. In the first instance, therefore, the blame for poor democratic performance lies first and foremost with the countries' president-parliamentary system.

The final criticism in the literature on semi-presidentialism is the problem of hyper-presidentialism. This problem was tested by the inclusion of a presidential power variable in all the estimations. Here, the results were more encouraging for the standard wisdom. In the event-history estimation, the Polity $\geq$+6 model did suggest a negative association between presidential power and democratic survival. That said, the form of semi-presidentialism was a much stronger predictor. In the other two event-history models, no significant association between presidential power and democratic survival was found. By contrast, across the range of estimation techniques in Chapter 4, presidential power was consistently found to be a strong predictor of democratic performance. In almost all of both the full and reduced models, there was a negative association between presidential power and democracy scores.

The findings in relation to presidential power are important to the central thesis of this book and in two ways. Firstly, the findings support the very foundation on which this book is built. In Chapter 2, it was argued that a reliable classification of semi-presidential countries requires a constitutional definition of semi-presidentialism. The drawback with such a definition is that the list of semi-presidential countries includes presidents with a very wide range of powers, ranging from Russia to Iceland. When this set of countries is taken as a discrete explanatory variable, the evidence suggests, reasonably enough, that semi-presidentialism has little predictive power (e.g. Cheibub and Chernykh, 2008, 2009). By contrast, this book starts from the premise that a reliable classification of semi-presidential countries is required and that only a constitutional definition can provide such a classification, but that semi-presidentialism should not be operationalized as a discrete variable. Instead, the variation within semi-presidentialism needs to be systematically captured and the effects of such variation need to be identified. The presidential power variable provides one way of capturing such variation. The empirical results suggest that, contrary to the expectations of the hyper-presidentialist critics, presidential power has only limited predictive capacity in relation to the collapse or survival of democracies. However, controlling for all other factors, variation in presidential power is a strong predictor of democratic performance within the set of semi-presidential democracies. Thus, even though this way of capturing the variation within semi-presidentialism is different from the one operationalized in this book, the fact that variation is shown to have discernible effects is consistent with the general thesis presented here.

Secondly, the inclusion of the presidential power variable in the various estimations provided a necessary and important test of the central argument of this book. Controlling for presidential power, it has been shown that the form of semi-presidentialism is a strong predictor of democratic outcomes. To put it another way, the inclusion of the presidential power variable in all of the estimations shows that the distinction between premier-presidentialism and president-parliamentarism is not merely a proxy for variation in presidential power. Distinguishing between premier-presidentialism and president-parliamentarism is not simply another way of distinguishing between weaker presidents and stronger presidents respectively. The causal mechanism presented in Chapter 2 emphasized why this was the case. Even though the distinction between the two forms of semi-presidentialism is very simple – whether or not the president has the power to dismiss the prime minister and the cabinet – the implications of this distinction are much broader. Under premier-presidentialism, the president can govern only through the legislature. Therefore, the president is encouraged to cooperate with the legislature. By contrast, under president-parliamentarism, the president and the legislature may have an incentive to govern against each other. This variation in incentive structure has far-reaching implications. Certainly, under president-parliamentarism, it can lead to a prime ministerial merry-go-round as presidential governments succeed legislative governments. However, the presence or absence of a political deal between the president and the legislature goes much farther. It will involve the partisan composition of the government, the distribution of political posts broadly, agreement on institutional and policy reform, and so on. These are factors that are not necessarily captured by an index of presidential power and certainly not by a single indicator.

This point can be illustrated very neatly by revisiting the case studies of Mali and Senegal. Presidents in both countries enjoyed similar constitutional powers, scoring 7 on the Siaroff (2003) scale. However, one country was premier-presidential and the other was president-parliamentary and both were governed in quite different ways. In premier-presidential Mali, President Touré did not enjoy majority support in the legislature. In this context, the president negotiated a wide-ranging coalition that lasted for the duration of his first term of office from 2002 to 2007. By contrast, in president-parliamentary Senegal, President Wade did have a majority after 2001 and there was no inclusive political deal. Consequently, not only was there prime ministerial instability, there was also general ministerial, constitutional, and political instability. The different outcomes were neither the result of any variation in the overall powers of the two presidents nor, indeed, the result of the simple power to dismiss the prime minister in one case but not the other. After all, in 2004, President Touré made it plain to Prime Minister Hamani that he should step down and the prime minister did so. In other words, in premier-presidential Mali, the president actually did have the *de facto* power to replace the prime minister. The key point is that he was able to do so because the decision was made in the context of a more wide-ranging political deal that permitted this course of action. Instead, the difference lies in the foundation upon which general political deals were made in the two countries. In Mali, they were relatively broad and deep and they were able to resist difficulties that occurred within the legislature. In Senegal, the political deals were very shallow, leading the president to revise them repeatedly.

Overall, the central insight of Shugart and Carey's distinction (1992) between premier-presidentialism and president-parliamentarism was not that the power to dismiss the prime minister and cabinet makes presidents generally more powerful, nor was it that dismissal power is, by itself, somehow more important than any other presidential power. Instead, it was the intuition that this power has much broader implications for the dynamics of governance. Building on their insight by specifying a precise causal mechanism and by systematically testing for the impact of the distinction on democratic performance while controlling for presidential power, this book has shown that institutional variation within semi-presidentialism does have a significant effect on democratic outcomes.

WHERE TO FROM HERE?

Having revisited the standard criticisms in the light of the material presented in this book, the question arises: where to from here? Three types of issues are relevant in this regard: definitional and operational issues, empirical issues, and theoretical issues.

An operational issue concerns the identification of minority government. In the statistical models, this book operationalized the concept of minority government very reliably by way of the MAJ variable in the World Bank's Database of Political Institutions (DPI). However, in one instance there was a mismatch between the coding of this variable by the DPI and the evidence from the in-depth case studies. In Guinea-Bissau, President Yalá was elected in January 2000 and formed a majority coalition government between his Social Renewal Party (*Partido da renovação social* – PRS) and the *Resistência Guiné-Bissau/Movimento Bafatá* (Resistance of Guinea-Bissau-Bafatá Movement – RGB-MB). However, in January 2001 the RGB-MB party left the coalition, leaving the PRS in a minority position. Arguably, the president continued to enjoy a *de facto* majority for some months by gaining the support of dissident deputies from other groups in the legislature. Even so, by September 2001 there was a clear majority against the president. All the same, the DPI records a value of 0.77 in Guinea-Bissau from 2000 to 2003 inclusive, implying that the government enjoyed the support of more than three-quarters of the deputies in the legislature during this time. Yet, when democracy collapsed, this was evidently not the case, the president dissolving the assembly in November 2002 precisely because there was an opposition majority there. In the absence of any other comprehensive cross-national time-series database of political institutions that captures coalition changes such as the one that occurred in Guinea-Bissau, the DPI still constitutes the most reliable record of the presence or absence of minority government and many other variables. However, the DPI's coding of this case is manifestly incorrect after a certain point. Even if the DPI had coded Guinea-Bissau as a case of minority government in 2002 and 2003, it is unlikely that the statistical results for this variable would have altered significantly. Moreover, the in-depth case studies clearly showed that events in Guinea-Bissau were entirely consistent with a president-parliamentary interpretation of events there. It is nonetheless possible that there are equivalent examples that have not been identified, especially in new democracies where party allegiances are often very fluid. Thus, while the creation of the DPI's database is a great advance for students of comparative politics, the accuracy of the database does need to be considered and future studies do need to take this example and any others like it into account.

A definitional issue relates to non-partisanship.[2] In this book, the partisanship of presidents and prime ministers was, again, operationalized very reliably by reference to the details recorded at 'worldstatesmen.org'. This source, like any equivalent one, identifies certain leaders as non-partisan. This affiliation, or non-affiliation, had an important consequence for this study because it meant that a period of cohabitation or a divided executive could not be recorded. Here, both concepts required an explicit partisan affiliation. While the details recorded at 'worldstatesmen.org' are accurate, the consequences of identifying a non-partisan affiliation may be problematic. For example, for East Timor from 2002 to 2006, 'worldstatesmen.org' records Xanana Gusmao as a non-partisan president and Mari Alkitiri as a FRETILIN prime minister. Therefore, for the purposes of this book there was neither a period of cohabitation nor a divided executive. However, Ben Reilly (2011: 125) refers explicitly to a divided executive during this period, arguing that the resulting power struggle between the two actors 'clearly hampered democratic consolidation' (Ibid.: 120). Dennis Shoesmith (2007: 227) goes one further, referring to a period of 'conflictual cohabitation' during this time. Quite possibly, the use of the term 'divided executive' and 'cohabitation' in these cases reflects the absence of any systematic definition of these terms by the writers in question. By contrast, this book has provided a reliable definition of each term and has operationalized them rigorously. Even so, if, for example, a non-partisan president enjoys the support of a certain voting block in the legislature, then a rule that cannot generate a period of cohabitation or a divided executive may underestimate the negative effects of these variables because, in practice, the supporters of the 'non-partisan' president may be consistently opposed to those other partisans. Again, recoding East Timor as a period of cohabitation or a divided executive would not have made any significant difference to the results for either of these variables in the statistical models, but if the identification of non-partisanship by 'worldstatesmen.org' or any similar database was unwittingly introducing large-scale and systematic bias into the coding of particular concepts, then the results of any statistical study may be compromised. Thus, the consequence of recording presidents and prime ministers as non-partisan does need to be considered. Ideally, a database that recorded the level of support for 'non-partisan' presidents and prime ministers would be extremely helpful.

An empirical issue concerns the impact of other institutional variables. This book has demonstrated that the distinction between premier-presidentialism and president-parliamentarism has a broad impact on government, affecting the nature of coalitions generally, policy platforms, and so on. However, a number of the case studies showed that lower level institutional rules had an impact on executive/legislative relations too. For example, in Russia and Taiwan the automatic dissolution of the legislature that would result from a vote of no-confidence in the prime minister and cabinet was a strong disincentive for the assembly to bring the government down. This rule did not alter the fundamental dynamics of president-parliamentarism in the two countries – there was still prime ministerial turnover, non-partisan presidential governments, impeachment votes, and so forth. All the same, it did have a substantive effect on the political process by reducing the likelihood of a vote of no-confidence. Similarly, the presence or absence of a specific investiture vote was shown to affect the nature of the political game. In Guinea-Bissau, there was no requirement for an immediate investiture vote. Therefore, the president could appoint a non-partisan prime minister who had time to try to construct a majority in support of the government's general programme. This gave the president a certain liberty in prime ministerial appointments. By contrast, in Portugal the constitution requires a vote on the government's programme shortly after the prime minister's appointment. When President Eanes tried to appoint non-partisan presidential governments, he found that the legislature was able to stymie this strategy. Again, the president-parliamentary regime created the incentive for both presidents to adopt the same strategy, but the presence of different subsidiary rules meant that in practice it was easier for the president to do so in one case than the other. Finally, Lin (2011: 79) has recently shown that the electoral system may have an important effect on the dynamics of semi-presidentialism, arguing that proportional systems may allow the president 'to override a fragmented legislature and [make] governing parties insensitive to the outcome of parliamentary election'. Thus, a proportional electoral system may exacerbate the problems already inherent in a president-parliamentary system. All of these factors, and no doubt others, have the potential to reinforce or weaken existing dynamics and need to be considered in future work.

Finally, two theoretical issues need further exploration. The first concerns the effect of variation within semi-presidentialism on other types of outcomes. While this book has focused on democratic performance, it is reasonable to speculate that the premier-presidential/president-parliamentary distinction may have a wider impact. For example, there is a general finding that cabinet size affects the level of the fiscal performance. Specifically, there is strong evidence to show that there is a positive correlation between the number of parties in government and the level of the fiscal deficit (De Haan et al., 1999). The logic of this volume is that premier-presidentialism generates a greater incentive for presidents and legislatures to cooperate relative to president-parliamentarism. Therefore, all else equal, there is likely to be a greater number of parties in government in premier-presidential countries than in their president-parliamentary counterparts. If so, then the level of the fiscal deficit may also be greater under premier-presidentialism than under president-parliamentarism. This proposition could be tested. Generally, the political economy literature has studied the effects of variation in the separation of powers for many years, including studies about the relative effects of presidentialism vs. parliamentarism. For example, Gerring et al. (2009) identified a strong relationship between parliamentarism and good governance, particularly economic development and human development. What is the likely impact of the distinction between premier-presidentialism and president-parliamentarism in this regard? To date, no theoretical propositions exist. This book has demonstrated that the two forms of semi-presidentialism generate very different theoretically grounded propositions about their relative impact on democratic performance and has shown that there is strong empirical evidence to support those propositions. In this context, it is almost inconceivable that the distinction between premier-presidentialism and president-parliamentarism will not generate further theoretically grounded propositions that could be tested in an equally rigorous way. Thus, even if Samuels and Shugart (2010) have already demonstrated that the distinction has a profound impact on the nature of party politics, plenty of other propositions remain to be tested.

The second theoretical issue remains the incorporation of the premier-presidential/president-parliamentary distinction alongside the standard distinction between presidentialism and parliamentarism in comparative studies of democratic performance. Shugart and Carey's study (1992) again provides the foundation for such a comparison. However, nearly two decades on, the theoretical propositions contained in their book need to be revisited and the implications of those propositions need to be tested. What expectations would such a comparison generate? Does the theory suggest that president-parliamentarism is as dangerous for democracy as presidentialism, or somewhat less so? Premier-presidentialism is likely to be less dangerous for democracy than presidentialism, but is it more dangerous than parliamentarism? Again, Samuels and Shugart's work (2010) provides some clues as to what contemporary expectations might be. However, no theoretically rigorous set of propositions has been generated and no empirically robust test of any such propositions has been undertaken. This gap in the comparative politics literature needs to be filled as soon as possible.

CONCLUSION

The study of semi-presidentialism has been transformed in recent years. Scarcely more than a decade ago, studies of semi-presidentialism were mainly confined to parochial debates about whether or not country *x* was 'really' semi-presidential. This is because there was no agreement as to how semi-presidentialism should be defined and because definitions of semi-presidentialism were inherently unreliable, allowing different writers to argue that their particular country did or did not fit a preferred definition. To the extent that the effects of semi-presidentialism were studied, the received wisdom about, for example, the negative effects of cohabitation lacked any rigorous theoretical foundation and was supported by purely anecdotal evidence from a small number of mainly West European countries. Now, there is an emerging paradigm in semi-presidential studies. In a recent review article, David Lake (2009) has sketched the development of an equivalent paradigm in the area of international political economy. He makes the point that real-world events in the 1960s and 1970s forced scholars to deal with issues that had previously been ignored or that, at least, were long forgotten. With a strong empirical focus, an emphasis on deductive rigour, and a willingness to draw upon broader bodies of theory (Ibid.: 231), gradually a paradigm emerged that made it 'easier to connect pieces of research and, in turn, to build cumulative knowledge' (Ibid.: 220). This is the essence of the scientific method. While the new paradigm in semi-presidential studies is not so advanced, there are parallels. The wave of constitution building in the early 1990s forced scholars to examine the politics of countries with 'mixed' constitutions with a renewed energy. Gradually, a common definition of semi-presidentialism emerged that now allows the reliable identification of countries with a semi-presidential constitution. Increasingly, scholars are using deductive methods to identify the implications of the various institutional arrangements within this set of countries and they are subjecting the resulting propositions to empirical testing. Relative to the study of international political economy, the study of semi-presidentialism is confined to a relatively small number of scholars. Nonetheless, semi-presidential studies is an increasingly vibrant field precisely because parochial and intrinsically uninteresting debates have been all but abandoned and because the scientific accumulation of knowledge has begun.

This book is part of the emerging paradigm of semi-presidential studies. It has adopted a reliable definition of semi-presidentialism and it has identified a comprehensive list of countries with semi-presidential constitutions since the first examples in 1919. Within that set of countries, it has operationalized Shugart and Carey's distinction (1992) between premier-presidentialism and president-parliamentarism, identifying systematic variation within a set of otherwise heterogeneous countries. It has used a deductive method to build on Shugart and Carey's logic and, in so doing, identified various expectations about the relative impact of the two forms of semi-presidentialism on democratic performance. It has then subjected those expectations to empirical analysis, using a mix of research methods and a mix of research designs within each method. The findings are unequivocal. As expected, premier-presidentialism and president-parliamentarism do have different effects on democratic performance, the former being associated with much better performance than the latter. In so doing, this book has shown that the study of variation within the set of semi-presidential countries alone is a justifiable research topic, in the same way that some scholars focus purely on presidential countries in Latin America or purely on parliamentary countries in Europe. While comparisons of semi-presidential, presidential, and parliamentary regimes are necessary, plenty of questions remain unanswered solely within the domain of semi-presidential studies. This book has provided the answers to some of those questions. It has also provided a research agenda for semi-presidential studies in the future. In this way, this book is not merely part of the emerging paradigm of semi-presidential studies, it also aims to shape the future development of such a paradigm.

NOTES

1. The others are three years in Weimar Germany and two in Sri Lanka.
2. Thanks to Ben Reilly for raising this point in various discussions.

Bibliography

Acemoglu, Darren, Simon Johnson, James A. Robinson, and Pierre Yared (2008), 'Income and Democracy', *American Economic Review*, vol. 98, no. 3, pp. 808–42.

Aghrout, Ahmed (2008), 'Parliamentary and Presidential Elections in Mauritania, 2006 and 2007', *Electoral Studies*, vol. 27, pp. 385–90.

Akokpari, John, and Elisabete Azevedo (2007), 'Post-Conflict Elections in Africa: Liberia and Guinea-Bissau in Comparative Perspective', *African Journal of International Affairs*, vol. 10, nos. 1 & 2, pp. 73–92.

Alesina, Alberto, Arnaud Devleeschauwer, William Easterly, Sergio Kurlat, and Romain Wacziarg (2003), 'Fractionalization', *Journal of Economic Growth*, vol. 8, pp. 155–94.

Almond, Gabriel A., and Sidney Verba (1963), *The Civic Culture: Political Attitudes and Democracy in Five Nations*, Boston: Little, Brown.

Altman, David, and Aníbal Pérez-Liñán (2002), 'Assessing the Quality of Democracy: Freedom, Competitiveness and Participation in Eighteen Latin American Countries', *Democratization*, vol. 9, no. 2, pp. 85–100.

Amorim Neto, Octavio (2003), 'Portugal: Changing Patterns of Delegation and Accountability under the President's Watchful Eyes', in Kaare Strøm, Wolfgang C. Müller, and Torbjörn Bergman (eds.), *Delegation and Accountability in Parliamentary Democracies*, Oxford: Oxford University Press, pp. 552–72.

—— Marina Costa Lobo (2009), 'Portugal's Semi-Presidentialism (Re)Considered: An Assessment of the President's Role in the Policy Process, 1976–2006', *European Journal of Political Research*, vol. 48, pp. 234–55.

Andreev, Svetlozar A. (2008), 'Semi-Presidentialism in Bulgaria: The Cyclical Rise of Informal Powers and Individual Political Ambitions in a "Dual Executive"', in Robert Elgie and Sophia Moestrup (eds.), *Semi-Presidentialism in Central and Eastern Europe*, Manchester: Manchester University Press, pp. 32–50.

Araújo, António de (2003), 'El Presidente de la República en la Evolución del Sistema Político de Portugal', in António Barreto, Braulio Gómez, and Pedro Magalhäes (eds.), *Portugal: Democracia y Sistema Político*, Siglo XXI de España Editores, pp. 83–112.

Augel, Johannes, and Peter Meyns (2002), 'Processos de Transição na África Lusófona', *Soronda. Revista de Estudos Guineenses*, no. 5, pp. 7–50.

Avillez, Maria João (1996), *Soares. Democracia*, Lisbon: Público.

Azevedo, Elisabete (2009), 'O semipresidencialismo na Guiné-Bissau: inocente ou culpado da instabilidade política?', in Marina Costa Lobo and Octavio Amorim Neto (eds.), *O Semipresidencialismo nos Países de Língua Portuguesa*, Lisbon: Imprensa de Ciências Sociais, pp. 139–70.

—— Lia Nijzink (2007), 'Semi-Presidentialism in Guinea-Bissau. The Lesser of Two Evils?', in Robert Elgie and Sophia Moestrup (eds.), *Semi-Presidentialism Outside Europe*, London: Routledge, pp. 137–60.

Barro, Robert J. (1999), 'Determinants of Democracy', *Journal of Political Economy*, vol. 107, no. 6, pp. S158–83.

Barroso, José Durão (1986), 'Les conflits entre le Président portugais et la majorité parlemaentaire de 1979 à 1983', in Maurice Duverger (ed.), *Les régimes semi-presidentiels*, Paris: Presses Universitaires de France, pp. 237–55.

Bathily, Abdoulaye (1992), *Mai 68 à Dakar ou la révolte universitaire et la démocratie*, Paris: Karthala.

Baudais, Virginie, and Grégory Chauzal (2006), 'Les partis politiques et l'«indépendance partisane» d'Amadou Toumani Touré', *Politique africaine*, no. 104, pp. 61–80.

Bauer, Gretchen (2001), 'Namibia in the First Decade of Independence: How Democratic?', *Journal of Southern African Studies*, vol. 27, no. 1, pp. 33–55.

Beck, Nathaniel, and Jonathan N. Katz (1995), 'What to Do (and Not to Do) with Time-Series Cross-Section Data', *American Political Science Review*, vol. 89, no. 3, pp. 634–47.

Belmessous, Hacène (2000), 'Sénégal: L'inévitable alternance', *Politique Internationale*, no. 87 Spring, pp. 131–44.

Berg-Schlosser, Dirk (2004), 'Indicators of Democracy and Good Governance as Measures of the Quality of Democracy in Africa: A Critical Appraisal', *Acta Politica*, vol. 39, pp. 248–78.

Bernhard, Michael (2005), *Institutions and the Fate of Democracy: Germany and Poland in the Twentieth Century*, Pittsburgh: University of Pittsburgh Press.

—— Christopher Reenock, and Timothy Nordstrom (2004), 'The Legacy of Western Overseas Colonialism on Democratic Survival', *International Studies Quarterly*, vol. 48, pp. 225–50.

Beuve-Méry, Hubert (1987), 'De la dictature temporaire au régime semi-présidentiel', in Dominique Colas and Claude Emeri (eds.), *Droit, institutions et systèmes politiques. Mélanges en hommage à Maurice Duverger*, Paris: Presses Universitaires de France, pp. 533–40.

Birch, Sarah (2008), 'Ukraine: Presidential Power, Veto Strategies and Democratisation', in Robert Elgie and Sophia Moestrup (eds.), *Semi-Presidentialism in Central and Eastern Europe*, Manchester: Manchester University Press, pp. 219–38.

Blanco de Morais, Carlos (1997), 'As metamorfoses do semipresidencialismo portugues', *Revista Jurídica*, no. 22, pp. 141–59.

Blondel, Jean (1960), 'Constitutional Changes in Former French Black Africa', *Parliamentary Affairs*, vol. 14, pp. 507–17.

—— (1984), 'Dual Leadership in the Contemporary World: A Step Towards Executive and Regime Stability?', in Dennis Kavanagh and Gillian Peele (eds.), *Comparative Government and Politics. Essays in Honour of S. E. Finer*, London: Heinemann, pp. 73–91.

Boilley, Pierre (2002), 'Présidentielles maliennes: L'enracinement démocratique?', *Politique africaine*, no. 86, pp. 171–82.

Braga da Cruz, Manuel (1994), 'O Presidente da República na génese e evolução do sistema de governo português', *Análise Social*, vol. 29, nos. 125–6, pp. 237–65.

Brown, Ian Richard (2000), 'Clinging to Democracy: Assessing the Russian Legislative-Executive Relationship Under Boris Yeltsin's Constitution', *Vanderbilt Journal of Transnational Law*, 1 May, available at: http://www.thefreelibrary.com/Vanderbilt+Journal+of+Transnational+Law/2000/May/1-p5690 (accessed 7 October 2010).

Campinos, Jorge (1986), 'Le cas portugais de 1979 à 1983: le Président opposé à la majorité', in Maurice Duverger (ed.), *Les régimes semi-presidentiels*, Paris: Presses Universitaires de France, pp. 209–36.

Cardoso, Carlos (1995), 'A Transiçāo Democrática na Guiné-Bissau: Um Parto Dificil', *Lusotopie*, pp. 259–84.

Carey, John M. (2000), 'Parchment, Equilibria, and Institutions', *Comparative Political Studies*, vol. 33, nos. 6–7, pp. 735–61.

Chaisty, Paul (2008), 'The Legislative Effects of Presidential Partisan Powers in Post-Communist Russia', *Government and Opposition*, vol. 43, no. 3, pp. 424–53.

—— Petra Schleiter (2002), 'Productive but Not Valued: The Russian State Duma, 1994–2001', *Europe-Asia Studies*, vol. 54, no. 5, pp. 701–24.

Chan, Steve (2006), 'Taiwan in 2005: Strategic Interaction in Two-Level Games', *Asian Survey*, vol. 46, no. 1, pp. 63–8.

Chandler, Andrea (2001), 'Presidential Veto Power in Post-Communist Russia, 1994–1998', *Canadian Journal of Political Science*, vol. 34, no. 3, pp. 487–516.

Cheibub, José Antonio (2007), *Presidentialism, Parliamentarism, and Democracy*, Cambridge: Cambridge University Press.

—— Svitlana Chernykh (2007), 'Constitutions and Democratic Performance in Semi-Presidential Democracies', *Japanese Journal of Political Science*, vol. 9, no. 3, pp. 269–303.

———— (2009), 'Are Semi-Presidential Constitutions Bad for Democratic Performance?', *Constitutional Political Economy*, vol. 20, nos. 3–4, pp. 202–29.

—— Adam Przeworski, and Sebastian M. Saiegh (2004), 'Government Coalitions and Legislative Success under Presidentialism and Parliamentarism', *British Journal of Political Science*, vol. 34, pp. 565–87.

—— Jennifer Gandhi, and James Raymond Vreeland (2010), 'Democracy and Dictatorship Revisited', *Public Choice*, DOI 10.1007/s11127-009-9491-2.

Clark, Andrew F. (1995), 'From Military Dictatorship to Democracy: The Democratization Process in Mali', *Journal of Third World Studies*, vol. 12, pp. 201–22.

Clark, David H., and Timothy Nordstrom (2005), 'Democratic Variants and Democratic Variance: How Domestic Constraints Shape Interstate Conflict', *Journal of Politics*, vol. 67, no. 1, pp. 250–70.

Clark, John F. (2008), *The Failure of Democracy in the Republic of Congo*, Boulder, CO: Lynne Rienner.

Collier, David, and Robert Adcock (1999), 'Democracy and Dichotomies: A Pragmatic Approach to Choices about Concepts', *Annual Review of Political Science*, vol. 2, pp. 537–65.

Collier, Paul, Anke Hoeffler, and Dominic Rohner (2009), 'Beyond Greed and Grievance: Feasibility and Civil War', *Oxford Economic Papers*, vol. 61, no. 1, pp. 1–27.

Colton, Timothy J., and Cindy Skach (2005), 'The Russian Predicament', *Journal of Democracy*, vol. 16, no. 3, pp. 113–26.

Committee on Evaluation of USAID Democracy Assistance Programs (2008), *Improving Democracy Assistance: Building Knowledge Through Evaluations and Research*, Washington, DC: The National Academies Press.

Copper, John F. (2008), 'Taiwan's Failed President', *Asian Affairs*, vol. 34, no. 4, pp. 179–92.

Coulibaly, Abdou Latif (2003), *Wade, un opposant au pouvoir. L'Alternance piégee*, Dakar: Les Éditions Sentinelles.

Creevey, Lucy, Paul Ngomo, and Richard Vengroff (2005), 'Party Politics and Different Paths to Democratic Transitions: A Comparison of Benin and Senegal', *Party Politics*, vol. 11, no. 4, pp. 471–93.

Cumming, Duncan Cameron (1953), 'The Disposal of Eritrea', *Middle East Journal*, vol. 7, no. 1, pp. 18–32.

de Haan, Jakob, Jan-Egbert Sturm, and Geert Beekhuis (1999), 'The Weak Government Thesis: Some New Evidence', *Public Choice*, vol. 101, pp. 163–76.

Desai, Raj M., Anders Olofsgård, and Tarik M. Yousef (2003), 'Democracy, Inequality, and Inflation', *American Political Science Review*, vol. 97, no. 3, pp. 391–406.

Diamond, Larry (1996), 'Is the Third Wave Over?', *Journal of Democracy*, vol. 7, no. 3, pp. 20–37.

—— Leonardo Morlino (2004), 'The Quality of Democracy: An Overview', *Journal of Democracy*, vol. 15, no. 4, pp. 20–31.

—— Juan J. Linz, and Seymour Martin Lipset (1995), 'Introduction: What Makes for Democracy?', in Larry Diamond, Juan J. Linz, and Seymour Martin Lipset (eds.), *Politics in Developing Countries. Comparing Experiences with Democracy*, 2nd ed., Boulder, CO: Lynne Rienner, pp. 1–66.

Diarra, Abdoulaye (2010), *Démocratie et droit constitutionnel dans les pays francophones d'Afrique noire. Le cas du Mali depuis 1960*, Paris: Karthala.

Diarra, Eloi (1995), 'Constitution et état de droit au Mali', *Revue juridique et politique, indépendance et coopération*, vol. 49, no. 3, pp. 252–84.

Diaw, Moussa (1998), 'Elections et pouvoir tribal en Mauritanie', *Politique africaine*, no. 71, pp. 156–64.

Diop, Abdoul Aziz (2009), *Une succession en démocratie. Les Sénégalais face à l'inattendu*, Paris: L'Harmattan.

Diop, Momar-Coumba (2006), 'Le Sénégal à la croisée des chemins', *Politique africaine*, no. 104, pp. 103–26.

—— Mamadou Diouf, and Aminata Diaw (2000), 'Le baobab a été déraciné. L'alternance au Sénégal', *Politique africaine*, no. 78, pp. 157–79.

Docking, Timothy W. (1997), 'Mali. The Roots of Democracy's "Success"', *L'Afrique politique 1997*, pp. 191–212.

Dunning, Thad (2008), 'Improving Causal Inference. Strengths and Limitations of Natural Experiments', *Political Research Quarterly*, vol. 61, no. 2, pp. 282–93.

Duverger, Maurice (1967), *Les Partis politiques*, 6th edn., Paris: Armand Colin.

—— (1970), *Institutions politiques et Droit constitutionnel*, 11th edn., Paris: Presses Universitaires de France.

—— (1978), *Echec au roi*, Paris: Albin Michel.

—— (1980), 'A New Political System Model: Semi-Presidential Government', *European Journal of Political Research*, vol. 8, no. 2, pp. 165–87.

Elgie, Robert (1998), 'The Classification of Democratic Regime Types: Conceptual Ambiguity and Contestable Assumptions', *European Journal of Political Research*, vol. 33, no. 2, pp. 219–38.

—— (1999), 'The Politics of Semi-Presidentialism', in Robert Elgie (ed.), *Semi-Presidentialism in Europe*, Oxford: Oxford University Press, pp. 1–21.

Elgie, Robert (2007), 'Varieties of Semi-Presidentialism and Their Impact on Nascent Democracies', *Taiwan Journal of Democracy*, vol. 3, no. 2, pp. 53–71.

—— (2010a), 'Semi-Presidentialism: An Increasingly Common Constitutional Choice', in Robert Elgie, Sophia Moestrup, and Yu-Shan Wu (eds.), *Semi-Presidentialism and Democracy*, London: Palgrave.

—— (2010b), 'Semi-Presidentialism, Cohabitation and the Collapse of Electoral Democracies, 1990–2008', *Government and Opposition*, vol. 45, no. 1, pp. 29–49.

—— Francesco Cavatorta (2010), 'The Impact of Semi-Presidentialism on Governance in the Palestinian Authority', *Parliamentary Affairs*, vol. 63, no. 1, pp. 22–40.

—— Iain McMenamin (2008), 'Semi-Presidentialism and Democratic Performance', in *Japanese Journal of Political Science*, vol. 9, no. 3, pp. 323–40.

—— Petra Schleiter (2011), 'Variation in the Durability of Semi-Presidential Democracies', in Robert Elgie, Sophia Moestrup, and Yu-Shan Wu (eds.), *Semi-Presidentialism and Democracy*, London: Palgrave Macmillan, pp. 42–60.

—— Sophia Moestrup (2008), 'Semi-Presidentialism: A Common Regime Type, But One That Should Be Avoided?', in Robert Elgie and Sophia Moestrup (eds.), *Semi-Presidentialism in Central and Eastern Europe*, Manchester: Manchester University Press, pp. 1–13.

Fall, Alioune Badara (2006), 'La démocratie sénégalaise à l'épreuve de l'alternance', *Afrilex*, no. 5, pp. 3–63.

Fall, Ismaïla Madior (2009), *Évolution constitutionnelle du Sénégal. De la veille de l'indépendance aux élections de 2007*, Paris: Karthala.

Fatton, Robert (2000), 'Constitution without Constitutionalism: Haiti and the Vagaries of Democratization', *New West Indian Guide*, vol. 74, nos. 1/2, pp. 5–32.

Fish, M. Steven (2001), 'The Inner Asian Anomaly: Mongolia's Democratization in Comparative Perspective', *Communist and Post-Communist Studies*, vol. 34, pp. 323–38.

—— Matthew Kroenig (2006), 'Diversity, Conflict and Democracy: Some Evidence from Eurasia and East Europe', *Democratization*, vol. 13, no. 5, pp. 828–42.

Forrest, Joshua (2002), 'Guinea-Bissau', in Patrick Chabal et al. (eds.), *A History of Postcolonial Lusophone Africa*, Bloomington: Indiana University Press, pp. 236–63.

—— (2005), 'Democratization in a Divided Urban Political Culture. Guinea-Bissau', in Leonardo A. Villalón and Peter VonDoepp (eds.), *The Fate of Africa's Democratic Experiments: Elites and Institutions*, Bloomington: Indiana University Press, pp. 246–66.

Foweraker, Joe, and Roman Krznaric (2003), 'Differentiating the democratic performance of the West', *European Journal of Political Research*, vol. 42, pp. 313–40.

Freedom House (2010), *Freedom in the World 2010. Erosion of Freedom Intensifies. Selected Data from Freedom House's Annual Survey of Political Rights and Civil Liberties*, available at: www.freedomhouse.org/uploads/fiw10/FIW_2010_Overview_Essay.pdf (accessed 5 March 2010).

Freeman, Mark (2000), 'Constitutional Frameworks and Fragile Democracies: Choosing Between Parliamentarism, Presidentialism and Semi-Presidentialism', *Pace International Law Review*, vol. 12, no. 2, pp. 253–82.

Frison-Roche, François (2005), *Le 'modèle semi-présidentiel' comme instrument de la transition en Europe post-communiste. Bulgarie, Lituanie, Macédoine, Pologne, Roumanie et Slovénie*, Brussels: Bruylant.

Galvan, Dennis (2001), 'Political Turnover and Social Change in Senegal', *Journal of Democracy*, vol. 12, no. 3, pp. 51–62.

Gaye, Mandiaye (2010), *Le Sénégal sous Abdoulaye Wade: Banqueroute, corruption et liberticide*, Paris: L'Harmattan.

Geddes, Barbara (1999), 'What Do We Know About Democratization after Twenty Years?', *Annual Review of Political Science*, vol. 2, pp. 115–44.

Gerring, John, Strom C. Thacker, and Carola Moreno (2009), 'Are Parliamentary Systems Better?', *Comparative Political Studies*, vol. 42, no. 3, pp. 327–59.

Herspring, Dale R. (2000), 'Civil–Military Relations in Post-Communist Poland: Problems in the Transition to a Democratic Polity', *Communist and Post-Communist Studies*, vol. 33, no. 1, pp. 71–100.

Hesseling, Gerti (1985), *Histoire politique du Sénégal. Institutions, droit et société*, Paris: Karthala.

Horowitz, Donald L. (1990), 'Comparing Democratic Systems', *Journal of Democracy*, vol. 1, no. 4, pp. 73–9.

—— (1993), 'Democracy in Divided Societies', *Journal of Democracy*, vol. 4, no. 4, pp. 18–38.

Huang, Thomas Weishing (2006), 'The President Refuses to Cohabit: Semi-Presidentialism in Taiwan', *Pacific Rim Law and Policy Journal*, vol. 15, no. 2, pp. 375–402.

Huber, Evelyne, Dietrich Rueschemeyer, and John D. Stephens (1993), 'The Impact of Economic Development on Democracy', *Journal of Economic Perspectives*, vol. 7, no. 3, pp. 71–86.

Huskey, Eugene (1996), 'Democracy and Institutional Design in Russia', *Demokratizatsiya*, vol. 4, no. 4, pp. 453–73.

Ibrahim, Jibrin, and Abdoulaye Niandou Souley (1998), 'The Rise to Power of an Opposition Party: The MNSD in Niger Republic', in Adebayo O. Olukoshi (ed.), *The Politics of Opposition in Contemporary Africa*, Uppsala: Nordiska Afrikainstitutet, pp. 144–70.

Indridason, Indridi H. (2005), 'A Theory of Coalitions and Clientelism: Coalition Politics in Iceland, 1945–2000', *European Journal of Political Research*, vol. 44, pp. 439–64.

Issa Abdourhamane, Boubacar (1996), *Crise institutionnelle et démocratisation au Niger*, Bordeaux: Centre d'Etude d'Afrique Noire.

Jalali, Carlos (2010), 'The President is not a Passenger: Portugal's Evolving Semi-Presidentialism', in Robert Elgie, Sophia Moestrup, and Yu-Shan Wu (eds.), *Semi-Presidentialsm and Democracy*, London: Palgrave.

Jasiewicz, Krzysztof (1997), 'Poland: Wałęsa's Legacy to the Presidency', in Ray Taras (ed.), *Postcommunist Presidents*, Cambridge: Cambridge University Press, pp. 130–67.

Karasimeonov, Georgi (1996), 'The Legislature in Post-Communist Bulgaria', *Journal of Legislative Studies*, vol. 2, no. 1, pp. 40–59.

Keefer, Philip (2007), 'Clientelism, Credibility, and the Policy Choices of Young Democracies', *American Journal of Political Science*, vol. 51, no. 4, pp. 804–21.

Kirschke, Linda (2007), 'Semipresidentialism and the Perils of Power-Sharing in Neopatrimonial States', *Comparative Political Studies*, vol. 40, no. 11, pp. 1372–94.

Kono, Daniel Y. (2006), 'Optimal Obfuscation: Democracy and Trade Policy Transparency', *American Political Science Review*, vol. 100, no. 3, pp. 369–84.

Kopstein, Jeffrey S., and David A. Reilly (2000), 'Geographic Diffusion and the Transformation of the Postcommunist World', *World Politics*, vol. 53, pp. 1–37.

Kouvibidilia, Gaston-Jonas (2000), *Histoire du multipartisme au Congo-Brazzaville: Les débuts d'une crise attendue 1992–1993*, Paris: L'Harmattan.

Kristinsson, Gunnar Helgi (1999), 'Iceland', in Robert Elgie (ed.), *Semi-Presidentialism in Europe*, Oxford: Oxford University Press, pp. 86–105.

Kucera, Ondrej (2006), 'Is Taiwan a Presidential System?', *China Perspectives*, no. 66: http://chinaperspectives.revues.org/document1036.html (accessed 5 November 2009).

Lake, David A. (2009), 'Open Economy Politics: A Critical Review', *Review of International Organizations*, vol. 4, pp. 219–44.

Laski, Harold J. (1944), 'The Parliamentary and Presidential Systems', *Public Administration Review*, vol. 4, no. 4, pp. 347–59.

Leeson, Peter T., and Andrea M. Dean (2009), 'The Democratic Domino Theory: An Empirical Investigation', *American Journal of Political Science*, vol. 53, no. 3, pp. 533–51.

Lijphart, Arend (1999), *Patterns of Democracy. Government Forms and Performance in Thirty-Six Countries*, New Haven: Yale University Press.

—— (2004), 'Constitutional Design for Divided Societies', *Journal of Democracy*, vol. 15, no. 2, pp. 96–109.

Lin, Jih-Wen (2011), 'The Rules of Electoral Competition and the Accountability of Semi-Presidential Governments', in Robert Elgie, Sophia Moestrup, and Yu-Shan Wu (eds.), *Semi-Presidentialism and Democracy*, London: Palgrave, pp. 61–80.

Linz, Juan J. (1990a), 'The Perils of Presidentialism', *Journal of Democracy*, vol. 1, no. 1, pp. 51–69.

—— (1990b), 'The Virtues of Parliamentarism', *Journal of Democracy*, vol. 1, no. 4, pp. 84–91.

—— (1994), 'Presidential or Parliamentary Democracy: Does It Make a Difference?', in Juan J. Linz and Arturo Valenzuela (eds.), *The Failure of Presidential Democracy. Comparative Perspectives*, Baltimore: Johns Hopkins University Press, pp. 3–87.

—— (1997), 'Introduction: Some Thoughts on Presidentialism in Postcommunist Europe', in Ray Taras (ed.), *Postcommunist Presidents*, Cambridge: Cambridge University Press.

—— Alfred Stepan (1996), *Problems of Democratic Transition and Consolidation. Southern Europe, South America, and Post-Communist Europe*, Baltimore: The John Hopkins Press.

Lipset, Seymour Martin (1959), 'Some Social Requisites of Democracy: Economic Development and Political Legitimacy', *American Political Science Review*, vol. 53, no. 1, pp. 69–105.

Lissouck, Félix François (2004), 'L'évolution politique et institutionnelle récente au Mali: Les leçons d'une expérience démocratique', *Revue juridique et politique des états francophones*, vol. 58, no.1, pp. 21–42.

Lopes, Pedro Santana, and José Durão Barroso (1980), *Sistema de Governo e Sistema Partidário*, Lisbon: Livraria Bertrand.

Magone, José M. (2000), 'Portugal. The Rationale of Democratic Regime Building', in Wolfgang C. Müller and Kaare Strøm (eds.), *Coalition Governments in Western Europe*, Oxford: Oxford University Press, pp. 529–58.

Maignan, Jean-Claude (2000), *La difficile démocratisation au Niger*, Paris: Centre des hautes études sur l'Afrique et l'Asie modernes.

Mainwaring, Scott (1993), 'Presidentialism, Multipartism, and Democracy. The Difficult Combination', *Comparative Political Studies*, vol. 26, no. 2, pp. 198–228.

—— Matthew S. Shugart (1997), 'Juan Linz, Presidentialism, and Democracy: A Critical Appraisal', *Comparative Politics*, vol. 29, no. 4, pp. 449–71.

March, James G., and Johan P. Olsen (1984), 'The New Institutionalism: Organizational Factors in Political Life', *American Political Science Review*, vol. 78, no. 3, pp. 734–49.

Marshall, Monty G., and Keith Jaggers (2009), *Polity IV Project. Political Regime Characteristics and Transitions, 1800–2007. Dataset Users' Manual*, Center for Systemic Peace (www.systemicpeace.org/polity).

Massicotte, Louis (2009), 'Mapping the Road to Democracy. The National Conference of Mali 29 July to 12 August 1991', Paper presented at the Conference "Changer la Donne Politique. Nouveaux Processus Constituants", available at: http://www.democratie.chaire.ulaval.ca/Upload/mali._27082009_161330.pdf (accessed 11 May 2010).

Matsuzato, Kimitaka (2005), 'Semipresidentialism in Ukraine: Institutionalist Centrism in Rampant Clan Politics', *Demokratizatsiya: The Journal of Post-Soviet Democratization*, vol. 13, no. 1, pp. 45–60.

Mazo, Eugene (2005), *Constitutional Roulette: The Russian Parliament's Battles with the President Over Appointing a Prime Minister*, CDDRL Working Papers, no. 35, available at: http://fsi.stanford.edu/people/eugenemazo/ (accessed 7 October 2010).

Mbow, Penda (2008), 'Senegal: The Return of Personalism', *Journal of Democracy*, vol. 19, no. 1, pp. 156–69.

McMenamin, Iain (2008), 'Semi-Presidentialism and Democratisation in Poland', in Robert Elgie and Sophia Moestrup (eds.), *Semi-Presidentialism in Central and Eastern Europe*, Manchester: Manchester University Press, pp. 120–37.

Metcalf, Lee Kendall (2000), 'Measuring Presidential Power', *Comparative Political Studies*, vol. 33, no. 5, pp. 660–85.

Millard, Frances (1994), 'The Polish Parliamentary Election of September, 1993', *Communist and Post-Communist Studies*, vol. 27, no. 3, pp. 295–313.

—— (2008), 'Executive–Legislative Relations in Poland, 1991–2005: Institutional Relations in Transition', *Journal of Legislative Studies*, vol. 14, no. 4, pp. 367–93.

Miranda, Jorge (1984), 'O sistema semipresidencial português entre 1976 e 1979', *Revista da Faculdade de Direito da Universidade de Lisboa*, vol. 25, pp. 193–220.

Mission d'Observation électorale de l'Union européenne en Mauritanie (2007), *Elections municipales, législatives 2006 et présidentielles 2007. Rapport final*, http://ec.europa.eu/external_relations/human_rights/election_observation/mauritania/final_report_fr.pdf (accessed 21 September 2009).

Moestrup, Sophia (1999), 'The Role of Actors and Institutions: The Difficulties of Democratic Survival in Mali and Niger', *Democratization*, vol. 6, no. 2, pp. 171–86.

—— (2007), 'Semi-Presidentialism in Young Democracies. Help or Hindrance?', in Robert Elgie and Sophia Moestrup (eds.), *Semi-Presidentialism Outside Europe*, London: Routledge, pp. 30–55.

—— (2011), 'Haiti: Semi-Presidentialism in a Fractured Society', in Robert Elgie, Sophia Moestrup, and Yu-Shan Wu (eds.), *Semi-Presidentialism and Democracy*, London: Palgrave.

Morais, Isaltino A., José Mário Ferreira de Almeida, and Ricardo Leite Pinto (1984), *O Sistema de Governo semipresidencial. O Caso Português*, Lisbon: Notícias.

Moreira, Vital (2005), 'Evolução Democrático em Portugal (1974–2002): Traços e Impasse', in Vital Moreira (ed.), *Crise e Reforma Da Democracia. V Curso Livre de História Contemporânea, Lisboa, 11 a 16 Novembro de 2002, organizado por Fundação Mário Soares e Instituto de História Contemporânea de Faculdade de Ciências Sociais e Humanas da Universidade Nova de Lisboa*, Lisbon: Ediçoes Colibri, pp. 11–34.

Morgan-Jones, Edward, and Petra Schleiter (2004), 'Governmental Change in a President-Parliamentary Regime: The Case of Russia 1994–2003', *Post-Soviet Affairs*, vol. 20, no. 2, pp. 132–63.

Morlino, Leonardo (2004), '"Good" and "Bad" Democracies: How to Conduct Research into the Quality of Democracy', *Journal of Communist Studies and Transition Politics*, vol. 20, no. 1, pp. 5–27.

M'Paka, Albert (2005), *Démocratie et administration au Congo-Brazzaville*, Paris: L'Harmattan.

—— (2007), *Démocratie et vie politique au Congo-Brazzaville*, Paris: L'Harmattan.

Müller, Wolfgang C. (1992), 'Austrian Governmental Institutions: Do They Matter?', *West European Politics*, vol. 15, no. 1, pp. 99–131.

—— (1999), 'Austria', in Robert Elgie (ed.), *Semi-Presidentialism in Europe*, Oxford: Oxford University Press, pp. 24–50.

Munck, Gerardo L., and Jay Verkuilen (2002), 'Conceptualizing and Measuring Democracy: Evaluating Alternative Indices', *Comparative Political Studies*, vol. 35, no. 5, pp. 5–34.

Murray, D. Christie (1875), 'A Scrap of Crimean History', *The Gentleman's Magazine*, vol. 14, Jan.–June, pp. 171–83.

Nalewajko, Ewa, and Włodzimierz Wesołowski (2007), 'Five Terms of the Polish Parliament, 1989–2005', *Journal of Legislative Studies*, vol. 13, no. 1, pp. 59–82.

N'Diaye, Boubacar (2009), 'To "Midwife" – and Abort – A Democracy: Mauritania's Transition from Military Rule, 2005–2008', *Journal of Modern African Studies*, vol. 47, no. 1, pp. 129–52.

Negretto, Gabriel L. (2006), 'Minority Presidents and Democratic Performance in Latin America', Latin American Politics and Society, vol. 48, no. 3, pp. 63–92.

Niang, Mody (2004), *Me Wade et l'Alternance: le rêve brisé de Sopi*, Paris: L'Harmattan.

—— (2006), *Qui est cet homme qui dirige le Sénégal?*, Paris: L'Harmattan.

Nóbrega, Álvaro (2003), 'Desejo de 'Cambança': o Processo Eleitoral de 1999', *Soronda. Revista de Estudos Guineenses*, no. 6, pp. 7–82.

Nogueira Alcalá, Humberto (1986), *El Regimen Semipresidencial. ¿Una Nueva Forma de Gobierno Democrático?*, Santiago: Andante.

Norris, Pippa (2008), *Driving Democracy. Do Power-Sharing Institutions Work?*, Cambridge: Cambridge University Press.

Novais, António Jorge Reis (2007), *Sistema de Governo da Guine'Bissau: na Constitução e na pratica*, Dissertação de Mestrado em Ciências Jurídico-Politicas, Faculdade de Direito, Universidade de Lisboa.

Nzouankeu, Jacques Mariel (1993), 'The Role of the National Conference in the Transition to Democracy in Africa: The Cases of Benin and Mali', *Issue: A Journal of Opinion*, vol. 21, no. 1/2, pp. 44–50.

O'Loughlin, John, Michael D. Ward, Corey L. Lofdahl, Jordin S. Cohin, David S. Brown, David Reilly, Kristian S. Gleditch, and Michael Shin (1998), 'The Diffusion of Democracy, 1946–1994', *Annals of the Association of American Geographers*, vol. 88, no. 4, pp. 545–74.

O'Neil, Patrick (1993), 'Presidential Power in Post-Communist Europe: The Hungarian Case in Comparative Perspective', *Journal of Communist Studies*, vol. 9, no. 3, pp. 177–201.

Opello, Walter C. (1990), 'The Transition to Democracy and the Constitutional Settlement as Causes of Political Instability in Post-Authoritarian Portugal', *Luso-Brazilian Review*, vol. 27, no. 2, pp. 77–94.

Ostheimer, Andrea E. (2001), 'The Structural Crisis in Guinea-Bissau's Political System', *African Security Review*, vol. 10, no. 4, pp. 1–8.

Pasquino, Gianfranco (2007), 'The Advantages and Disadvantages of Semi-Presidentialism: A West European Perspective', in Robert Elgie and Sophia Moestrup (eds.), *Semi-Presidentialism Outside Europe*, London: Routledge, pp. 14–29.

Peceny, Mark (1999), 'Forcing Them To Be Free', *Political Research Quarterly*, vol. 52, no. 3, pp. 549–82.

Pereira, André Gonçalves (1984), *O Semipresidencialismo em Portugal*, Lisbon: Ática.

Pierce, Roy (1991), 'The Executive Divided Against Itself: Cohabitation in France, 1986–1988', *Governance*, vol. 4, no. 3, pp. 270–94.

Pimont, Yves (1993), 'La Constitution de la République de Mali', *Revue juridique et politique, indépendance et coopération*, vol. 47, no. 3, pp. 462–91.

Plümper, Thomas, and Vera A. Troeger (2007), 'Efficient Estimation of Time-Invariant and Rarely Changing Variables in Finite Sample Panel Analyses with Unit Fixed Effects', *Political Analysis*, vol. 15, pp. 124–39.

Power, Timothy J., and Mark J. Gasiorowski (1997), 'Institutional Design and Democratic Consolidation in the Third World', *Comparative Political Studies*, vol. 30, no. 2, pp. 123–55.

Price, Don K. (1943), 'The Parliamentary and Presidential Systems', *Public Administration Review*, vol. 3, no. 4, pp. 317–34.

Pridham, Geoffrey (2005), *Designing Democracy: EU Enlargement and Regime Change in Post-Communist Europe*, Palgrave: Macmillan.

Pringle, Robert (2006), 'Mali's Unlikely Democracy', *Wilson Quarterly*, vol. 30, no. 2, pp. 30–9.

Protsyk, Oleh (2003), 'Troubled Semi-Presidentialism: Stability of the Constitutional System and Cabinet in Ukraine', *Europe-Asia Studies*, vol. 55, no. 7, pp. 1077–95.

—— (2004), 'Ruling with Decrees: Presidential Decree Making in Russia and Ukraine', *Europe-Asia Studies*, vol. 56, no. 5, pp. 637–60.

—— (2005), 'Prime Ministers' Identity in Semi-Presidential Regimes: Constitutional Norms and Cabinet Formation Outcomes', *European Journal of Political Research*, vol. 44, pp. 721–48.

—— (2006), 'Intra-Executive Competition between President and Prime Minister: Patterns of Institutional Conflict and Cooperation under Semi-presidentialism', *Political Studies*, vol. 54, pp. 219–44.

Przeworski, Adam, Michael E. Alvarez, José Antonio Cheibub, and Fernando Limongi (2000), *Democracy and Development. Political Institutions and Well-Being in the World, 1950–1990*, Cambridge: Cambridge University Press.

Pugačiauskas, Vykintas (1999), 'Semi-Presidential Institutional Models and Democratic Stability: Comparative Analysis of Lithuania and Poland', *Lithuanian Political Science Yearbook 1909*, pp. 1–26.

Raynal, Jean-Jacques (1993), *Les institutions politiques du Niger*, Saint-Maur: Sépia.

Reilly, Benjamin (2000), 'Democracy, Ethnic Fragmentation, and Internal Conflict: Confused Theories, Faulty Data, and the "Crucial Case" of Papua New Guinea', *International Security*, vol. 25, no. 3, pp. 162–85.

—— (2011), 'Semi-Presidentialism and Democratic Development in East Asia', in Robert Elgie, Sophia Moestrup, and Yu-Shan Wu (eds.), *Semi-Presidentialism and Democracy*, London: Palgrave, pp. 117–33.

Reiter, Dan, and Erik R. Tilman (2002), 'Public, Legislative, and Executive Constraints on the Democratic Initiation of Conflict', *Journal of Politics*, vol. 64, no. 3, pp. 810–26.

Remington, Thomas F. (2001), 'The Evolution of Executive-Legislative Relations in Russia since 1993', *Slavic Review*, vol. 59, no. 3, pp. 499–520.

—— (2008), 'Patronage and the Party of Power: President–Parliament Relations Under Vladimir Putin', *Europe-Asia Studies*, vol. 60, no. 6, pp. 959–87.

Roper, Steven D. (2002), 'Are All Semipresidential Regimes the Same? A Comparison of Premier-Presidential Comparison Regimes', *Comparative Politics*, vol. 34, no. 3, pp. 253–72.

Rudebeck, Lars (2001), *On Democracy's Sustainability. Transition in Guinea-Bissau*, Sida Studies, no. 4, Gothenburg: Swedish International Development Cooperation Agency.

Salgado de Matos, Luís (1992), 'O sistema político português e a Comunidade Europeia', *Análise Social*, vol. 27, nos. 118–19, pp. 773–87.

Samuels, David (2007), 'Separation of Powers', in Carles Boix and Susan C. Stokes (eds.), *The Oxford Handbook of Comparative Politics*, Oxford: Oxford University Press, pp. 703–26.

—— Matthew Shugart (2010), *Presidents, Parties, Prime Ministers: A Framework for Analysis*, Cambridge: Cambridge University Press (all chapters available at http://dss.ucsd.edu/mshugart/samuels-shugart.html (accessed 22 July 2009)).

Sanford, George (1993), 'Delay and Disappointment: The Fully Free Polish Election of 27 October 1991', *Journal of Communist Studies and Transition Politics*, vol. 9, no. 2, pp. 107–18.

Sartori, Giovanni (1994), 'Neither Presidentialism Nor Parliamentarism', in Juan J. Linz and Arturo Valenzuela (eds.), *The Failure of Presidential Democracy. Comparative Perspectives*, Baltimore: Johns Hopkins University Press, pp. 106–18.

—— (1997), *Comparative Constitutional Engineering: An Inquiry into Structures, Incentives and Outcomes*, 2nd edn., London: Macmillan.

Schiller, Arthur A. (1953), 'Eritrea: Constitution and Federation with Ethiopia', *American Journal of Comparative Law*, vol. 2, no. 3, pp. 375–83.

Schleiter, Petra, and Edward Morgan-Jones (2009), 'Review Article: Citizens, Presidents and Assemblies: The Study of Semi-Presidentialism beyond Duverger and Linz', *British Journal of Political Science*, vol. 39, pp. 871–92.

Seck, Mamadou (2006), *Les scandales politiques sous la présidence d'Abdoulaye Wade*, Paris: L'Harmattan.

Sedelius, Thomas (2006), *The Tug-of-War between Presidents and Prime Ministers. Semi-Presidentialism in Central and Eastern Europe*, Örebro Studies in Political Science 15, Örebro universitet, Sweden.

Shoesmith, Dennis (2003), 'Timor-Leste: Divided Leadership in a Semi-Presidential System', *Asian Survey*, vol. 43, no. 2, pp. 231–52.

—— (2007), 'Timor-Leste: Semi-Presidentialism and the Democratic Transition in a New, Small State', in Robert Elgie and Sophia Moestrup (eds.), *Semi-Presidentialism Outside Europe*, London: Routledge, pp. 219–36.

Shugart, Matthew Soberg (1993), 'Of Presidents and Parliaments', *East European Constitutional Review*, vol. 2, no. 1, pp. 30–2.

—— (2005), 'Semi-Presidential Systems: Dual Executive and Mixed Authority Patterns', *French Politics*, vol. 3, no. 3, pp. 323–51.

—— John M. Carey (1992), *Presidents and Assemblies. Constitutional Design and Electoral Dynamics*, Cambridge: Cambridge University Press.

Siaroff, Alan (2003), 'Comparative Presidencies: The Inadequacy of the Presidential, Semi-Presidential and Parliamentary Distinction', *European Journal of Political Research*, vol. 42, no. 3, pp. 287–312.

Sidibé, Doudou (2006), *Démocratie et alternance politique au Sénégal*, Paris: L'Harmattan.

Silva, António E. Duarte (2006/2007), 'O Constitucionalismo da Guiné-Bissau (1973–2005)', *Direito e Cidadania*, vol. 8, nos. 25/26, pp. 63–100.

Skach, Cindy (2005), *Borrowing Constitutional Designs. Constitutional Law in Weimar Germany and the French Fifth Republic*, Princeton: Princeton University Press.

Smith, Herbert Arthur (1923), *Federalism in North America: A Comparative Study of Institutions in the United States and Canada*, Clark, NJ: The Lawbook Exchange Ltd.

Smith, Zeric Kay (2001), 'Mali's Decade of Democracy', *Journal of Democracy*, vol. 12, no. 3, pp. 73–9.

Stepan, Alfred, and Cindy Skach (1993), 'Constitutional Frameworks and Democratic Consolidation. Parliamentarism versus Presidentialism', *World Politics*, vol. 46, no. 1, pp. 1–22.

Stock, Maria José (1986), 'O centrismo político em Portugal: evolução do sistema de partidos, génese do «Bloco Central» e análise dos dois parceiros da coligação', *Análise Social*, vol. 21, no. 85, pp. 45–82.

Strom, Kaare (1990), *Minority Government and Majority Rule*, Cambridge: Cambridge University Press.

Thiam, Assane (2007), '«Une Constitution, ça se revise!» Relativisme constitutionnel et état de droit au Sénégal', *Politique africaine*, no. 108, pp. 145–53.

Thomas, Melissa A., and Oumar Sissokho (2005), 'Liaison Legislature: The Role of the National Assembly in Senegal', *Journal of Modern African Studies*, vol. 43, no. 1, pp. 97–117.

Tirera, Lamine (2006), *Abdou Diouf: biographie politique et style de gouvernement*, Paris: L'Harmattan.

Troxel, Tiffany A. (2003), *Parliamentary Power in Russia, 1994–2001: President vs Parliament*, London: Palgrave.

Van Der Meer Krok Paszkowska, Ania (1999), 'Poland', in Robert Elgie (ed.), *Semi-Presidentialism in Europe*, Oxford: Oxford University Press, pp. 170–92.

Villalón, Leonardo A. (1994), 'Democratizing a (Quasi) Democracy: The Senegalese Elections of 1993', *African Affairs*, vol. 93, no. 371, pp. 163–93.

—— Abdourahmane Idrissa (2005), 'The Tribulations of a Successful Transition. Institutional Dynamics and Elite Rivalry in Mali', in Leonardo A. Villalón and Peter VonDoepp (eds.), *The Fate of Africa's Democratic Experiments. Elites and Institutions*, Bloomington: Indiana University Press, pp. 49–73.

—— —— (2005), 'Repetitive Breakdowns and a Decade of Experimentation. Institutional Choices and Unstable Democracy in Niger', in Leonardo A. Villalón and Peter Von Doepp (eds.), *The Fate of Africa's Democratic Experiments. Elites and Institutions*, Bloomington: Indiana University Press, pp. 27–48.

Wilson, Woodrow (1884), 'Committee or Cabinet Government?', *Overland Monthly*, January, series 2, vol. 3, pp. 17–33.

Wing, Susanna D. (2008), *Constructing Democracy in Transitioning Societies of Africa. Constitutionalism and Deliberation in Mali*, London: Palgrave.

Woldendorp, Jaap, Hans Keman, and Ian Budge (2002), *Party Government in 48 Democracies (1945–1998): Composition-Duration-Personnel*, Dordrecht: Kluwer.

Wright, Gordon (1950), *The Reshaping of French Democracy*, 2nd edn., New York: Reynal and Hitchcock.

Wu, Yu-Shan (2005), 'Appointing the Prime Minister under Incongruence: Taiwan in Comparison with France and Russia', *Taiwan Journal of Democracy*, vol. 1, no. 1, pp. 103–32.

—— (2007), 'Semi-Presidentialism – Easy to Choose, Difficult to Operate: The Case of Taiwan', in Robert Elgie and Sophia Moestrup (eds.), *Semi-Presidentialism Outside Europe*, London: Routledge, pp. 201–18.

Wyrzykowski, Mirosław, and Agnieszka Cielen (2006), 'Poland – Semi-Presidentialism or "Rationalised Parliamentarianism"?', *European Constitutional Law Review*, vol. 2, pp. 253–67.

Zielonka, Jan, and Alex Pravda eds. (2001), *Democratic Consolidation in Eastern Europe. Volume 2. International and Transnational Factors*, Oxford: Oxford University Press.

Zisenwine, Daniel (2007), 'Mauritania's Democratic Transition: A Regional Model for Political Reform?', *Journal of North African Studies*, vol. 12, no. 4, pp. 481–99.

Index

The manufacturer's authorised representative in the EU for product safety is Oxford University Press España S.A. of el Parque Empresarial San Fernando de Henares, Avenida de Castilla, 2 – 28830 Madrid (www.oup.es/en or product.safety@oup.com). OUP España S.A. also acts as importer into Spain of products made by the manufacturer.

www.ingramcontent.com/pod-product-compliance
Lightning Source LLC
LaVergne TN
LVHW011818200926
848484LV00005B/1237
* 9 7 8 0 1 9 9 5 8 5 9 8 4 *